Restoration
The Rebuilding of Windsor Castle

Restoration

The Rebuilding of Windsor Castle

Adam Nicolson

MICHAEL JOSEPH
LONDON
in association with
THE ROYAL COLLECTION

MICHAEL JOSEPH LTD
in association with
THE ROYAL COLLECTION

Published by the Penguin Group
Penguin Books Limited, 27 Wrights Lane, London w8 5tz
Penguin Putnam Inc., 375 Hudson Street, New York, New York 10014, USA
Penguin Books Australia Ltd, Ringwood, Victoria, Australia
Penguin Books Canada Ltd, 10 Alcorn Avenue, Toronto, Ontario, Canada m4v 3b2
Penguin Books (NZ) Ltd, 182–190 Wairau Road, Auckland 10, New Zealand

Penguin Books, Registered Offices: Harmondsworth, Middlesex, England

First published 1997
10 9 8 7 6 5 4 3 2

Text copyright © Royal Collection Enterprises Ltd and Adam Nicolson, 1997
The picture credits on p. 280 constitute an extension of this copyright page.

The moral right of the author has been asserted

Set in 12/15pt Monotype Sabon
Designed in Quark Xpress on an Apple Macintosh
Printed in Great Britain by Butler & Tanner Ltd, Frome and London

A CIP catalogue record for this book is available from the British Library

ISBN 0718I 4192 X

Endpapers: *Part of Giles
Downes's design for the
new stone floor in the
Lantern Lobby. For a
description of its symbolic
significance see page 242.*

Frontispiece: *One of the
so-called wall corbels,
on which suits of armour
usually stand, lining St
George's Hall, immediately
after the fire in 1992. In the
restoration, the original
candlestick branches on
either side, one of them
broken here by falling
timber, were removed
and lights installed within
the crown.*

Preface

November the 20th 1992 was the forty-fifth anniversary of the Queen's wedding to the Duke of Edinburgh. It was also the day of the fire which devastated the north-eastern corner of Windsor Castle. The restoration of the damage and the reinstatement of the contents of the rooms were originally scheduled to be complete by the spring of 1998. Towards the end of 1996, however, those in the Royal Household who were in charge of running the restoration project realized that, with a little squeezing of the programme and a little pressure being applied to the works in hand, it could all be finished earlier. The target on which they settled had a neat concordance about it: 20 November 1997, the fifth anniversary of the fire and the Golden Wedding of the Queen.

Everything to which the project had been devoted became heightened by that choice of completion date: a precision and even panache in execution; a certain air of theatricality which sets it apart from more mundane building projects; and a desire to do well by the Queen, who was after all the client, the person to whose use, finally, Windsor Castle is dedicated.

In large part because of those qualities – high standards aimed for by highly qualified people – writing this book has been an enormous stimulus and pleasure. It is, essentially, a picture of an organization confronted by a crisis and overcoming it. On such a large job, involving over 4000 men and women on many highly technical, sensitive and complex issues, the whole story could never have been told in a book of this length. Nevertheless, it is certainly not and was never designed to be anything resembling a company report. The bland laying out of a sequence of triumphs, easily arrived at in a glitch-free process without argument or agony, this it is not. There are wrinkles to the fabric here, difficult moments, disagreements, failures, mistakes and U-turns. Nevertheless, despite all of that, the dominant impression I am left with, as a complete outsider both to the building industry and to the Royal Household, is of something extraordinarily well done, with a systematic rigour and dedication towards clearly identified ends of rare quality.

A book like this is inevitably an exercise in parasitism. It takes whatever life it has from those it describes. A full list of acknowledgements can be found at the back, but there are four people I would like to thank here for the assiduous care they have taken in guiding me though the interlocking labyrinths of the Castle itself, the restoration project and the task of describing it with clarity. Michael Peat, at first Director of the Royal Household Property Section and then Keeper of the Privy Purse; Hugh Roberts, first Deputy Surveyor of the Queen's Works of Art and then Director of the Royal Collection; Chris Watson, Project Manager for Gardiner and Theobald Management Services at Windsor itself; and John Thorneycroft, Head of the Government Historic Buildings Advisory Unit at English Heritage: these four have ushered me carefully through the process and, but for that service, which has taken many hours of their time, this book would not be half what it is.

John Thorneycroft, in particular, played a crucial part in the first chapter, which describes the fire. He interviewed participants, established the sequence of events and wrote an account of it on which I have drawn so heavily that the text of the chapter as it stands is in effect a collaborative effort between the two of us. I am immensely grateful to him.

Finally, I would like to thank my wife Sarah Raven, to whom this book is dedicated, and who knows how much I love and owe to her.

ADAM NICOLSON

Contents

1 The Fire

Windsor Castle lies roughly east–west along its chalk hill above the river Thames. It is divided into three distinct parts. In the centre, visible from many miles away as the highest point of the famous silhouette, is the Round Tower, an early nineteenth-century romantic adaptation of an earlier keep, raised on the mound which William the Conqueror first built here soon after the Conquest.

On each side of that central boss is a large enclosure or ward, looping out from the Round Tower like the two halves of a slightly bowed figure of eight. To the west is the Lower Ward, dominated by St George's Chapel and its precincts. This lower half of the Castle, which is nearer the town of Windsor whose houses used to lap up against its walls, has always been, at least since the late twelfth century, the more open and more accessible part.

On the other side of the Round Tower, to the east of it, through a narrow gateway in which the Constable and Governor of the Castle now lives, is the Upper Ward. The atmosphere here is quite different. If the Lower Ward has a sort of urban busyness about it, almost like the extended piazza of an Italian hill town, the Upper Ward has an air of removal and profound quiet. There is none of the toing and froing between the offices, houses and shops that you find lower down.

From the windows of the Upper Ward you look out over gardens and what still might be mistaken for the open country of the Home Park. This end of the Castle has always been the more removed from public gaze. Here, again from the twelfth century onwards, the Kings and Queens of England have had their private apartments. A palace within a castle has for many centuries existed in the north-east corner of the

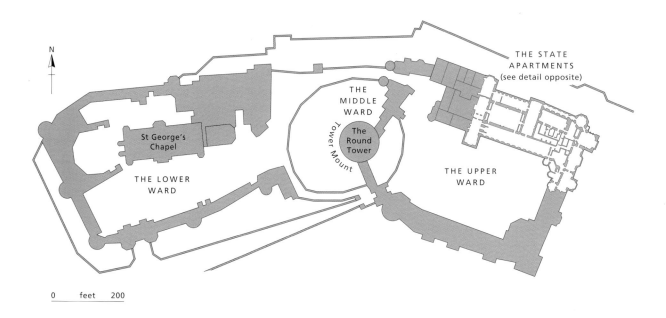

N

THE STATE
APARTMENTS
(see detail opposite)

THE
MIDDLE
WARD

The
Round
Tower

Tower Mount

St George's
Chapel

THE LOWER
WARD

THE UPPER
WARD

0   feet   200

ward. It is there that most care has been taken and most expense devoted to the creation of beautiful rooms with rich and comfortable inter-iors. Edward III in the fourteenth century, Charles II in the seventeenth and George IV in the early nineteenth all made of this north-eastern corner the finest series of rooms in the country at the time.

This palace within a castle has been occupied by the Royal Family for at least 800 years. In that way, Windsor Castle, and particularly this corner of it, is more than merely a symbol of the Crown's immense depth of continuity; these buildings are the physical embodiment of it. In many ways, nowhere in the country is richer, either historically or symbolically. Chance had it that it was precisely here, in this corner of the Upper Ward, that the disastrous fire of 20 November 1992 broke out.

It was a Friday. For over four years, since June 1988, the Upper Ward had been subjected to a comprehensive works programme, in which the wiring and the heating were being replaced. This project, known as Kingsbury, had been working its way around the Upper Ward, disrupting life in one section after another. It was necessary. The Castle had last been rewired in the fifties and the system was unreliable. Fire compartmentation, preventing the spread of any future blaze, and a new automatic fire-detection system were being installed at the same time, but no sprinklers, as it was calculated that the damage to important historic interiors which the installation of sprinklers would involve, let alone what they might do if they went off by mistake, would not be worth the reduction in fire risk which they would bring. The fire of 1992 did not in any way alter this judgement.

The Kingsbury work had already travelled along the south and east sides of the Upper Ward. It had been concentrated in the north-eastern corner since the middle of 1991. On 20 November 1992 most of the rooms there were due for completion in a couple of weeks. The State Apartments on the principal floor, the staff accommodation in the towers above them and the service rooms on the ground floor below were all virtually finished. The new automatic fire-detection system would have been in operation ten days later. On the day of the fire it was not yet working.

The Kingsbury works involved partial dismantling of the rooms they affected. Everything had to be taken out of these rooms and a special store in the California Gardens in the Home Park had been built to house the furniture and works of art while the job was being done. It was a rolling programme. As Kingsbury moved on, works of art from the completed rooms were moved back in from store and those from the

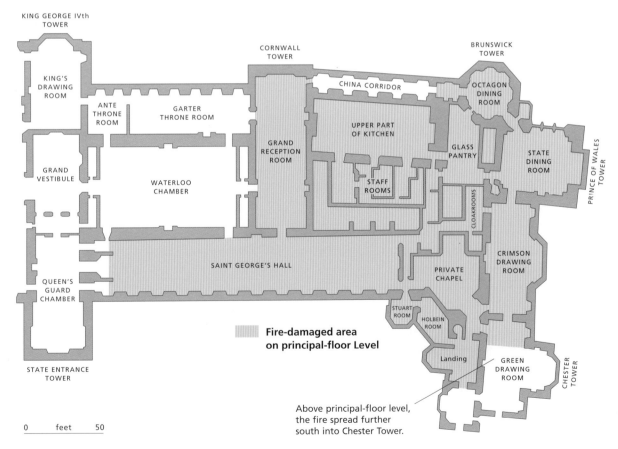

rooms which were now being rewired and had to be decanted took their place.

This emptying and refilling of rooms was a complex, highly phased process, so that side by side you found rooms that had been rewired and refurnished with those which had yet to be touched. In mid-November 1992, on the north side of the Upper Ward, the Private Chapel and the Grand Reception Room had been finished, while work on St George's Hall was just about to begin.

The Private Chapel, which the fire utterly destroyed, was at the north-east corner of the Upper Ward, on the first-floor level, the piano nobile. Surrounding it on the same level are the other State Apartments. The Private Chapel occupied a strategic position. To the west was St George's Hall, the Grand Reception Room, Waterloo Chamber and the other State Apartments running along the range towards the Royal Library. To the north of it was the complex labyrinth of offices, service rooms and food-preparation areas flanking the Great Kitchen. To the east was the great sequence of George IV drawing rooms, leading to the State and Octagon Dining Rooms in the north-eastern corner of the Castle. Further to the south lay the Queen's Private Apartments, connected to the chapel by the Grand Corridor which houses one of the greatest collections of paintings, furniture and sculpture in the world.

Because of its key position, the Private Chapel had been handed back early by Wallis's, the contractors working on the Kingsbury project, so that the Royal Collection could use it as a 'decant', a place to inspect and store paintings which had been removed from the rooms that were next due for rewiring.

On the day before the fire, eleven huge pictures of British monarchs lining St George's Hall, with Lelys and Knellers among them, had been taken down, dusted off and placed in the Holbein Room next to the Private Chapel. They were to be wrapped there before being shipped off to the California Store. Some twenty-four other, mostly very large, pictures remained in the Private Chapel, stacked against self-supporting A-frames that stood on the chapel floor. Some of the pictures, including a couple of oversize paintings by Benjamin West – portraits of George III's sons – had been there since 30 July, when they had been removed from the landing on the Equerries' Staircase, just south of the Chapel.

These Benjamin Wests were leant against the wall on either side of the Sanctuary, an alcove in the north wall of the Chapel which contained the altar and which was screened off by a pair of heavy white and gold-coloured curtains about nineteen feet tall. The curtains had been

The Private Chapel was designed by Edward Blore in the 1840s and painted and gilded by Sir Hugh Casson in 1976. This is where the fire began. On 20 November 1992, as usual, the curtains in front of the altar were drawn and the fire may well have been started by a spotlight behind them overheating the fabric. Compare this scene with the photograph on page 37.

closed for months, during which time the Private Chapel had at least been in occasional use.

Little natural light, at least during the dimmer days of winter, came into that chapel and anyone who used the room would have turned on the electric lights. Since 1976, when the room was refurbished, they had been operated from more than one bank of light switches, where the switches were arranged in four ranks of three. The switches were not labelled and so it was the natural habit of anyone wanting to use the room to turn them all on.

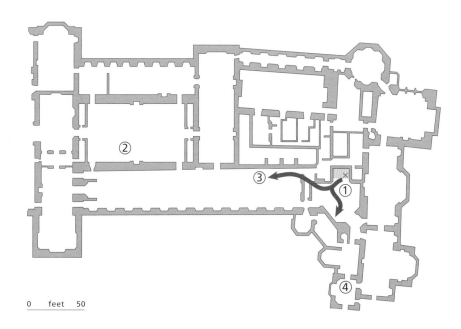

0   feet   50

c. 11.15 am

① c. 11.15 am Fire in Sanctuary of Private Chapel.
② 11.20 am Workman on roof of Waterloo Chamber spots smoke from vents in roof of
③ St George's Hall.
④ 11.30 am Telephone used to raise alarm.

×   Spotlight behind curtain in Sanctuary

◄   Movement of fire at high levels in roof voids

Two of those twelve switches operated spotlights in the altar alcove, one on either side, about eleven feet above the floor. Those spotlights, which were fitted with mirror-backed tungsten bulbs, were intended to throw light on the altar when it was needed for Easter services, attended by the royal family and members of the Household. They were meant to point away from the curtains and towards the altar.

Various suggestions have been made about the part these spotlights played in causing the fire, although none of the suggestions precisely fits the facts. It was conjectured, in the official report later made by Sir Alan Bailey and others to the Secretary of State for National Heritage, that 'one of [the large Benjamin West pictures] may have leaned against the curtain pushing it slightly closer to the spotlight. The curtains were so close to the spotlight track (not more than a few centimetres) that only a small movement of bulb or curtain would have brought the two into contact, creating the conditions for a smouldering fire.'

Although this is is a perfectly possible explanation, conservators employed by the Royal Collection continue to maintain that it is unlikely. They would not dream of allowing valuable paintings to be left in any way touching a curtain. More importantly, by late November 1992, those paintings had been there for three and a half months during which the room had been occasionally used and the lights turned on without any disaster taking place. The room had been in full use the day before

and the Benjamin Wests had not been touched during that day nor on the day of the fire itself.

A cumulative effect might well have occurred. Perhaps on 19 and 20 November 1992 these lights were on for longer and more continuously than before. It may be that the spotlights, on for that unusual length of time, gradually overheated the back of the curtains in the altar recess to the point where the heat finally ignited them. There may well be no need for the extra factor of an intruding picture frame to be added to the explanation. All that can safely be said is that it will never be known precisely why one of those spotlights ignited the curtains at the time and on the day it did.

On that Friday morning the picture specialists had put their coats and bags down in the Private Chapel when they had arrived at about nine before starting work. The lights had been turned on as usual. There were builders in St George's Hall, pulling up the first of the floorboards and removing one or two sections of panelling as the first investigative moves of that phase of the Kingsbury works. There was still a large picture to get down from high off the wall in the Queen's Guard Chamber and they had arranged for three fine art handlers to be with them to do the lifting.

After working with the paintings for about an hour and a half, two of the picture specialists, Charles Noble and Cliona Bacon, went to have coffee in the Library Coffee Room. By about 11.10 they had returned to the Private Chapel where Viola Pemberton-Pigott, Senior Paintings Conservator for the Royal Collection, was inspecting one of the St George's Hall pictures, a large Mytens of Charles I. It needed a new frame and the three of them began to measure the painting and discuss what the new frame should be like. After about a quarter of an hour, at about 11.26, Charles Noble said, 'Can you smell burning?' As Cliona Bacon remembers, 'We all looked at each other and looked around the place. And I thought, Oh my God, probably some of my hair … because we had a lamp on.'

In the middle of the room they had a tungsten photographic lamp on a tripod, to provide the sort of illumination needed to look carefully at paintings. But there was nothing touching the lamp, and Cliona Bacon joked that 'it must be somebody's lunch'.

They went back to examining the Mytens for perhaps two or three minutes. The time was now about 11.28. Viola Pemberton-Pigott looked up from their work and noticed that in the beam of their light there was a large number of dust particles from the work going on in St

The portrait by Benjamin West of George, Prince of Wales, and Frederick, Duke of York, was stored in the Private Chapel as the fire began and was hurried out of there with its plastic bubble-wrap already alight.

The portrait by Daniel Mytens of Charles I, which usually hangs in St George's Hall, was being measured up for a new frame in the Private Chapel when the picture restorers spotted the first flames.

George's Hall and as she turned back from the lamp towards the painting, she shouted out, 'Oh my God! Look! Fire!'

At the extreme top right corner of the right-hand curtain in front of the altar alcove, she saw a triangle of flame, about six inches across the top and eighteen inches down the right-hand side. It was just flickering over the top of the curtains and spreading rapidly both sideways and downwards. As later experiments at the Department of the Environment's Fire Research Station showed, the small amount of flame she saw was probably only the outer edges of what was already a substantial fire burning across the whole width of the back of the curtain, whose very thickness had obscured the fire until now. Even before those flames had appeared, a plumber working on the roof had seen white smoke coming from the vents on the roof of St George's Hall, to the west of the Private Chapel. That was at about 11.20. By the time the flames were spotted by the picture specialists, the fire was already finding its way into the roof voids of the Castle.

Viola Pemberton-Pigott ran for the phone to raise the alarm. Charles Noble ran for the packers in a nearby room. Cliona Bacon ran for the workmen in St George's Hall. 'I screamed down the hall, "FIRE!" and nobody reacted. "FIRE!" They all looked at me. I shouted, "What shall I do?"'

The six or seven men in the Hall then came running towards her. Two of them grabbed extinguishers and tried to squirt them at the flames nineteen feet or so above them. The jets didn't reach. Steve Humphreys, one of the fine art handlers, tried to pull the curtains down but they would not come. Someone screamed, 'Get the paintings out!'

Meanwhile Viola Pemberton-Pigott had dialled the Castle's emergency number, 222. The operator answered after two rings and the alarm was given. Predetermined instructions now swung into place. The operator called the Police Lodge, the Guard Room, key figures in the salvage squad and the Fire Control Room in Windsor Castle's own fire station. The call to the fire station was logged there a few seconds before 11.35.

The Fire Control Room summoned its own fire engine, at that time two miles away in the Home Park, disposing of chemicals, and paged the Castle's men on personal pagers. The siren was activated throughout the Castle.

At 11.36 a call was put in from the Castle's Fire Control Room on a dedicated line to the Royal Berkshire Fire and Rescue Service Fire Control in Reading. In their Control Room a button which says simply

WINDSOR CASTLE flashed red. Marshall Smith, Chief Officer of the Castle Fire Brigade, came on the line: 'We've got a fire in the Private Chapel at Windsor Castle. Come to the Quadrangle as arranged.'

'Is this a fire alarm or an actual fire?' the Berkshire officer asked him.

'Fire has been reported in the Private Chapel,' Smith replied. 'Come to the Quadrangle as arranged.'

On the Berkshire officer's computer screen the predetermined response flashed up: 'Special Address One: 2 water-tender ladders, 1 water tender, 1 salvage pump, 1 hydraulic platform.' The stations at Windsor, Slough and Langley were automatically notified.

In the Private Chapel, it was clear that hand-held fire extinguishers could do nothing about the fire which was already running out of control. By the time Viola Pemberton-Pigott returned from raising the alarm on the telephone, which had taken no more than a minute or two, flames had spread twelve feet or more down the right-hand curtain and across the altar recess on to the left-hand curtain.

As she came into the Private Chapel and saw this horrifying sight in front of her, she glimpsed out of the corner of her eye a painter in the doorway to the Crimson Drawing Room still calmly painting the panelling as part of the final finish being applied to that room at the end of the Kingsbury works. She shouted 'FIRE!' at him and he and other workmen came to help with taking the paintings stacked in the Private Chapel out of the danger zone southwards into the Grand Corridor. About thirty-five paintings were saved in a desperately hurried removal from the Chapel. The fire seemed to be surrounding them. 'We all lifted things we didn't know we could possibly manage that day,' one of them remembers. The only loss in the Private Chapel was a large eighteenth-century frame in the manner of William Kent from which the canvas had already been removed. One of the Benjamin Wests which had been leaning next to the altar alcove caught fire as the burning curtain dropped on to its packaging. The hot plastic burned the hands of an electrician, Dean Lansdale, as he helped carry it to safety.

The last of the pictures were rescued in extraordinarily dangerous conditions. The picture specialists, painters, art handlers and electricians came back into the Chapel three or four times. As Cliona Bacon wrote the following week, 'The last time I entered, the fire was quite advanced and black smoke was very choking and pieces of burning cloth were raining down on our heads. Both curtains were ablaze and the heat was intense. The man behind me shouted "Get out, the ceiling's falling."' The Chapel was crowned by a glass lantern and they

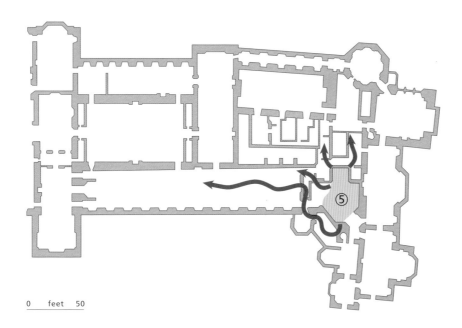

c. 11.45 am

⑤ c. 11.45 am Private Chapel alight. Fire migrating at high levels into Saint George's Hall, Vestry and north towards Kitchen Court.

◄━ Migration of fire at high levels

▨ Areas burnt or burning

could hear the glass cracking in the panes. The following day their faces would feel burned, as if by a hot sun.

As the workmen, picture specialists and removal men at last got out of the burning Chapel, where the curtains had fallen to the floor and begun to burn the packers' jiffy foam and foam pads as well as the carpet on the floor itself, they slammed the doors shut behind them. Beyond that fragile barrier, they could hear the fire roaring.

At about 11.40 the Windsor Castle Fire Brigade, under the command of Marshall Smith, reached the fire. Smoke was coming through the roof as they arrived at the Equerries' Entrance immediately below the Chapel. Marshall Smith recognized that this was already a major incident. A crew wearing breathing sets and with a hose already charged with water ran up to the first floor. The whole of the inside of the Private Chapel was red. Marshall Smith was appalled at what he saw. 'Beams were falling. They were coming down from above. The whole of that decorated ceiling was going. The fire was whirling round and it was coming down over our heads. There was lots of smoke and I couldn't distinguish everything but as you came from the Equerries' Staircase into the Chapel, the beams were falling which must mean it had been burning for quite a while.'

'I was panicking,' he says. 'We didn't have a strong enough pump. I requested "Where the bloody hell is Berkshire?" I put it in my bluntest.

I had to. They hadn't arrived. They had bigger pumps. I knew we didn't have a big enough pump. I knew that straight off.'

The Windsor Castle Fire Brigade log says: '11.40 Enter the building with jets via the Equerries' Entrance. Whereabouts are Berkshire?'

Smith knew that the fire engine from the Windsor fire station should already have been there. Its expected response time was two minutes. But that morning it was out in South Ascot conducting familiarization exercises. The fire engine based in Windsor didn't arrive until 11.55, nineteen minutes after Berkshire had first been alerted.

Almost certainly that delay had no effect on the progress of the fire. Within two minutes of the alarm being sounded, the fire had already broken through the roof of the Private Chapel and as David Plunkett, Clerk of Works at Windsor, saw from a tower on the other side of the building 'clean flames were burning in the open air'. As the first fire engines from Slough made their way across the Thames, a tall plume of grey-black smoke was already climbing in a steady diagonal above the Castle, blown by the south-west wind.

As the first fire engine from Slough came through the Castle gate at 11.44, its commander radioed Fire Control in Reading: 'Windsor Castle: make pumps 10.' As soon as that call for ten fire engines to attend a fire is received by the Control Room, either the Deputy Chief or the Assistant Chief of the fire brigade has to take control. It is the mark of a major disaster in progress. David Harper, Deputy Chief of Berkshire at the time, was at a conference the other end of the county when he got the message.

'Make pumps 10,' the Control Officer said.

Harper said 'What, Windsor Castle?'

'Yes.'

'You're joking.'

'I'm not joking. It's in the Upper Ward.'

Harper left immediately but was unable to arrive until about one o'clock that afternoon. Until then the fire was in the hands of Lynn Ashfield, Operations Commander of the brigade. As soon as Ashfield arrived at about 11.50, it was clear that a very large number of firefighters was required. Gradually the number of pumps requested, and the support systems to sustain their fight against the fire, was increased: make pumps 15 at 11.56; Breathing Apparatus Support Team and Air Cylinder Support Team at 12.03. 'Make pumps 20,' Ashfield requested at 12.12.

Around the streets of Windsor, with the Christmas decorations already strung between the buildings, people stood in tears as the dirty thunderclouds of black and brown smoke rose from the far end of the Castle. Fire engine after fire engine screamed past the the statue of Queen Victoria and up Castle Hill. Two hundred bewildered tourists were shepherded out of the precincts. Under the grey winter sky, plane-loads of visitors constantly passing low overhead were being treated to an extraordinary spectacle of destruction. On landing, many of them hurried to Windsor, swelling the traffic chaos in and around the town.

The press was already in overdrive. Calls had been coming into the Buckingham Palace Press Office since 11.40, little more than ten minutes after the fire was discovered. Soon the cars and vans of reporters and news teams were to clamp the centre of Windsor into gridlock. On every bridge across the M4 long lenses focused on the sight of the Castle on fire. Donald Insall, the architect, remembers that afternoon, even from his car, 'the dreadful stench of burning oak and scorched upholstery, sweeping in thin, acrid wreaths across the London motorway'.

Before 12 o'clock the news was around the world. Even as residents of the Castle were learning about the fire themselves, they were being rung up by worried relatives in Australia, South Africa, Hong Kong and the United States, who had heard what was happening on radio or TV.

To understand the progress of the fire, even now, is extremely difficult. Its precise development will in fact never be known. Too much occurred in areas that became too dangerous to enter. Nevertheless, certain aspects are more than clear. As Major Jim Eastwood, Superintendent of Windsor Castle, has said, 'Fire is like an animal, looking for the easiest way to go. You have to think of it as a hungry animal. But this beast is different from others: the more you feed it, the hungrier it becomes.' By the time the fire brigade had begun to build up its resources, Major East-wood's consuming beast had already been let loose for too long. It had escaped and would not be caged again for many hours.

The very reasons that had made the Private Chapel such a convenient place for the picture specialists of the Royal Collection also meant that a fire starting there had its own terrifying strategic possibilities. Because, in particular, the roof void of the Chapel was connected to the roof voids of adjoining areas and to spaces behind panelling and between floors in all directions, the fire had the chance of moving in all ways at once.

This is almost precisely what it did. The only direction in which it made virtually no progress was southwards. To the north, east and west, on up to six floors, prowling around this large and complex build-

In the early afternoon, the fire is burning at high level, in staff rooms above the Green Drawing Room.

ing over the next fifteen hours or so, it devastated a total of 115 rooms, an area of damage five times what had been destroyed at Hampton Court in 1986 and perhaps twenty times the total area of Uppark, the National Trust house in Sussex that was famously devastated by fire in 1989. It had done about £35 million of damage. There were four reasons it was not any more: most of the rooms it burned had no furniture or works of art in them, because they had been cleared for the Kingsbury rewiring project; some fire compartmentation had been installed as part of Kingsbury, which had got as far as the south of the Private Chapel and helped stop the fire spreading south; the salvage operation in those rooms that were furnished was a model of its kind; and the fire brigade managed to hold the fire where it did.

There were essentially three phases to the fire brigade's strategy: the initial attack; the withdrawal to defensible boundaries; and the final extinction.

The first crews that arrived went into the heart of the building, pouring water, at 1000 litres a minute from each of six and then ten jets into the Private Chapel itself, up at the roof of St George's Hall from the floor of the Hall and from aerial platforms parked in the Quadrangle.

None of this was able to contain the fire. It had taken hold in the enormous roof void of St George's Hall, 180 feet long and six feet high at the apex. By about 12.30 fire had travelled the entire length of this space and was beginning to break through the armorial plaster ceiling into the room below. The mid-nineteenth-century Father Willis organ which formed the screen between St George's Hall and the Private Chapel had already disappeared in flame. It was difficult to believe that this enormous instrument with all its zinc pipework had been vaporized.

John Coleman, one of the architects responsible over many years for the Kingsbury project, looked into the Hall, 'to see the fire rolling along the ceiling, from one end to the other, high up along the tops of the windows, in long rolling flames . . . I was very, very upset. It was shattering, absolutely numbing.'

Meanwhile, the fire had already travelled north from the Chapel, through the roof of the Vestry and into the confusing web of the Kitchen Courtyard, filled with a mass of interlocked and muddled buildings. Fire teams were in there, and in the Great Kitchen, but the fire was licking and searching all around them, in ways they could neither suspect nor predict. By about one o'clock, it had become clear that this way of attacking the fire was inherently hazardous and putting fire crews in constant danger of being outflanked by flames that had travelled quickly through hidden voids and passages, suddenly erupting into rooms and corridors, cutting them off.

Soon after one o'clock, when the Deputy Chief David Harper took over the firefight, crews were pulled back from the burning areas. Those who had been cutting holes in the lead, outer skin of St George's Hall roof, in order to vent the flames upwards, were reluctant to leave their task. It was fortunate they did. Within twenty minutes of their withdrawal from that roof, it began to collapse in a chaotic burning mass on to the floor of the hall sixty feet below them. The lead of the roofs and windows had started to run like molten wax.

While the firefighters' focus had largely been on the area of the fire itself and on a desperate attempt to contain it near its source, another vast and parallel operation had been under way since the first siren had sounded in the middle of the morning.

There was no guarantee, as long as the fire was uncontained, that it would stop anywhere. The Berkshire Fire Brigade commanders had advised complete evacuation of the contents of the Upper Ward. If the fire spread southwards into the Queen's Private Apartments, or westwards into the still furnished state rooms and then on into the Royal Library and Print Room, the damage to works of art could easily have amounted to £500 million or more.

Major Eastwood, the Castle Superintendent and Fire Officer, was in the Lord Chamberlain's Lower Stores at the time the siren first sounded. The Duke of York was asking him what furniture might be available for his house. 'As soon as the alarm went,' Major Eastwood remembers, 'I said, "I'm off." We went up together and could see black smoke coming out above the Equerries' Entrance. It was frightening.'

As part of the pre-arranged response to the fire, a 25-strong salvage squad was contacted as soon as the first emergency call had been made. They were to rendezvous with Major Eastwood in the centre of the Upper Ward Quadrangle. Many of them were there to meet him. Eastwood realized within a few minutes that both the eastern side of the Quadrangle, which housed the Private Apartments, and the western end of the northern side, with the State Apartments and the Library, were in equal danger. The sheer scale of the salvage that was required was obviously beyond the capacities of his 25-man squad. 'I told my secretary to get hold of every removal man and his van she could. Six months earlier, I had been reading a book about Queen Victoria and it had mentioned the fire in the Castle that occurred in 1853. It was almost in the same place as this one, in the Prince of Wales Tower, and it said

there, "The very first thing the Superintendent did was get the army in."
Of course, I thought, what couldn't I do with a load of soldiers? Get the
cavalry in.'

Major Eastwood, a Grenadier to his bones, got in touch with the
Commanding Officer at Combermere Barracks in Windsor and ordered
up 'as many vehicles, as many soldiers in Bedford vehicles as he'd got.
That's something I'm used to, with a commanding officer, his second-
in-command, his company commanders, his platoon commanders. So
they turned up. "Here we are. What do you want us to do?"

'I said, "You start there, emptying that corridor. Top priority. Don't
let's stop."' By then the removal men had started to arrive and with lorries parked at the entrances, the contents of the Grand Corridor and
then the Private Apartments themselves were decanted first on to the
grass and then on to lorries, which took these precious things first to the
California Store in the Home Park and then, as that filled up, to the Riding School in the Mews. It was an extraordinary sight, the great collection of ebony and ormolu, of Boulle and pietra dura, of scagliola and
bronze and marble being manhandled by the Life Guards and construction workers from the Kingsbury project in ways that would normally have horrified the staff of the Royal Collection. Sir Geoffrey de
Bellaigue, Director of the Royal Collection, saw one Life Guard walk
manfully up to a large marble bust, wrap his arms around it, and begin
to stride off down the corridor before totally collapsing under the
unsuspected weight.

Canalettos, Zoffanys, Zuccarellis, the great Riesener jewel cabinet
for the Comtesse de Provence, busts of Germanic sovereigns, Pugin
chairs, Sèvres porcelain bowls and figures, the wonderful set of Gainsborough portraits of George III and his family, all came rolling on to the
Quadrangle lawn. Inside the rooms and corridors, it looked as disorga-
nized as a country sale, with the constant shrieking whine of the alarms
echoing through rooms where electric torches were the only illumination. One of the greatest pieces of luck was the absence of rain on that
particular day, and outside on the grass you might have mistaken it for
an elaborate picnic, as these enriched exotica found themselves for the
first time in their lives standing about on an open lawn. A glance at the
north side of the Quadrangle would have convinced you otherwise. The
long range of windows in St George's Hall glowed orange and red, while
smoke and flame bubbled and flicked above them.

Almost nothing was broken and nothing went missing. Unknown
to many of the people there, the Thames Valley police had thrown a

cordon around the entire Castle, in case anyone imagined this might be an opportunity for looting, but nothing of the kind occurred. The only things that went astray were a pair of Sèvres biscuit porcelain busts of Louis XVI and Marie Antoinette which usually stand in the Queen's dressing room. The following morning, a little shamefacedly, one of the removal men returned with them to the Castle, saying he had failed to notice them in the dark of the evening before, lurking among the blankets in the far corner of his van.

At the other end of the Quadrangle, quantities of material, including the vast Lawrences from the Waterloo Chamber, Rubenses and van Dycks, much of it marshalled with great enthusiasm by the Duke of York, was pouring out of the State Entrance and into yet more vans. The most dramatic of all was the vast Agra carpet rescued from the Waterloo Chamber by the men employed by Wallis's under Les Broome. This enormous, ungainly, magnificent and heavy thing was manoeuvred downstairs by the Wallis team and then handed over to the Life Guards for them to march to the Lord Chamberlain's Lower Stores.

The smoke was thick and black in the Grand Reception Room and firefighters in breathing apparatus were removing element after element of the enormously rich furnishing of that room, receiving instructions from members of the Royal Collection at the doorways. Incredibly, almost every single thing was rescued from the room in this way, including the incalculably valuable Gobelins tapestries which lined the walls. They were attached with Velcro and poppers and came bundling down with one sharp tug. The only things that were left were the recently restored bronze and crystal chandeliers and the vast Russian malachite urn in the window at the northern end. It had been a present to Queen Victoria from Tsar Nicholas I in 1841, was taller than a man, with a mouth almost five feet wide, and weighed two tons. In these circumstances it was immovable.

Yet another evacuation process was occurring alongside these other two. Oliver Everett, the Royal Librarian, had come up to Major Eastwood in the middle of the Quadrangle and said, 'Jim, what do we do now?'

Major Eastwood turned to him and said, 'Oliver, how long would it take to evacuate the Library?'

Everett said it would take three hours.

Major Eastwood said, 'You've got an hour before it hits there if it gets through.'

The Library and the Print Room hold some of the most valuable things in the world, including the great collection of Leonardo and

In the afternoon, smoke
continues to tower away
from above the Private
Chapel. Water is poured
into the building from
hoists by the Equerries'

Entrance and another
next to St George's Hall.
Tarpaulins are laid out on
the grass of the Quadrangle
as part of the salvage operation and timber track-

ways are laid to prevent
fire-engines sinking into
the grass. Removal lorries
queue for the contents of
the Castle.

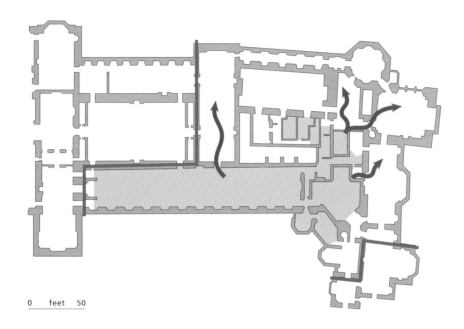

c. 1.00 pm

▦ Rooms alight at 1pm

◄ Migration of fire at high levels 1–1.30pm

— Boundaries to fire-ground established by 1pm at all levels

0   feet   50

other Old Master drawings, medals, coins, miniatures and illuminated manuscripts. All of it came out.

Joanna Palmer, the wife of General Sir Patrick Palmer, the Constable and Governor of the Castle and in 1992 recently retired as Commander-in-Chief Allied Forces Northern Europe, was deeply involved in the Library salvage and her diary for the day describes the operation:

Finally the cry came – 'Clear the Print Room.' It was what the Library Staff gathered around had been waiting for and there was immediate ACTION. I ran after them into the Print Room and within seconds one of the girls who works there [it was Henrietta Ryan, Deputy Curator of the Print Room] had found the 'Salvage List', which reads something like A 1–6, B 7 & 8, C17–19. These are the catalogue numbers clearly printed on the outside of the red boxes – each approximately 3 feet by 2 feet by 3 inches – and containing any number of drawings. The point of the salvage list is to get out the most valuable drawings (Leonardo da Vinci, Holbein etc.) first and under any conditions. As she read the catalogue numbers, she pulled a box off the shelf and passed it to someone who ran and passed it to me who ran and passed it to Cpl Cooke [a member of the Palmers' staff] and before we knew it there was a human chain – but we were doing an awful lot of running and there was certainly a sense of urgency in the air if not actual panic.

A jumble of furniture and pictures evacuated from the State Apartments emerges into Engine Court before it is transferred into waiting removal vans.

The Persian carpet from the King's Drawing Room needed six men to carry it.

The bust by Louis-François Roubiliac of Handel, usually in the Queen's Presence Chamber, sits (bottom right) on the tarmac of Engine Court. Italian baroque torchères (centre) from the King's Drawing Room are partly obscured by a single coat-hanger. In the background on the left, a William III silver mirror sits precariously on its matching table.

On Lady Palmer's initiative, the contents of the Print Room and then of the Library itself were directed into her own house in the Norman Tower, clear of any danger. The word came that every single thing had to be decanted from both the Library and the Print Room. Three chains of people began to siphon all this material into the Palmers' house. Her diary continues:

It was an amazing sight – this line of people passing three or four books at a time – the Dean to an electrician to the elderly wife of a Military Knight to a Keeper (they brought a lot of people in from the Great Park) to a Gurkha (they were on Guard at the time) to a Lay Clerk to a painter to a Military Knight to a Minor Canon to one of the girls who works in the shop to a 'wag' who announced what he was passing on ('here's Germany … a bit of history … was it Egypt, you wanted Pete? … sorry … here's something on "sand", will that do? … oh, nice portrait of Cleopatra coming up … ')

Gaiety was not the mood of the moment at the firefight. It is an inevitable fact that, because of the distances involved, the build-up of firefighting crews will, as time goes by, slow down. The more you want, the further they will have to come and the longer they will take to get there. They had summoned all they could. By 1.03 in the afternoon, it was 'Make pumps 25'. An hour and a half later, the battery of fire-fighting equipment had reached its maximum: 36 pumps, 200 men, 25 officers controlling them, using 31 water jets on the fire, three of them from high-rise hydraulic platforms. Fire engines and crews had come from London, Surrey, Hampshire, Wiltshire, Oxfordshire and Buck-inghamshire, as well as every single fire appliance in Berkshire. Never-theless, it was clear to both Lynn Ashfield and David Harper, the two senior Berkshire commanders, that some difficult choices had to be made. There were more things to do, and more fires to fight, than men to do them.

Ashfield had already divided the fire ground, as firefighters call it, into four sectors, two in the Quadrangle, one on the northern side of the building and one on the roof. Each sector had its own commander and they were, at least in theory, in constant communication with each other on the eight-channel fire-ground radios. In fact, the sheer noise of alarms and water pumps and of the fire itself at times made it difficult to hear what was being said.

By about one o'clock, as the salvage operation was in full swing, Harper and Ashfield had made their decision. Because of the danger, the scale of the fire, the depth of the building in plan and the limited resources they had, the decision was taken to withdraw to defensible boundaries and to concentrate everything they could on not allowing the fire to get past those lines. As Ashfield puts it: 'It had to be "For goodness sake, define it and then push it in." Of course this meant that one area may indeed have been denuded of firefighting resources at one time or another, but that would only have been because there was a greater need elsewhere. Any fireman will tell you that their first instinct is to draw the line and then push it to the extreme ends.' It was in many ways a courageous decision, involving a recognition that large parts of Windsor Castle had to be allowed to burn if the rest of it were to be saved.

At the western end, the line they chose ran along the west of St George's Hall, around the Waterloo Chamber and along the west side of the Grand Reception Room. The ceiling of that room was still intact when this decision was made, but the fire had already migrated into the roof void above it. Even then, the collapse of the Grand Reception Room ceiling was an inevitability.

Unknown to the fire commanders at the time, the line they had chosen was particularly strong. The Waterloo Chamber had been built in 1831 inside what until then had been an open courtyard, ringed by immensely thick, largely medieval walls. On each floor there were one or two openings through that barrier, at each of which a fire crew was positioned, prepared to hold it against anything the fire might offer.

At the other end of the fire-ground, the situation was nothing like as simple. The disposition of many small rooms on many floors was complex. The decision was taken to destroy large sections of the ornate plasterwork in both the Crimson and the Green Drawing Rooms and in the rooms above them. Walls and ceilings were stripped so that any fire that came through there could be seen as it arrived and stopped before it took hold. As they hacked the plaster down, smoke was already travelling through the voids, not fire but the precursor of fire. As yet, there was no flame.

This was the second crucial firebreak and up to ten fire crews were permanently deployed at this line, two on each floor and on the roof pouring out a curtain of water the full height and width of the building. Large holes were cut in the roof here too for the same reason. Below them, at the northern end of the Grand Corridor, Wallis's men, under instructions from Major Eastwood, erected a barrier of fireproof material to stop the fire bursting into the corridor, down which it would have travelled in a fireball.

The firefighting tactics were not, even at this stage, purely passive. A

London crew entered the Crimson Drawing Room, well within the fire area, to hose a localized fire spot. At that moment, with fire already well alight on the floor above, large pieces of plaster fell from the ceiling, breaking one of the firemen's legs. The crew was immediately withdrawn and the man sent to hospital.

At about 2.20, deep in the warren of the ground-floor rooms, a crew embarked on an unauthorized entry. The Sector Commander, fearing he might have lost men in a roof collapse that occurred at the same time and unable to account for everyone, ordered a total evacuation of the fire-ground by all men. Within eight minutes of the whistle signal being given, the men were found, given a severe reprimand and the firefight resumed. A second evacuation was to occur later in the evening when a crew wearing breathing apparatus went missing. Again within eight minutes it was established that they had reported to the wrong control point. Each time the crews were withdrawn, the fire seemed to grow in intensity.

By about three o'clock the Queen had arrived from London. After being told of the overall situation and going to the Waterloo Chamber from where she could see what had happened in St George's Hall, she went with Sir Geoffrey de Bellaigue to sort out her belongings in her own rooms in the south-eastern corner of the ward. Her shock and distress were quite apparent to all who saw her. There were many people in the Quadrangle that afternoon who simply wept at what confronted them.

By 3.30 that afternoon the Deputy Chief Fire Officer David Harper was content that the fire was now surrounded. The firebreaks were holding and the beast had been caged. A quarter of an hour later, when about 250 press people had been gathered on the mound beneath the Round Tower, Harper was to tell them, after the Duke of York had given them his briefing, 'The fire is now controlled. You must remember that there is a difference between controlled and extinguished. It isn't going anywhere. What you are seeing is as bad as it is going to get. It won't spread; it might consume where it is at the moment.'

There was elation, among the firefighters anyway. It was what they call 'a good stop'. They had shut the fire within the boundaries they had drawn and were confident that those boundaries would not now come under threat.

Others, even officers from other fire brigades under Berkshire's temporary command, were not quite so content. Why not attack the fire now from the far side? Surely with the capacity to pour 22,000 litres

At about three o'clock the Queen arrives from London, and Prince Andrew, who had been there since the first minutes of the fire, guides her through a Quadrangle busy with the evacuation from the Upper Ward.

of water a minute on to the fire, they could make some inroads into the fire in the north-east corner, at the Brunswick and Prince of Wales Towers?

Vigorous discussions were held on this point but the original Berkshire policy was maintained. The chance of a crew being surrounded and cut off by a fire coming insidiously towards them was too great to risk. It was known in the middle of the afternoon that the fire would in the end vent itself through those towers and that would allow the firefighters to push in towards the north-east corner, coming from the south-west, behind the fire, pushing the fire before them.

There can be no doubt about the passion and commitment of the men and women involved. There were 200 firefighters there from seven brigades. Eighty of them wore breathing apparatus. Each cylinder lasts forty-five minutes and some went in six or seven times in succession on new cylinders. That would represent more than five hours of intensely hot, sweaty and exhausting work. The sector commanders' experience was of crews refusing to be relieved until ordered to do so.

Nevertheless, as the winter night drew in, cold but not wet, and as the floodlights came on in the Upper Ward, the destruction continued. At about 6.30, with the daylight gone and filled with an overwhelming sense of helplessness and foreboding, Geoffrey Parnell – by coincidence it was his last day as English Heritage Inspector of the Castle – left the frantic scenes of firefighting and salvage that filled the Upper Ward and made his way down through the building on to the North Terrace. Here, in strange contrast, there was an eerie atmosphere of complete emptiness and quiet. The Terrace was not strong enough to take the weight of fire engines, nor was the gate on to it from the Lower Ward big enough for them to pass through. From this side, it seemed almost as if the fire was in another building. Apart from the reflected glow of the fire on the clouds, no flames could be seen. Now and again, from deep within the towering mass of the State Apartments, came terrible hollow rending sounds as steel and timber crashed on to the floors below.

The climax of the fire seen from the North Terrace: the floors of the Brunswick Tower finally give way and the flames burst through the roof into the night sky. What looked like the ultimate catastrophe was in fact the moment when the intensity of the fire began to lessen. For the effect of this fire see the photograph on page 38.

A dull red sunset began to suffuse the many panes of the tall Gothic window of the Cornwall Tower; glancing to the unbroken greyness of the horizon, Parnell suddenly understood, with a shock, that this glow came from within. The fire was breaking through the magnificent rococo ceiling of the Grand Reception Room.

High above, firefighters could dimly be seen in the growing swirl of sparks and smoke, falling back as warning whistles blew the retreat, to regroup behind the parapets above the Waterloo Chamber. It was an unforgettable sight; in what seemed only a matter of minutes, the structure of the roof had collapsed, carrying with it almost the whole of the enormous and elaborate white and gold ceiling and reducing one of the most important interiors of the nineteenth century to ruins.

Along with the Waterloo Chamber, this was the one state room that had been completely refitted and furnished ready for opening to the public the following week. Less than an hour before, the Lord Chamberlain, Lord Airlie, had been in charge of the systematic removal of everything that could be salvaged. Now, from the terrace below, only the huge and immensely heavy malachite urn could clearly be seen, silhouetted against the flames.

Leaving the fire, Parnell walked back through the Lower Ward of the Castle, untouched by the fire, where lights shone out in the dusk from windows of deserted offices that were silent except for the frantic ringing of unanswered telephones, while fax after fax fell unheeded, as they had done for hours, from brimming trays.

In the early evening the Prince of Wales arrived, having driven down

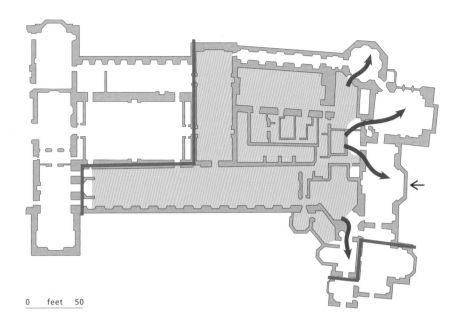

c. 6.30pm

▧ Burnt or burning
at 6.30pm

← Fire well established at
upper levels at 6.30pm

— Held boundaries to
fire-ground

← Bay window in danger
of collapse

0   feet   50

from Sandringham. 'It was appalling,' he says. 'The Quadrangle was covered in fire engines and people and hoses and everything else. St George's Hall was steaming and smouldering, the smoke billowing out and steam hanging over it. In one or two places, there was fire coming out of the windows. I went up on to the roof above the Clock Tower – a terrible view, a great gaping hole. It was shattering, awful.'

By then, the fire was making its way into the far north-eastern corner of the Castle. Some of the State Apartments there were surrounded by fire on all sides but had yet to burn. Soon after 6.30 Marshall Smith, the Castle fire chief, walked through the abandoned, threatened rooms in the company of Maurice Doyle, a Berkshire officer. As they crossed the Crimson Drawing Room, they could hear the roaring and crackling of the fire burning among the tightly packed mass of staff rooms immediately above them. In the nearby cloakrooms, jets of flame could be seen flaring incongruously from each basin waste after the inferno in the service rooms below had melted the old lead pipework.

To the north of the Crimson Drawing Room, in the still darkness of the State Dining Room, the scaffolding stood ready for the painters who were due to return on Monday morning to add their finishing touches to the ceiling. In that room were the two objects which had been so large that they had not been removed from the Kingsbury work area but had been carefully boxed up: the giant portrait by Sir William Beechey of

George III on horseback at a review and a Gothic rosewood sideboard designed by the young A. W. N. Pugin for George IV's great rebuilding of Windsor in the 1820s.

The Duke of York offered to go in and cut the Beechey from its frame but was advised against doing so. Both picture and sideboard were eventually consumed in the fire when it broke through from above perhaps at about 7 that evening.

The officers of the Fire Brigade always knew that the burning of the north-east corner of the Castle would be the final, violent and dramatic event. The more violent it was, in fact, the more effectively it would draw the fire from the rest of the fire-ground.

Few, however, were prepared for what happened to those two north-eastern towers at about eight o'clock in the evening. One by one the floors within them burned and collapsed, so that eventually the Brunswick Tower in particular became a massive hollow chimney through which the rage of the fire and all the pressure within it could be vented into the night sky.

First the Brunswick and then the Prince of Wales Tower, whose burning had been slowed by thick, nineteenth-century, supposedly fireproof floors, erupted like giant bunsen burners into the night. Both towers became Roman candles in which every window was a panel of flame and above which the fire roared half as high as the towers again into the night sky. At the foot of the Brunswick Tower, analysis afterwards of the vitrified surface of the bricks showed that the temperature there had reached 820° C (1508° F).

It was a horrifying Vesuvian spectacle. But for the firefighters, the eruption through the north-eastern towers was the signal to begin their move into the fire-ground. Cautiously at first, they began to push the fire before them, driving it north-eastwards through the wreck of the building, with a moving curtain of water and water vapour.

It was a slow and meticulous process. Many dangerous fires were still alight throughout the building. But the energy was going out of it and the fire's appetite had finally been sated. Only at 2.30 the next morning did David Harper feel able to leave the Castle, content that the crisis was over. He had been controlling it for thirteen and a half hours without a break. He felt exhilarated, the adrenalin still pumping around his body. 'I walked to my car,' he remembers, 'and I bent down to pull my fire boots off and I couldn't get them off. I was exhausted, I hadn't realized. I suddenly got cramp in my hamstrings. I hadn't realized what a long day it had been.'

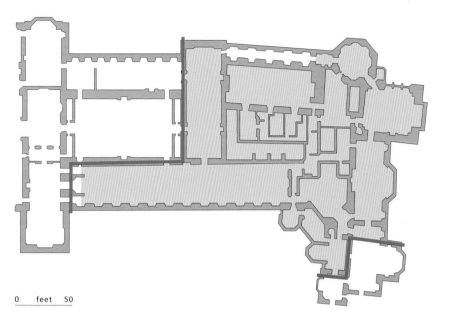

c. 8.30pm

▦ Areas of devastation
   by 8.30pm

▬ Held boundaries

0   feet   50

Behind him smoke and steam towered away north-eastwards under the glare of the arclights. A hundred firefighters were still there maintaining their vigilance on a fire that had burned for fifteen hours, destroying part of one of the great buildings of the world, at the rate of about £2.3 million an hour, or £38,000 for every single minute it had lasted. At least no one had died.

At home in London, in the small hours of the morning, Suresh Dhargalkar, the Royal Household's Superintending Architect, sat down at his desk and began typing the agenda for the next morning's meeting. '9 am. Action Committee,' he wrote. '1.0 Assessment of Structure. Make safe. Recording of Details. Report.' The road stretched a long way ahead.

From a hoist parked in the Quadrangle, the firemen attempt to douse the fire. Part of the problem in containing it was the sheer depth of the building – 140 feet from the Quadrangle to the North Terrace (see page 73). No water jets could cover that distance. Royal Berkshire commanders decided there was no option but to let the inner recesses of the fire burn themselves out.

2 The Aftermath

Overleaf: *Smoke still rises from the building on the morning after. Soot marks the openings in the Brunswick Tower where the flames had burnt through them.*

In the first light of Saturday morning the mist lay wrapped around the smoking hulk, filling the Quadrangle like a quilt. Smoke and steam were still rising from the open rooms. Firefighters were picking their way across the site, turning over smouldering timbers, hosing down embers that the light breeze was still fanning into life.

From the sky, the burnt area no longer seemed like rooms and corridors but had come in parts to resemble natural forms, crags bordering on canyons, a blackened landscape over which a bush fire had carelessly driven. The light seemed to sink into the blackened surfaces, so that even in the rooms that had now been exposed to the sky, the impression was of darkness. Those who ventured on to the site were tempted to use their torches even in the open air. Everywhere was the unique smell, familiar enough to those who had been at Uppark and Hampton Court, of an old house devastated by fire. It is a disturbingly sweet smell, almost caramelized, mixed with something that reminds you of burnt hair, perhaps from the singeing of cloth and carpet. Above that, dominating it, was the steamy, charred, chemical smell of water on hot wood.

The firefighters in their yellow helmets, dragging their red hoses behind them, were almost the only points of colour in what had been the most gorgeously and richly coloured apartments at Windsor. In places, fragments of what had been there survived. On the walls of the Crimson Drawing Room, the silk panels, held there by gilded fillets, remained in a room whose floor was a chaos of burnt timber and shattered plaster, fallen from above. The huge bay window, overlooking the East Terrace, had developed a crack an inch wide that ran the whole height of the building. The engineers, who had gone round to the East

Terrace as the fire was burning through the night, had seen what was happening. 'It was obviously in distress,' Clive Dawson says. 'You could see it moving. It was opening as you watched it. We thought it might well go. You can tell just by looking at these things. Once you've got an eye for them, you know when it doesn't look right.'

What had happened was quite simple. The Government's Property Services Agency had renewed the staff accommodation above the Crimson Drawing Room in the 1970s. As part of the general improvements they installed a new steel roof. The fire had burned long and hard in those staff rooms and the steel of the roof had expanded with the intense heat. On one side the steel trusses were anchored to the enormously thick medieval wall that bordered the Kitchen Court. That wall was utterly immobile and so the expansion in the metal could have had only one effect: pushing out the whole eastern face of the Crimson Drawing Room. The bay window was the weakest part; that is where the crack had developed and it worried the engineers. The entire façade of the room was now in danger of collapse.

Nevertheless, within it, the chandelier still hung there, broken and bedraggled, like a shot grouse poised in mid-air. A fire extinguisher stood poignantly and absurdly among the debris. High above it, the new steel roof still dangled from its bearings, its parts twisted but attached, and the purlins sagging between the trusses like draped steel swags.

Next to the Crimson Drawing Room, in the Green Drawing Room

In the drizzle of the following morning, Lynn Ashfield, Operations Commander for the Royal Berkshire Fire Brigade, accompanies the Queen across the Quadrangle to inspect the damage.

just to the south of it, the ceiling was still there. Meetings between members of the Household, the engineers and representatives of English Heritage were held beneath it on the sodden floor. No one was aware that the four levels of the Chester Tower that rose above it had all collapsed on top of each other during the fire. Hundreds of tons of debris, made heavier by a swimming pool of water poured in there by the Fire Brigade, was now resting directly on the ceiling. It could have come down at any moment.

Almost everywhere else that you looked on the principal floor, the elements were the same: the complete removal and incineration of whole sections of the building; the lingering of unexpected parts; the ever-present danger of collapse. In what had been the Private Chapel, where the fire had begun, almost nothing was left. The blind Gothic tracery panels and the reredos behind the altar were still where the architect Edward Blore had installed them in the 1840s when he converted George IV's band room into a chapel for Queen Victoria. Nothing else remained beyond the sodden, undulating field of ash and debris, thick with nails and broken glass that stretched from room to room underfoot. Above the Equerries' Entrance, a huge bath lay incongruously on that surface, where it had fallen through from the floor above.

In St George's Hall, at the eastern end, where the fire had been at its most furious, the steel framework for the huge Henry Willis organ was there, gaunt and bearing the marks of intense heat, but the whole body of the instrument, its zinc tubes and valves, the whole screen of which it had been a part and the doors through into the Private Chapel, had all vanished. What had been two rooms was now one.

In the body of the Hall, some of the roof had collapsed on to the floor and some of the trusses remained precariously in position. There were stiffened puddles of lead among the ash, where it had dripped from the burning roof. A builder's ladder leant askew against the wall where it had been placed the morning before. In the centre of the room, with timber and ash lapping up against them, stood a neat row of stone plinths on which the marble busts of sovereigns had once sat. On Friday the builders had moved them away from the panelled walls so they could begin their first investigations of how to install the new wiring.

Room by room, members of the Household and of the Kingsbury design team poked among the ruins. It was all more dangerous than they realized but still, in the numbed shock of what had happened, some consolation was to be had. Most of the rococo plaster ceiling had collapsed in the Grand Reception Room but one of the chandeliers, so

The blind tracery panels and north window of Blore's Private Chapel survived the fire but scarcely resemble their condition before it (see page 7).

The iron girders of Wyatville's Brunswick Tower were all that survived the fire, which in this part of the building was found, by analysis of its effects on the bricks, to have reached temperatures approaching 820°C (1508° F). For the scene at the foot of the tower see page 42.

recently restored, remained hanging in situ. Much of the deep cove of the ceiling was still there with its decoration intact. In the window embrasure, the giant Russian malachite urn looked, at first sight, untouched but closer inspection revealed that a strange and unforeseeable sort of damage had occurred. The malachite is no more than a thin veneer on a body that is carved from a limestone block. In the heat of the fire, these two layers had remained miraculously bonded together. Deep in the night, however, as the firefighters had made their way into the heart of the building, pushing the fire before them, hosing down everything they came to, it was inevitable that cold water would fall on to the great malachite urn. The effect was instantaneous: as the malachite skin received the sudden shock of cold water, and while the limestone body behind it remained hot, the glue could no longer hold the two together and the malachite veneer, particularly around the upper rim, shattered explosively off the surface of the vase, jumping like popcorn into the surrounding room. This morning you could see tiny jewel-flakes of it glittering among the ash.

In the Great Kitchen, much of the ceiling had collapsed on top of about £150,000 of equipment that had been installed there two weeks before. The fire had gutted the labyrinth of food-preparation areas in the Kitchen Court next to it. The area they had occupied would over the next few weeks become known to the scaffolders and the demolition men simply as 'The Void'. The base of the Brunswick Tower was inaccessible, twelve feet deep in the debris of the four floors that had collapsed down through the tower itself. The Prince of Wales Tower, partly rebuilt by Salvin after the fire in 1853, was too dangerous for anyone to enter. Salvin's fireproof floors, consisting of brick jack arches resting on flanged iron joists, had in part been successful. They had not collapsed and burned through as the timber floors in other parts had done. But it was that partial success which made the Prince of Wales Tower so exceptionally dangerous. The iron joists had moved and buckled in the heat, which, precisely because it had been contained within these brick ovens, was more intense here than anywhere else. No one could be certain which of the jack arches were still securely supported by the joists and which were not. Bricks were falling out of them from time to time. Any one of them could have killed someone. Whole floors might be teetering on the edge of collapse. It was quite clear that the Prince of Wales Tower in its present condition was a death trap.

In the rest of the ground floor it was dark – the electricity had not yet been turned on – but accessible with torches. Below the Private Chapel the giant blower for the Father Willis organ was still there. The fire had travelled down the zinc air tube from above and destroyed it, leaving its stub like a gut torn away. Here, in many ways, was the strangest of all the post-fire landscapes. In these stone vaulted spaces, the fire itself had not penetrated but the water had.

One and a half million gallons, which had flowed into the building at up to 4000 gallons a minute at the peak of the fire, was still there, soaked into the immense thicknesses of the medieval walls and vaults. It was the equivalent of the entire weight of the Niagara Falls descending on the building for a full two seconds. This was to be one of the great problems for the restoration team. In the silver pantries and hamper rooms below the Green Drawing Room, where the Fire Brigade had created their curtain of water to prevent the fire spreading south into the Private Apartments, bricks were still found to be 80 per cent saturated in August 1994, almost two years after the fire. The walls were still so wet that it was impossible to take a core from them.

This Saturday morning the Fire Brigade was still pouring water in, attempting to cool the mass of fallen and still burning material at the foot of the Brunswick Tower. Everywhere else, the water was draining down from above, through the floor of the Grand Reception Room and through the stone vaults below St George's Hall. The corridors in the ground floor slope this way and that and in the dark, seen only with torches, the water was running in streams several inches deep along them, making miniature cataracts in doorways, bubbling up around the boots of anyone who ventured in there. They felt like speleologists, exploring the dark, wet chambers and arteries of a limestone cave. People who were there that day, expecting to shudder as drips fell down the back of their necks, found at least one pleasant surprise: the water, as it dropped down through the masonry above, became warm.

At nine o'clock that Saturday morning, in an atmosphere that mixed shock and dismay with a resolve to get things going again, to establish the structures by which decisions could be made, the first of many thousands of meetings was convened in the Saxon Tower in Windsor Castle. Suresh Dhargalkar, the Royal Household's Superintending Architect, had contacted people the afternoon before, while the fire was burning, but others came and the room was crowded. Members of the Royal Household Property Section, architects, structural engineers, mechanical and electrical engineers, quantity surveyors, people from Wallis's, the main contractor, and from Palmer's, the scaffolders, all were pushed into the room. There were not enough chairs for everyone to sit down.

The priorities were clear. The burnt building had to be held up and a temporary roof put on it. The wettest part of the winter was coming and the rain had to be kept out. Everyone knew that water was to become the main enemy. At the same time, it was perfectly clear that the eyes of the world would be on this job, both in the immediate aftermath and in the time it would take to restore the building. Everyone involved here would in some senses be on show. Already, at this first meeting, it was realized that what people on the job would come to call 'the Windsor factor' was in play. The fire had created the chance of a resounding triumph in the remaking of Windsor; and by the same measure, there was all the opportunity here for humiliation and failure.

As part of the Queen's Household, the Property Section was aware of the need to set high standards and of the consequences of falling short. The objective was to do something better than it ever had been done before, for less money and in less time. Those aims were quite explicitly stated by the Royal Household Property Section on the morning after the fire. There was to be no tolerance on this job of the second-rate, of slackness or sloppy thinking. The Royal Household intended to make clear that it could hold its own with any organization, however trim and efficient it might be.

Accounts of the way the aftermath of the 1986 fire at Hampton Court had been handled by the Government's Property Services Agency (PSA) were already circulating among the Household that weekend. The PSA had adopted a relaxed timetable. The fire had occurred on 31 March 1986. There was a clear-up and a tea-party was held in the ruins during the summer. Not until October was a Design Think Tank established and only in January the following year was a PSA team office set up. Building work began in the autumn of 1988, two and a half years after the fire, and the job was finally completed three years after that.

The burnt area at Windsor was five times the size of what had been destroyed at Hampton Court. The prospect of following the same sort of timetable, and the possibility of spending ten years or more on this job, sent shudders of alarm through the Royal Household.

This was the Queen's house, a working palace, to which she came almost every weekend, the natural place for state visits to be held, the focus for the ceremonies based on the Order of the Garter and for Ascot week. Disruption through the Kingsbury project had already lasted long enough. Of course urgency was required and the importance of both speed and rigour was communicated to everyone around that room in the Saxon Tower that Saturday morning. It is one signal of the mood at the time that the next phases of the Kingsbury rewiring project, moving along the north side of the Upper Ward, were not for a moment interrupted by the fire. The electricians and carpenters dealing with Kingsbury Phases IV/V resumed their work at eight o'clock on Monday morning.

Michael Peat, now Keeper of the Privy Purse but at that time Director of Property Services, was quite conscious of putting pressure on everyone involved: 'At the end of projects people always work hard and they are always committed. It is very easy to be committed because you have got your deadline coming up. Reality is staring you in the face. Where projects go off the rails and you lose it is at the beginning. People relax. They think they've got tons of time and they dribble around. If you are the manager, you have to motivate people and get them going early in a project and keep them under pressure, keep the buzz going and keep things spinning. People in my view enjoy working under a bit of pressure. They enjoy being involved in something that has a buzz to it. If you've got a team, you have really got to give that team a sense of purpose.' In this way, from the first moments, the tenor of the Windsor job was set. It was intended to be a highly demanding environment.

On Friday afternoon, as the fire was burning, English Heritage, which had wide experience of dealing with the aftermath of fires, particularly at Uppark and Hampton Court, offered its services to the Royal

In St George's Hall, debris was sifted into dustbins and anything of any value then carried away in skips suspended from a crane in the Quadrangle. The rest was shovelled out through a window and then down a slide into a series of skips.

The mound of debris in the Octagon Dining Room, fallen from the four floors of the Brunswick Tower above it, was twelve feet deep. Ironically enough, the debris saved crucial details in the dining room from the fire, allowing the architects to know what they had to reinstate.

Household. John Thorneycroft, then in charge of the section of English Heritage that was concerned with royal palaces and government buildings, attended the meeting at Windsor on that Saturday. The offer of help had been gratefully received by the Household and the meeting listened to Thorneycroft's account of what English Heritage had found necessary in a crisis of this sort: a careful sifting of the debris for any valuable remains that might be found there; a careful survey of the surviving fabric; and a meticulous working out of the philosophy of restoration. The very bins, 1000 of them, which the National Trust had used at Uppark were available and on offer. Arrangements were made for them to be delivered to Windsor.

Although English Heritage is the government agency that is charged with the protection of the nation's most important buildings, it had so far scarcely been involved at Windsor. This may seem surprising, given the historical significance of the Castle, but the planning situation is complex. The Castle is both a Grade 1 Listed Building and a Scheduled Monument. When it is considered as a Grade 1 Listed Building, the Windsor and Maidenhead District Council is the planning authority.

But when it is considered as a Scheduled Monument, the Secretary of State for Culture (or National Heritage as it was up to 1997), advised by English Heritage, is the planning authority. On top of that, in a building owned and occupied by the Crown, there is no requirement, formally at least, for works there to be subject to any kind of planning process or building regulation. It is 'Crown exempt'. In the early part of the Kingsbury works under the Property Services Agency, for example, no clearance had been sought.

Many government buildings are covered by a special advisory 'shadow procedure' which had been worked out in 1984, but even that had not, under the PSA, been applied here. Suresh Dhargalkar, the Superintending Architect, explains the PSA's position: 'Windsor was considered the Queen's house and if the monarch wanted to do some changes, it was up to her. It was not anyone else's business. Otherwise the building would never change. But it had to change, as it always had changed, right from William the Conqueror.'

When the Household took over from the PSA in 1991 and established its own Property Section, there was a deliberate change of attitude, more open and more sympathetic to the interests English Heritage represented. As a result, its archaeologists had been involved as observers in recent works to the Round Tower.

In the aftermath of the fire, the English Heritage inspectors were still desperately anxious to get into the Castle, knowing that it would have revealed parts of the structure that could only have been guessed at before and knowing equally well that the restoration works would be certain to cover up that evidence again.

The fire had the effect of accelerating the process of mutual accommodation that was already in train, a growing openness on both sides and a readiness to search for shared ground between what might have been conflicting interests. There was a job to be done. As the weeks of emergency clearance and stabilization works unfolded, the actions of the various agencies here were, on the whole, melded together. Needless to say, there were inevitably times when their different priorities came to the fore. The Department of National Heritage (DNH), through which both English Heritage and the Grant-in-Aid to the Royal Household Property Section were funded, was above all concerned with keeping costs down. The Household wanted speed and efficiency, a dynamic thrust to the programme, as well as ferociously tight cost controls. The Royal Collection, which was responsible for all the furniture and artefacts that were due to return to the restored rooms, was anxious that the

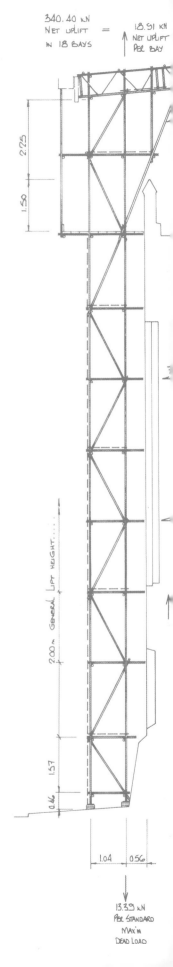

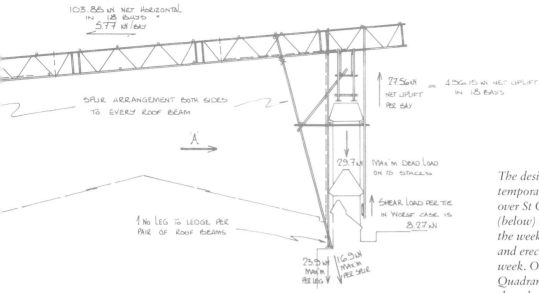

103.85 kN NET HORIZONTAL
IN 18 BAYS =
5.77 kN/BAY

SPUR ARRANGEMENT BOTH SIDES
TO EVERY ROOF BEAM

'A'

1 No LEG TO LEDGE PER
PAIR OF ROOF BEAMS

27.56 kN
NET UPLIFT
PER BAY   = 496.15 kN NET UPLIFT
            IN 18 BAYS

29.7 kN   MAX'M DEAD LOAD
           ON TO STACKS

           SHEAR LOAD PER TIE
           IN WORST CASE IS
           8.27 kN

23.9 kN   16.9 kN
MAX'M   MAX'M PER
PER LEG   SPUR

TYPICAL CROSS-SECTION

R TIE

2 TIE

PER TIE
CASE IS
00 kN.

The design (left) for a temporary scaffolding roof over St George's Hall (below) was made during the weekend after the fire and erected the following week. One side stood in the Quadrangle (see page 52), the other on the wall between St George's Hall and the Kitchen Courtyard.

quality of the work should be nothing but the highest, to provide the settings into which those pieces could go. English Heritage, treading carefully, knowing they were in here partly by right and partly by invitation, nevertheless had to fulfil their statutory requirement to protect the historic fabric, to go slowly, not to assume that what looked like rubbish and discardable debris was anything of the kind.

Alongside those official agencies, the contractors and their subcontractors, the architects, engineers, quantity surveyors and other consultants all had their own agendas and their own well-being to promote. And so the meetings proliferated. As Hugh Roberts, then Deputy Surveyor of the Queen's Works of Art, recalls, that was what it was like, 'meeting after meeting after meeting after meeting. In the end, one was in something of a blur.' The Property Section was meeting with the architects, the architects with the structural engineers, the engineers with the scaffolders, the scaffolders with English Heritage, English Heritage with the main contractors, the main contractors with the Property Section, the Property Section with the Department of National Heritage, and so on for weeks and weeks, to resolve the crisis.

The building was open to the sky, wobbling – or 'live' as the structural engineers describe it – and wet. It had to be covered, it had to be stabilized and it had to be dried. By Sunday night, two days after the fire, drawings had already been done for half the scaffolding that was to support the new roofs. Within a week the whole design for the temporary roofs was complete. It was a complex task. Scaffold roofs like this are designed from the top down. The engineer works out the area to be covered, the likely snow loads it might have to carry and the way in which rainwater is to be carried off. Then he considers the scaffold units, purlins and rafters necessary to support that roof and only thirdly works out how it is actually going to be held up.

These roofs, as usual after fire has devastated a building, could not rest on the castle walls, whose integrity and strength no one could yet guess at. The masonry was soaking wet and the mortar might well have been too soft to resist any strain that was put on it. In addition, the mortar joints at Windsor are full of flint gallets or chips, which makes drilling into them almost impossible.

Instead, then, the roofs had to be 'landed' on pillars that would come down on the floors below. There, with a whole variety of concrete blocks, anchors and bolts, the scaffold was pinned to the ground. A big roof, as Jack Jenner, the scaffold designer explains, 'is like a big kite, a big sail. It doesn't have the self-weight a building has. The wind, as it goes over it, has a suction effect and it can pick it up. That is when you get a disaster.'

The whole team was well aware of what had happened to the scaffold at Uppark, which the wind had picked up by one corner and dropped on two of the men working there. They had been killed. It was of supreme importance that nothing like that happened here and the temporary roof was drawn up within the design parameters that are usually applied to a permanent structure. The largest single element was a giant raking shore to hold up the cracked bay window in the Crimson Drawing Room, fixed to the East Terrace with resin anchors and, according to Jenner, 'big enough to hold up two Windsor Castles'.

Overall, the scaffold they created, with up to forty-six scaffolders on site at any one time, was enormous: 3700 square metres of corrugated iron roof, supported on 25 miles of scaffold pole (a figure that would triple over the course of the restoration) and 2 miles of prefabricated beams. The entire construction weighed just short of 1000 tons, all of it shipped into the Castle in convoys of giant articulated trucks. The monarflex polythene sheeting with which the whole structure was

The temporary roof goes up. Experience after the fire at Hampton Court showed the importance of having large numbers of translucent panels in the roof and at Uppark of designing it so that the wind would flow smoothly over shallow-pitched surfaces.

The painters' scaffold in the State Dining Room had softened and warped in the heat of the fire, only to stiffen into a tensed and highly dangerous condition as it cooled.

encased was constantly ripping on the exposed hilltop site and for the two years the scaffolding was up, needed constant replacement and repair. Although every single aspect of the scaffolding, apart from the very first few days' work, was put out to competitive tender from at least three companies, none of this was cheap. The cost of putting the scaffolding up had been over £280,000 and for every week it stood there the hire was another £4500.

Meanwhile, alongside it, sewn in with it, and just as urgent a priority, the demolition and clearance work had to go on. The more the engineers looked at the building, the more dangerous they understood it to be. People from the Household who in the very early days had casually wandered in with no helmet and in their pinstripe suits were gradually excluded or shepherded towards the safer parts.

It was perfectly clear from the start that one or two points were spectacularly dangerous. The painters' scaffold in the State Dining Room had softened to spaghetti in the fire and then resolidified in a warped and tensed condition. It was perfectly possible those sprung, stressed bars might suddenly flick loose, whipping out and firing scaffolding

One of the chandeliers in the Grand Reception Room before an attempt was made to salvage it.

clips in any direction they chose. Another scaffolding walkway still bridged St George's Hall. It also had the potential to kill.

Ron Edwards, working at the time for the Demolition Co-Partnership, had also worked on the demolition after the fire at Hampton Court. He brought twelve men with him, including a brother and several nephews, widely admired on site as a tightly bound team of brave and skilful men. The essence of their work was to get above the danger and handle the damaged building from wherever it could not hurt them. It might be, as in St George's Hall, by attaching themselves on safety harnesses to heavy-gauge wire bonds that were stretched across the gaping mouth of the roofless hall to scaffolding that had been erected on either side. From there they could dig out the brickwork that still supported the ends of the roof trusses and, once they were free, lash them with chains that were suspended from the booms of cranes parked in the Quadrangle.

One at a time the trusses were lifted out. Three of them at the west end were left in situ. The trusses were of an ingenious design by Sir Robert Smirke, the architect of the British Museum, and had originally

been assembled within the attic of the seventeenth-century roof they were designed to strengthen. The fire had been less intense at the west end of the hall, the trusses were still securely in place, they were considered an important part of the historical record and John Thorneycroft for English Heritage felt that if they did not have to be removed immediately they shouldn't be. For the time being, they stayed where they were.

'This was not a ball and chain job,' Ron Edwards says. 'It was a careful dismantling of damaged fabric.' In the centre of the Grand Reception Room, a chandelier was still hanging from the shattered ceiling. Its little candle lights were pointing in all directions as if blown about by the wind and the whole sad object had the air of a duchess who had been sleeping rough for a couple of nights. The chandelier clearly had to be rescued.

The demolition men's favoured method simply would have been to erect a scaffold tower beneath the object and take it down from below. But English Heritage archaeologists were set against too many people trampling across the debris field. They knew that it contained a large

English Heritage archaeologists do a fine sift on the debris surrounding the Grand Reception Room chandelier after it had crashed to the floor.

number of plaster fragments, many of them still gilded, which a careful sift would be able to rescue for future use. Demolition men's boots would crush the precious fragments to dust. They had to go in from above.

All day, they struggled to attach a line from a crane, positioned outside on the North Terrace, around the chandelier. Eventually the line was dogged, as the expression is, on to the chandelier chain. The crane driver then lifted it to take the weight and held it there for about forty minutes while the demolition men cut the surrounding timber away. The job was virtually done when, without warning, the chandelier's own chain suddenly snapped and the whole thing crashed on to the black, ashy debris of the floor, collapsing with its gilded skirts and hundreds of facets all around it. The chandelier's own chain, unnoticed by the rescuers, had stretched and weakened in the fire.

If that was a disappointment, elsewhere in the fire site there was an extraordinary and anomalous piece of good luck. The Glass Pantry was near the hottest part of the fire, at the foot of the Brunswick and Prince of Wales Towers. No one believed that anything could have survived there. It was now also one of the most dangerous parts of the building. At the height of the fire a fireman had come out to Major Eastwood, the Castle Superintendent standing in the Quad, and had told him 'There's a load of glass in there still.' Of course, Eastwood knew. There were several thousand pieces of the glassware used during state banquets.

On the day after the fire, Eastwood was anxious to find out what had happened to it all. The Health and Safety Officer told him 'There's no way you're going in there.'

Eastwood replied, mockingly 'What time's your coffee break?'

The safety officer said, 'I'm off now.'

Major Eastwood and one of the salvage officers then gingerly found their way to the Glass Pantry door. 'It was something out of a book,' he remembers. 'Steam, flickers of flame, a hell's cauldron in there. The door was just about hanging on. The salvage officer kicked it and when he kicked the door it was like pulling a cork out of a bottle: all the musty air came rushing out. It was a big oak-panelled door, but it had been charred and it fell to pieces like a crisp. I looked in and there was all the glass in the cabinets. The ceiling was sagging with the weight of the water and the debris above it but the glass was untouched.'

Major Eastwood brought the Master of the Household and the Deputy Master and they pushed an acro-prop under the sagging ceiling. 'We told the safety officer to go away and have his dinner,' Major

The sooty shelves of the Glass Pantry after the miraculously preserved glasses had been removed and rescued.

The cranes in the Quadrangle, one holding a bucket full of demolition men, the other a bucket into which they were putting hanging debris, reaching far over to the side of the building, were in constant danger of clashing or 'sword-fencing' as the crane-drivers put it. It never happened.

Eastwood says. 'We went in and we handed out the glassware one by one.' Not a single item was broken in the salvage. When the structural engineers heard what the glass party had been doing, their faces turned grey with the risk. While the glasses were being rescued, leaving neat white rings on their sooty shelves, two complete iron and brick floors hung unsupported above them, ready with the slightest nudge to collapse on their heads.

Ron Edwards's demolition team would never have played those odds. Nonetheless, their work was consistently near the edge. Five cranes were brought on to site. The East Terrace would not have been able to support their weight and to use one on the North Terrace was only possible by parking it on large steel plates to spread the load. Most of the time, the cranes remained in the Quadrangle, reaching over towards the body of the building just as the firefighters' tall white hoists had attempted to reach over during the course of the fire.

Picking away at the hanging debris in the far north-eastern corner of the burnt Castle was a hazardous business. The structural engineers, Clive Dawson and Cliff Nursey, would go up with Ron Edwards, the demolition man, in buckets dangled at the end of a giant crane arm. One bucket from one crane held the engineers and another, lowered into the same space, took the demolished material up and away to skips in the Quad. Neither crane driver could see where their buckets were going and were responding to walkie-talkie messages from the men they were dangling over the site. Worse still, the cranes were at full reach and in their cabs the buzzers and sirens were constantly going to indicate they were operating at the very edge of their capacity. Modern cranes are computer-controlled and will not allow the crane driver to lift something which would topple the crane over. All the same, there was always the risk that two cranes might lock their enormously long arms and engage in a terrifying form of 'sword-fencing' as they called it. It was, as Cliff Nursey, the site engineer, described it, 'dodgy stuff'.

While the building was being picked clean, the staff of the Royal Collection were busy relocating works of art and pieces of furniture that had been hurriedly transferred to houses and apartments around the Castle or to the Riding School in the Home Park. There, Canalettos were stacked six deep against the walls. The frame specialist Cliona Bacon remembers finding the pictures in the damp atmosphere 'bellying out like sails. We had to get them out of there.' Much of the material was going down to the California Store in the Home Park, but some already was going back into the great rooms from which it had been removed the day before. Polythene had been stretched over the sand of the Riding School floor but nevertheless, for weeks afterwards, grains of it were found dropping out of drawers and hinges on to the carpets of the State and Private Apartments.

While in these different ways the team on the ground was grappling with the challenges of a ravaged building and a disrupted collection, in the world beyond the Castle walls the fire had already thrown up some strange and unexpected phenomena of its own. Already, the offices of the Household Property Section were being inundated with offers of help and expertise from all over the country and the world. This was the pit of the recession and the building industry was on its knees. Anyone who thought they might have a skill or a service that would be of use at Windsor was sending in their brochures, their letters, their leaflets and their videos. Experts in timber treatment and the dehumidification of buildings called from the United States. Plumbers, craftsmen and carpenters from across the breadth of Europe suggested they came immediately. One man from the Midwest even presented himself at the Castle claiming that without him no one had any hope of restoring the Castle within the decade. In many senses, this craving of the construction industry for work was of enormous assistance to the restoration project. There was no shortage of manpower or materials, and companies in need of turnover were prepared to make keen offers for the work.

The flood of commercial offers, however, was of little significance compared to the political firestorm that blew up even on the afternoon and evening of the fire. The fire at Windsor summoned a public mood not of sympathy but of retribution. It had been what the Queen, in her Guildhall speech the following week, would call her 'annus horribilis'. From her point of view, the fire at Windsor was only the concluding piece of bad luck in a difficult year. No institution, she said, should expect to be free from the scrutiny of those who give it loyalty and support. But there was no reason why, in the light of these difficulties, such scrutiny should not be made with 'a touch of gentleness, good humour and understanding'.

For whatever reason, that was not the public mood. Peter Brooke, the Secretary of State for National Heritage, had come with his wife to Windsor on the afternoon after the fire. It was a damp and drizzly day. The mood was sombre. The reality of what had happened, which in some ways had been obscured during the crisis by the shared flood of adrenalin, was now felt more starkly. In this atmosphere, and confronted with the deeply depressing sight of the blackened building, Mr

Brooke said publicly and quite straightforwardly that the Government would now pay to restore what had been destroyed.

Such a categorical remark was thought, in parts of the press, a little impetuous and premature. But in making it, Brooke was doing no more than articulating the existing policy and legal position. The Government has been responsible for the funding, maintenance and repair of Windsor Castle, as for other Crown buildings, since 1760. This undertaking was first made on the accession of George III, in exchange for the surrender of the Sovereign's hereditary revenues. As each successive monarch has come to the throne, that agreement has been renewed. The Royal Collection has its own insurance policy, which pays for reparable damage to furniture and works of art. But the building and its fixtures and fittings, as the Government's own responsibility, have never been insured. When Hampton Court burned in 1986, the same policy applied and at that time there was no questioning of the principle. The Government would pay.

In 1992, however, the reaction was of a fiercely different kind. Perhaps it was precisely because of the loss of dignity which the Crown had suffered during the annus horribilis; perhaps because Windsor seemed, however erroneously, more of private castle-cum-palace than a public possession; perhaps because the recession, then at its worst with thousands of homes being repossessed by mortgage companies every month, had made the country less tolerant of the expenditure a monarchy necessarily involves. In terms of the overall government budget in the early 1990s of over £240 billion a year, the cost of the restoration scarcely figured. It would be perhaps £7 million a year, or 0.003 per cent of the total. But those were hardly the terms in which it was being discussed.

The newspapers on Saturday morning were dominated by two questions, each of them being asked with equal and, to some, disturbing vehemence: Whose fault is it? and Who's going to pay? In the absence of any real information, the hunt for the culprit soon settled on Viola Pemberton-Pigott, one of the picture specialists who had been in the Private Chapel when the flames were first spotted. Stories about inflammable liquids being squirted on to halogen lamps were devised, repeated, elaborated and confirmed in a spectacle of freewheeling fantasy and the mutual confirmation of invented facts. Journalists besieged Miss Pemberton-Pigott on her London doorstep, ringing the doorbell all night. Whenever she replaced the phone they would ring again to ask the one question they knew how to ask: 'What does it feel like to have burned down Windsor Castle?'

Part of Ron Edwards's demolition team take down some of the tower above the Equerries' Entrance after the iron beam below them was found to be cracked.

Meanwhile, the other question – Who's going to pay? – had been fuelled by the Secretary of State's confident assertion on the Saturday, repeated in the House of Commons on Monday afternoon, that the Government would honour its obligations to pay for the repairs. This appeared in Tuesday's headlines as 'It's a blank cheque for Windsor' and 'Taxpayer to foot Windsor bill'. English Heritage officers stirred the pot over the week-end by 'questioning the logic of providing public money for repairs to palaces that are not subject to planning legislation'. They 'raised doubts about an arrangement which in effect frees from public scrutiny work carried out by the Royal Household on Crown properties'. This was not strictly true: the Royal Household Property Section, as distinct from the Government's Property Services Agency that had preceded it, considered itself subject to the arrangements made by the Department of the Environment in 1984 by which so-called 'Crown-exempt' buildings were subject to planning control.

Spokesmen for Government and Household repeatedly pointed out that the Government received far more in revenues from the Crown estate than it distributed via the Civil List and the Grant-in-Aid. They repeatedly explained the basis on which the state had responsibility for the buildings. What building could be said to belong to the state more than Windsor Castle? Few, however, were in a mood to listen and telephone polls showed a large majority against the Government paying for the restoration.

Discussions, which remain confidential, were held during the Tuesday and Wednesday, which resulted in a statement by the Prime Minister to the House of Commons on Thursday afternoon to the effect that the Queen would, from the following 1 April, pay income tax. Parliamentary annuities to all members of the Royal Family except the Queen Mother and the Duke of Edinburgh would also now be refunded out of income derived from the estates belonging to the Duchy of Lancaster.

In some ways the hurry with which this announcement was made was not entirely fair to the process that had been going on behind the scenes. As part of a large-scale rolling programme to modernize its financial and administrative arrangements, the Household had been holding internal discussions since late 1990 on the possibility of the Queen paying income tax. Discussions with the Treasury and the Inland Revenue had been taking place since February 1992. By the time of the fire, most of the details for the way in which the Queen would pay income tax had already been worked out. The plan was to make the announcement early in the New Year. Coming, as it would have done, on Buckingham Palace's own initiative, integrated with the rest of the programme to introduce efficiencies and cost-saving measures in the management of the Royal finances, this would have been seen as a central pillar in the new arrangements.

It was unfortunate that the announcement about tax, precipitated by the crisis over the fire, came to be seen as a defence against a mood of public annoyance and uncharitableness. But as a political gambit it worked. At least for the time being, the heat went out of the question.

It was an adroit manoeuvre. The answer to the question 'Who's going to pay?' had not in fact changed since Mr Brooke's statement the previous Saturday. The Government, at this stage, was still going to honour the indemnity agreement. But the announcement over tax meant that the question which had given rise to the crisis was forgotten in the hubbub.

It did not go away. In the light of the Queen's decision over tax and the Civil List, the assumption in the Household over the winter was that the Government, through the Department of National Heritage, would fulfil its duty in paying for the restoration. Nevertheless, when the subject was raised again in the New Year, the grumbling resentment and objections returned, both in the press and in Parliament.

This time, the Household took the initiative. It was suggested to the Queen that she might consider opening Buckingham Palace to the public for the two summer months which were usually devoted to maintenance. The revenue from that and from charging for entry to the precincts of Windsor Castle itself, which until now had been free, could be devoted to the restoration of the burnt parts of Windsor. It was thought that ticket sales and shop income could account for 70 per cent of the overall cost. The other 30 per cent could be derived from the annual Grant-in-Aid which the Government makes anyway to the Royal Household Property Section to pay for the upkeep of the occupied palaces. The normal programme of the Property Section would be adjusted and various works postponed so that money would become available for Windsor. In that way, the fire would involve not a single extra penny of government money being spent. The Queen accepted the idea and that is the basis on which the works at Windsor have been funded.

The malachite urn presides over the Grand Reception Room en fête for the court of Queen Victoria, the image of regal sumptuousness bequeathed by George IV to his successors. The Grand Reception Room *from* Views of Windsor Castle *by Joseph Nash the Elder.*

At the building itself, the scaffolding shores were going up, the demolition men were slowly picking their way around the site and the temporary roofs were going on. One or two nasty surprises confronted the team. Above the Equerries' Entrance, an iron girder supporting a large part of the tower was found to be cracked and everything above it, hundreds of tons of stonework, had to be taken down. On the other side of the building, above the Great Kitchen, the scaffolders were clearing debris before erecting the temporary roof there. It was just before Christmas and five weeks had passed since the fire. A crane lifted the lead coping away from the top of the Great Kitchen wall. To the horror of Tony Mileham, the scaffolders' project manager, there was a beam under there, an upper wall plate, hidden until that moment by the lead, and it was still burning. The site was evacuated, the fire brigade called and the smouldering timber easily doused.

These were small hiccoughs. Before the project could move on to its next phase, two main tasks had to be tackled: the clearance of the debris; and the drying of a building which the fire brigade had soaked for fifteen hours.

English Heritage was well prepared to take on the task of sifting the debris for any valuable fragments that might survive in it. Both at Uppark and at Hampton Court they had achieved great success in salvaging fragments of roof trusses, structural ironwork, ornate plaster from the ceilings, panelling, carved woodwork, statues, chandelier glass and even jewellery, which had either been returned to its owners,

reinstated in the restored buildings, or used to provide the best possible models from which craftsmen could reproduce what had been there before.

At Uppark, the National Trust's insurance policy had covered them for the costs of total reinstatement. That provision of money had in effect decided their philosophy of 'authentic restoration' for them. At Windsor, no such insurance policy existed and no such presumption could be made. Although English Heritage had clearly developed the skills by which an Uppark-style authentic restoration could be based on the quality of fragments they could recover from the debris, the question still hung in the air whether that was worth doing. An archaeological sift was very expensive. English Heritage's first guesstimate of the cost was £1.11 million. Neither the Department of National Heritage, which would eventually have to pay for it, nor the Royal Household, which was worried about the time that painstaking archaeology involves, were entirely certain this was the route to go, particularly if the eventual style of restoration was not to be the kind that would require the many fragments such a careful sifting of the debris would recover.

The three organizations, each with their very different cultures, moved towards a solution. There were, inevitably, niggles between them. English Heritage was insistent on the need for an accurate survey of the fabric after the fire. Both the Household and DNH were concerned about the cost. The Household wanted the clearance done quickly but the security passes necessary for anyone working at Windsor were taking between four and six weeks to get through the system. English Heritage was 'being put through the mill' over the basis for its costs. These were teething troubles, to be expected as these very different organizations bedded down with each other.

As a result, there was some clearance before Christmas in St George's Hall and in other areas where space was needed for the legs of the giant scaffold that was to support the temporary roofs. But it took until the first week of January 1993 before the main team of thirty freelance archaeologists, drawn from a register which English Heritage holds for precisely such an occasion, had been vetted and the expense of their work authorized.

As a sign of their willingness to get on with the job, Wallis's team had decided to protect the giant malachite urn standing in the window of the Grand Reception Room. Although the urn was the responsibility of the Royal Collection, John Thorneycroft of English Heritage was dismayed at the result of Wallis's initiative. On 7 December he wrote to Suresh Dhargalkar, at that time the Royal Household's Superintending Architect, anxious about the flakes or spalls of the green stone that were scattered around the urn. 'The malachite spalls,' Thorneycroft wrote,

The malachite urn in the Grand Reception Room in the 'tight-jointed and unventilated plywood box' mistakenly built by the contractors in what English Heritage called 'a well-meaning but unscientific rescue bid'.

had fallen from the upper rim, but instead of lying as they had fallen where they could, with proper sifting, have been related to their original positions, we found that they had been grossly displaced and were heaped with the debris that had been shovelled aside to construct a tight-jointed and unventilated plywood box.

I had singled out this object for special urgent protection as it was largely intact but in danger and this unfortunate action by Wallis [the main contractors] gives little reassurance of their understanding of the relatively sophisticated and delicate issues of conservation that must be appreciated by any contractor dealing with such important and severely damaged historic interiors.

Since the pieces of the jigsaw have been scattered, it will prove hard now for conservators to reconstruct the complex whorl patterns typical of this type of veneer work and lost pieces are virtually irreplaceable.

It had been, Thorneycroft concluded mollifyingly, 'a well-meaning but unscientific rescue bid'. The source of Russian malachite is now exhausted and Thorneycroft was worried that no replacements could be found to match in colour and pattern any pieces that might have been lost. Despite these anxieties – and in the end the malachite flakes were not too difficult to retrieve – and despite the questions over the need to do a sift in these circumstances, the archaeology began to go ahead in earnest in the New Year. After what John Thorneycroft calls 'a symbiotic process', in which English Heritage, the Household and Royal Collection jointly established what were the most critical rooms and the most critical zones within rooms, different intensities of sifting were applied to different parts of the site. Brian Kerr and David Batchelor of English Heritage's Central Archaeology Service surveyed the whole site and recommended that the three finest rooms, the Grand Reception Room and the Crimson and Green Drawing Rooms, should be sifted very carefully indeed, as there was likely to be a great deal of reusable material in there. Other rooms, such as St George's Hall and the Great Kitchen, either did not have very sophisticated finishes or anything very much worth retrieving; or had been subject to such devastating fire that there would not be very much left there anyway. This was thought to be true of the Octagon and State Dining Rooms. These rooms would only be subject to a coarse sift.

That was the intention, but the nature of the site intervened. Archaeologists could not get into the Crimson Drawing Room nor the State and Octagon Dining Rooms because their insurance did not cover them for such hazardous working conditions. The distorted fireproof floors in the Prince of Wales Tower were still hanging dangerously. The steel roof above the Crimson Drawing Room could only be taken down from below, because cranes could not reach it. But this was the conundrum. It could not be demolished before the precious debris had been cleared. But the debris could not be cleared by archaeologists until the steel roof had been demolished.

The project team cut the knot: the contents of these rooms were shovelled by well-insured but unskilled workmen into dustbins, which were then transported in skips down to the Mushroom Farm. More than 8000 dustbins were filled from this room and others, causing enormous problems, both in transport and storage.

John Thorneycroft wrote to Suresh Dhargalkar on 5 January to explain what he called 'this indiscriminate binning'. 'The impression,' Thorneycroft wrote, 'that the Central Archaeological Service has been amassing alarming quantities of worthless, space-consuming detritus is indeed well founded.' But, as he explained, there was no other way around the problem. It was a classic of its kind. In the same way, the marquetry floor in the Crimson Drawing Room needed protection from anything that might fall on it. But to cover it up, in its thoroughly soused condition, would be to provide the ideal conditions for rot to begin its colonization. Neither solution was ideal, but in this case it was thought the danger of impact damage was worse than the prospect of rot and so the second route was followed.

In the Green Drawing Room, the huge carpet, 52 feet 2 inches long by 23 feet 9 inches wide, remained under the double layer of plywood and fibre-board under which it had been protected for the duration of the Kingsbury works. This incredible object had been woven at Wilton in 1851, one of Prince Albert's commissions to the design of Ludwig Grüner, described on the original bill as 'An Extra superfine Axminster Carpet in rich Crimsons, Greens & Chintz colours: £490'. It had a central circular motif with V&A monograms on either side, set against a red, cream and beige main field, gold, brown and coffee coloured borders and extra floral borders in green, coral, crimson, pink, blue and brown.

In about 1967 a latex backing was applied to the carpet to strengthen it, but in the twenty-five years since it was put there, the latex had stiffened so much that the Royal Collection had decided that to move the carpet might be damaging and it was safer to board the carpet over, leaving it where it was, all except for a narrow strip along the west wall of the room, which was rolled up and cased in a wooden box so that the electricians could get at the floorboards and skirting.

During the fire, timber and plaster in the north-west corner of the room had crashed on to the boards, which were scorched in places. The carpet underneath had been superficially burnt in long pencil-thin lines where the boards had not quite abutted. But the main worry was the wet. The whole sandwich of board, cotton protective cloth and carpet was wet through. If the carpet was to be saved from rot, it had to be moved out and dried. On 30 November, under the directions of the Castle Superintendent, with experts on hand from the Royal Collection and the Hampton Court Textile Conservation Studios, thirty-two men gathered in the desolate Drawing Room. The separately woven part of the carpet that extended into the bay window was detached and then the main body rolled up from west to east. As Hugh Roberts, then Deputy Surveyor of the Queen's Works of Art, describes it, 'This was done without too much apparent damage, the rubber backing proving surprisingly pliable, perhaps in part because of the inundation. The resulting sausage, over fifty feet long and weighing an incredible amount, was lifted by the thirty-two men, using rope slings, and in miserable cold, wind and rain eased out on to the upper area of the Terrace, then somehow down the steps on to the Terrace proper. There it was laid on four trolleys, on which it was wheeled/lifted round to the South Front, past the Dog Door, down the road to the Mews, through the Top Court and into the Riding School.' There it was laid on pallets and exposed to the drying effects of two industrial-capacity dehumidifiers. The textile experts remained anxious that the wettened latex was setting up a chemical reaction with the carpet which, it was thought at the time, would eventually destroy it.

Once the carpet had been removed, the ceiling in the Green Drawing Room, which had survived, could be attended to. An internal scaffold was erected, supporting a padded platform, lined with insulation quilt, precisely an inch below the plasterwork to catch it if clearance works on the floors above dislodged any fragments. As it happened, and through the meticulous care of those working above to remove debris and insert some massive new steel structures, nothing fell.

St George's Hall went straightforwardly enough. As the scaffolders put the temporary roof on, the English Heritage archaeologists followed them down the length of the room, ten metres or so behind. 'It's like sausage processing,' Brian Kerr now says. 'You start at one end and just work your way up this coal face which gradually recedes.' They managed to save many of the 200 carved oak shields which had decorated the ceiling but only small examples of the ceiling itself. It had been installed late in the 1820s, as George IV's and Sir Jeffry Wyatville's recreation of Windsor was reaching its climax. It was not oak panelling as had appeared, but made out of plaster on a string and nail backing. The parts they kept were taken in bread trays down to the disused Mushroom Farm in the Home Park and the rest was shovelled out down slides into skips waiting in the Quadrangle. The carpet which the builders had rolled up on the morning of the fire was found badly damaged beneath the ash which, paradoxically, had protected much of the floor, particularly as it was lying on a layer of polythene which had been rolled out on the day before the fire as part of the Kingsbury works in the Hall.

Next door in the Grand Reception Room, the ceiling had crashed through in the evening of the fire. The first job was to pick away the large timbers that had fallen after it and were now poking out of the debris like cocktail sticks. Then the team worked through the ash systematically, looking for the plasterwork. It was all still there on the floor and some of the pieces, still gilded, were as much as three feet across.

The three chandeliers and the area around the malachite urn, despite the earlier disturbance, were subjected to a micro-sift. The chandelier at Hampton Court had been pulled down early in the fire and had smacked on to a bare floor, scattering in all directions. The three chandeliers in the Grand Reception had come down very late. There was already a thick layer of ash and plaster on the floor and the chandeliers were cushioned as they fell. Virtually all the pieces remained gathered where they had first dropped.

This made the archaeologists' job easier. Everything from these four important grid squares was carefully shovelled into bins and taken down to the Mushroom Farm. There, in a technique learned from the police forensic specialists who had developed it in response to the aftermath of IRA bombing incidents, they had set up a wide conveyor belt. The material from the bins was carefully ladled on to the belt, which was about twenty feet long, running past up to eight archaeologists who stood on either side of it, picking out the significant fragments from the gritty mess. The end of the conveyor tipped the residue into a skip which was changed every day. Day after day, week after week, they stood there picking out malachite chips, fragments of chandelier, masses of plaster, for months and months, and the rescued material was transferred into climate-controlled storage in the old mushroom sheds. The last of the 8400 bins was sorted in June of 1993, more than seven months after the fire.

Large pieces of the Great Kitchen roof lie collapsed on the £150,000 worth of equipment installed there two weeks before the fire.

Alongside that salvage, another perhaps even more important enterprise was under way: the campaign to drive out the wet. The building environment specialist, Dr Brian Ridout, remembers his first visit to the site in the week after the fire. 'It was dripping with water, pools of it, swimming in water. Soot and muck and debris all over the place and water still dripping through everything. There were planks across the pools in some places to get over.'

On 4 December Ridout made his first report. Timber can be considered dry if it is below 12 per cent moisture, and brick below 5 per cent. Here most walls in the burnt area were well over 10 per cent. In the lower floors, as the moisture sank towards them, that figure was rising. The shallow vaulted ceilings in the basement and the bases of the deep vaults there were saturated, at up to 30 per cent. Some of the panelling on the ground floor was also at 30 per cent moisture.

Ridout advised that panelling should stay where it was, for the time being anyway. Warping in drying wood is minimized by keeping it in position and too rapid a drying regime – which removal would probably mean – can destroy the surface finishes. But sodden carpets, which were just pools of water in another form, should be taken away. Lino was to be removed from the basement. The builders' debris, especially piles of softwood, had to be taken elsewhere. They too were standing lumps of water. The baize cupboard linings in the silver pantry had to go.

Above all, the roofs had to be put on as soon as possible and an envelope had to be created around the site. Where doors had been removed, new barriers had to be installed. Heavy polythene fixed with Velcro was suggested. But there was a paradox here. The wet had to be kept out but in keeping it out, you reduced the movement of air through the building and so reduced the speed at which it was drying naturally. Fans and dehumidifiers were needed. Those that were powered by refrigeration units would scarcely operate in the winter temperatures. Desiccant-based machines were required. By mid-December, seventeen dehumidifiers and their ducting had been installed. Nothing, however, was more important than keeping the rooms sealed. There was no point in dehumidifying Berkshire.

Even so, within twelve days of the fire, as Dr Ridout reported 'primary colonizing growths of fungi are already evident'. Still air in humid voids is what the fungi love more than anything else, especially on what are called 'nutrient substrates', such as cabinet linings made of paper or fabric. There is something deeply alluring about the strange fungi which invade a burnt building. Their spores are always there, in the air and the spaces of old buildings, waiting for fire to create the habitat in which they can come into full life.

Environmental experts recognize a familiar progression in the fungi. 'You've created this entirely virgin habitat,' Dr Ridout explains. 'It's been blasted by fire and then soaked wet. It's waiting to be colonized.' First come the Ascomycetes, the plaster moulds, Peziza and Pyronema, which cause a mass of white fluffy growth and little bobbles of salmon-pink fruits. They appear in burnt woods after the fire has gone through, colonizing tree stumps. And they appeared in the burnt parts of Windsor.

Then, just as inevitably, come the moulds, Hyphomycetes like Aspergillus or Trichoderma, which are green and black. Then the decay fungi, the Basidiomycetes, the coppery one called Coprinus and then the one with the most beautiful name of all, Serpula lachrymans, better known as dry rot. This entire sequence emerged in the burnt wet parts of Windsor Castle although the dry rot was almost certainly reactivated rather than a new colonization.

Dr Ridout treats burnt buildings as natural environments and was anxious that no hurry should be applied to the drying-out process. He monitored the movement and intensity of damp in the walls by inserting wooden dowels in holes and looking at them from time to time to see if fungus of different sorts had colonized them and how damp they had become themselves. His timescale scarcely seemed to fit with the sense of urgency that the Household was keen to promote. He was reluctant to remove panelling because of the damage that is done in the removal, but by January he did agree that some of it should be taken off the walls and transferred to the stables in the Mews which had been swept for the purpose. Teak sinks in the basement were in danger of splitting if dried too fast and so they were filled with water but then sealed across the top with polythene and tape so that the walls around them could continue to be dried.

Dr Ridout pleaded simply 'to get rid of the rubbish, get the roof back on, then just blow air through it for a few years. Generally get the air belting though the place and then say, right, we'll leave it for three years.'

That approach, given the need to return Windsor to full working order and given the attention of Parliament and the world on what was being done here, could never have been taken up. It was inevitable, even as Dr Ridout was suggesting his long, slow ideal – his report suggested that the building would not be dry for ten years – that the Household should be turning its mind, in a rather less passive way, to the urgent questions that were confronting them: What should be done next? And precisely how should Windsor be restored?

A Kneeling Knight corbel from St George's Hall, later to be taken down, consolidated and repainted (see p 229).

3 Options
& Choices

Nothing is simple about Windsor. Complexity seeps from every stone. That famous outline, laid along the crest of its chalk ridge like the knobbled spine of a heraldic beast, is at the same time one of the most familiar and most opaque of all our national symbols. Far more than the bland, grey, 1913 façade of Buckingham Palace, whose features few people could easily bring to mind, Windsor Castle remains one of our core emblems. But what is it an emblem of?

It seems central and at the same time marginal, set back from the hubbub around its feet. It is a monument to continuity but also to a willingness at various moments in its history to engage in radical change. It is one of the great medieval buildings, but it looks from the outside like a giant nineteenth-century toy, a play-castle. Osbert Lancaster said that Windsor wouldn't deceive a four-year-old into thinking it was real. But it is both real and unreal, a real fortress and a romantic fantasy of a fortress, which nevertheless has rather too hard and material an air for the word 'fantasy' to fit. It can seem rather off-putting and even ugly at first, but its beauty creeps up on you.

Windsor is a relic of a previous world in which Castle dominated town and yet it is clearly a busy, occupied place, the home for three hundred people and filled with their offices too. It is a setting for constitutional ceremonial and in many ways on state visits acts as a hotel. It has an identifiable coherence but is a mishmash of different ages, manners and means of construction. It is a barrack, a museum, a country house, an archaeological site and a tourist attraction, a palace, a picture gallery, private, public, ours and not ours at the same time.

It was scarcely surprising that a flood of contradictory responses should appear after the burning of this mille-feuilles of a building. Almost any attitude could be said to have some validity. A break with the past, an extension of the past or a re-creation of the past: all had their precedents here. Symbolism ran rampant. The fire was seen in some quarters as a symptom of national decline. Others thought it a metaphor for the threat to the monarchy. The *Sunday Telegraph* quoted Edmund Burke after the French Revolution: 'As long as the British monarchy, like the proud keep of Windsor girt with the double belt of its kindred and coeval towers, as long as these endure, we are all safe together, the high from the blights of envy, the low from the iron hand of oppression.'

Others relished the sheer excitement of destruction. Watching the fire, Hugh Pearson of the republican *Sunday Times* saw 'Sir Jeffry Wyatville's distinctly dull late-Georgian interiors at last putting on something of a show, converting themselves into greenhouse gases with all the energy and visual magic of a professional firework display'. Rowan Moore, the architectural journalist, and others wanted St George's Hall left as a ruin, with wild flowers covering the floor and and a memorial flame burning there for ever. This, according to Moore, was the 'revenge of nature' on a Royal Family that had 'suppressed nature, pretended to be sexless and surrounded themselves with artifice'. His solution was a form of punishment. Robin Nicholson, Vice-President of the Royal Institute of British Architects, joined the ranks of the Ruinists and managed to say 'It's no great shakes as a building. It isn't that old and we've got plenty of really wonderful castles around. Rather than build a bland replacement, I would prefer it just left charred.' *The Times* brought in an ecological analogy: 'Just as old forests can renew themselves by fire, so can old castles. It was ever thus.' It wasn't – burnt roof trusses do not sprout new versions of themselves – but, at these poetic outer margins of the response, the metaphorical had clearly taken over.

At the other end of the spectrum, and in an almost equally symbolic way, the assumption was made that the only possible route was precise and total replacement of everything that had been there before the fire. This had been the approach both at Hampton Court and at Uppark, even to the extent that hidden elements, such as the riven oak laths on which the plaster was to be laid or the way of fixing the timbers in the roof trusses, should carefully and exactly follow what had been lost. For these Replicationists, modern architects were vandals who had destroyed so much that was valuable that they should not be allowed anywhere near something as sensitive as Windsor. Any idea of a new design was anathema to them. Nicholas Paget-Brown, writing in the *Independent,* encapsulated the view: 'The sad fact is that in the late twentieth century, there is very little suitably modern either in fixtures and fittings or in constitutional structures which is other than laughably ugly, uncomfortable and designed to crack up after minimal pressure.' The duty of the loyal and the faithful was a loyal and faithful reproduction.

Between the Ruinists and the Replicationists, at least in this largely theoretical public debate, the ground was held by the modernists, who came in a variety of forms. There were the Purists. For them restoration was an impossibility, on the purely intellectual ground that a restoration of something was not the same as the thing it aimed to restore. For them, the only pure option was to build something in contemporary style. Their position was reinforced by that of the Moralists. The Wyatville interiors, according to them, had been 'fakes' – pretending to be medieval or French eighteenth-century rooms when they were neither – and what could be more reprehensible, they asked, than 'refaking fakes'? What kind of signal of moral degeneracy would that send out? Again, for them only an overtly modern solution would be good enough.

The Moralists, who were of course descendants in line direct from the Pugin–Ruskin school of honesty in architecture, fringed into a group who might be called the Vitalists. For them the fire was not a disaster but an opportunity. It was a chance to demonstrate not only the vitality of the monarchy at the end of the twentieth century but to be a showcase of everything that British architecture could be or had become.

For the more extreme among the modernists, Windsor was 'a Regency theme-park' which deserved demolition. The fire had only begun the work which any right-thinking Vitalist would happily complete. The Royal Family should be 'patrons not pasticheurs' and anyone interested in the past was doing nothing more than 'wandering befuddled in the miasma of history'. There was an almost Hygienist element to some of this. According to the *Independent,* for example, 'It would be far more healthy were the Palace and the Department of National Heritage to follow the example of King George IV and announce their intention to have the gutted interiors rebuilt to the best of confident, contemporary British design.' There were complicating facts: most of the interiors were not entirely gutted; virtually all of the furniture survived; and George IV's work, while undeniably contemporary and confident, had nevertheless itself largely been a *pastiche*, in the technical sense of that term, a combination of old and new elements sewn together to make a new whole. Nearly all of this passed without comment.

The drama over, the fire-damaged part of the Castle presented the Household with a vast, intractable, sodden, complex bulk of a building.

The President of the Royal Institute of British Architects, Richard MacCormac, trod carefully. 'There is no question of returning to an authentic design for the Castle,' he said, 'since one doesn't exist. A good solution would be to allow contemporary architects to design sensitively around the historical fabric.' His Vice-President, Robin Nicholson, went further, urging 'an architectural competition be held for the rebuilding of Windsor Castle. An architectural competition would be a far more positive assertion of tradition than the slavish re-creation of Victorian pastiche.'

This met with an excoriating response from Colin Amery of the *Financial Times*: 'Apart from the breathtaking ignorance that tries to suggest that good Regency architecture is Victorian pastiche, I wonder whether any member of the RIBA has recently been to Windsor or taken the slightest interest in English artistic and architectural history.'

Within the Household, thinking was running along rather different if parallel lines. Two things were clear: an accurate report was needed on the state of the building, on what had and had not survived and on the costs of the different methods of rebuilding; and an effective decision-making structure had to be set up which would take into account the tides of opinion that were ebbing and flowing around the Castle walls. With those two things in place, decisions could then be made about what to do, when and how.

Before the end of November 1992, within a week of the fire being put out, Michael Peat, the Royal Household's Director of Finance and Property Services, had outlined to the Permanent Secretary at the Department of Heritage at least the questions that needed answering: to restore or not to restore, to be authentic in the restoration or to use equivalent means to produce the same effect, to 'decide which rooms we might rationalize and fashion in a more contemporary manner'. He suggested 'a small group including figures such as the Chairman of the Arts Council should be set up to consider the matter'.

From the beginning, the Household's focus was on how the Castle would function as a living and working building. Unlike most of the points of view expressed in the outside world, where symbolism ruled,

the Household's functional approach could consider the possibility of treating different parts in different ways. 'Windsor Castle is a living building which has evolved over time,' Peat emphasized to the DNH in these early days. 'It may be thought to be a pity to miss the opportunity to give the main state rooms some twentieth-century imprint. It is a *living* building used for state and official purposes rather than an historic monument or museum.'

As for the question of how to restore what had been burnt, Peat's memorandum to the DNH was even-handed: 'Some will say that little is achieved by pretending that this has not happened. Some people will ask why we should reconstruct the roof supports for St George's Hall using nineteenth-century techniques if the only people who will go into the roof voids are maintenance staff? Others will say that past techniques and materials should be replicated for the sake of historical correctness and to ensure that our heritage is not diminished.'

The Household was moving fast – it was hoped at this stage to have completed the restoration within two years, although no one could be certain about timing yet – and by early December it was decided that the Duke of Edinburgh should chair the Advisory Committee to consider these questions. By the 7th the Duke himself had written 'Some Thoughts on the Restoration of Windsor Castle'. His analytical method did not take into account the wilder shores of symbolism, but looked at the burnt parts of Windsor in the way anyone would consider a damaged building which they knew well.

'It is important to bear in mind,' the Duke wrote, 'that all the furniture (other than the Pugin sideboard), pictures (other than the Beechey in the Dining Room), all the carpets and all the works of art (other than parts of the chandeliers), from the rooms affected by the fire are safe and intact. This implies that it would be difficult to make a case for the complete redesign of the Grand Reception Room, St George's Hall and the Red and Green Drawing Rooms.'

The furniture for the State Dining Room was still intact but as a room it was not as important as the others. There was no furniture directly associated with the Chapel. 'In effect,' the Duke went on, 'the only "public" area which could be radically redesigned, and where it would be possible to introduce "contemporary styles", is the Chapel and, to a lesser extent, the Dining Room. The Chapel area has always posed a problem of movement between the public rooms along the east wing and St George's Hall and the other rooms along the north wing. There would now be an opportunity to change the general layout of this area to allow the two wings to be connected in a more convenient manner.'

Apart from that, the Duke said, the fire had given them an opportunity to redesign the staff rooms in the upper floors and 'the rabbit warren of glass and china pantries, the vestry, two sets of back stairs and access to the gold and silver pantries and to the kitchen area as a whole. The question will be how to do this within the limitations imposed by the outside walls and "historic" nature of the structure within the area.'

The question of St George's Hall ceiling was not addressed and the fate of the Dining Room was left hanging. Apart from that, this rapidly sketched strategy – replicating the State Apartments, rationalizing the service areas, and both rationalizing and redesigning what had been the Private Chapel area – is, in broad outline, the route which the restoration would take over the next five years.

A few days later it was decided that the Duke's Advisory Committee, whose members had yet to be appointed, should spawn a sub-committee, chaired by the Prince of Wales. This committee would have the responsibility for those parts of the Castle which might be subject to new designs. It would make recommendations to the Duke's Restoration Committee, which would consider them without necessarily being bound to follow them.

This division of functions was devised to reflect the different priorities and roles of Duke and Prince: architectural design was obviously an area in which the Prince, more than any other member of his family, has great interest and expertise, but Windsor was not his house. It was clear that the Prince should be integral to the process but that the Duke and the Queen should, after all the consultations had been made, have the final decision on what was done. Necessarily more formalized than most, it was very much the sort of arrangement which any family would have come to in the circumstances.

At the same time, on the recommendation of the Lord Chamberlain, Lord Airlie, it was decided that the Royal Household itself via its Property Section should be solely responsible for the design and rebuilding of all the back parts: the Kitchen, Kitchen Court and staff rooms. The public would never go there and they were not, Lord Airlie felt, 'matters of public concern, other than cost'. The Duke agreed that there should be no consultative committee for those designs. English Heritage was necessarily concerned with the historic fabric but neither the Design nor the Restoration Committee was to be involved. These arrangements were discussed by the Duke with Peter Brooke, Secretary of State for National Heritage, before Christmas.

This early decision to keep the back of house away from any overseeing committee of taste, which seemed at the time so obvious and so anodyne, was indirectly to lead to one of the more difficult moments in the project, two years later, when, as will be described in Chapter 5, designs that had been approved, at least in outline, within the Property Section for the Kitchen, Kitchen Court and staff areas were subsequently changed in mid-course.

As these early strategic decisions were being made, the Property Section set about preparing its report on the fire-damaged area. Fierce time pressures were applied. Throughout December and the first part of January, with no more than a single day off for Christmas, and with long hours being worked, John Tiltman, then Deputy Director of the Property Section, orchestrated a team of quantity surveyors, structural engineers, architects and architectural historians.

On 26 January 1993, the Options Report, by then in its eighth draft and having cost £44,000, was finally produced by this Steering Group and delivered to the Queen, the Duke of Edinburgh, the DNH and English Heritage. It was not published, because it was an internal document and perhaps because it was felt that public attitudes to the different options which the report described would bring distorting pressures on the decision-making process. At this stage, the decision to fund 70 per cent of the project from the entry fees to Buckingham Palace had not been made and it was likely, given the mood of the time and the general tightening of government finances, that public opinion would have pressed for the cheapest of all options. Although the Department of National Heritage was always looking for cost savings, that was not necessarily the route the Household wanted to follow.

The Options Report is the key document in the whole restoration project. It formulates and amplifies most of the assumptions made by the Duke of Edinburgh after the fire and subtly steers the reader towards his conclusions. That, at least, is the sub-text. Superficially, the report maintains a cool distance from any particular preference, and portrays itself as an impartial laying out of all the available options. In fact, it has a clear agenda of its own and signals its intentions early on. 'There is a wide range of options for reconstruction,' it says smoothly. 'Some, it may be felt, are more for theoretical than practical consideration.' Three of them are dismissed straight away. The romantic, Ruinist idea of leaving part of the Castle unrestored is dismissed as impractical because Windsor 'is a living and working building for the Head of State'. It could not function without the accommodation that was burnt.

Restoration in substitute materials, such as fibreglass mouldings instead of plasterwork, which might be suitable 'for new interiors of luxury hotels', was thought too tawdry and cheapskate for Windsor.

A total redesign of the burnt corner of the Castle, along the lines some of the Vitalists had suggested, was rejected because the stone shell of the Castle has survived intact. 'It was thought inappropriate to consider an option embracing partial or total demolition of the surviving shell . . . Any adjustment to the external fabric,' the report says, 'will be limited to possible remodelling of small areas of roofscape.'

This early assumption that the external profile would remain virtually untouched meant, for example, that no outside staircase could be introduced to the Quadrangle at the Equerries' Entrance, even though that would have solved a whole set of difficult circulation problems in bringing the Queen's guests up on to the first floor.

More importantly, this decision also meant that the roof of St George's Hall was always going to be at a lower pitch than the aesthetics of the room required. Wyatville's flat ceiling had given the room, which is 180 feet long, something of the look of a railway carriage. A steeper and more sculptural pitch would have heightened the room in proportion to its length inside and would have been more in keeping with any medieval antecedents but would have changed its appearance from the Quad. This early veto on any externally visible alteration made a very much steeper roof impossible.

Why, then, was this decision made? If the work was to progress at the speed required, some sort of cap had to be placed on the options available. There is something alarmingly all-consuming about the manner of modern architecture, which many clients feel the need to keep at bay. One devastatingly radical scheme for Windsor, for example, floated in a Sunday newspaper, had envisaged a 180-foot-high glass and steel cylinder, in the form of an alembic with little cauldron legs, where the Brunswick Tower used to be. The Household's closing of the envelope, although no part of the Windsor tradition – the silhouette has changed over the centuries as much as anything else – should perhaps be seen as a symbol of independence from fashion and as part of the urge to get on. Whatever the real virtues and beauties of which modern architecture is capable, it was inconceivable, given the nature of the client and the purposes to which this building must be put, that any of the more radical solutions could ever have been entertained here.

The Options Report group could then turn to the three more mainstream alternatives. These they called Authentic Restoration, Equivalent Restoration and Contemporary Redesign. Authentic Restoration was by far the most expensive. The quantity surveyors estimated that to restore the burnt area to its previous condition, using precisely the same techniques and materials as those which had been destroyed, would cost £41–2 million. In the time and the circumstances that could be little more than a guesstimate, and the figure included £5.1 million for contingencies. Nevertheless, a beam-by-beam, truss-by-truss reconstruction of the nineteenth-century roofs, for example, was estimated at £5.5 million, almost double the estimated cost of a roof using modern techniques and materials.

The report wrinkles its nose at the idea of Authentic Restoration. It had been the method used at Uppark, but the insurers there had paid for it. At Windsor there was no insurer and both the Royal Household and the Department of National Heritage did not like the idea of spending many millions of pounds on historical authenticity, a large part of which no one would ever see. Although the cost of Authentic Restoration was gone into in great detail in the report, room by room throughout the burnt area, it was never a runner. At least in part, costing the option was useful to demonstrate that the next alternative, Equivalent Restoration, was not the most expensive available.

The guesstimate for Equivalent Restoration gave a figure of £32 million for the job. Savings on the Authentic approach were to be achieved everywhere, chipping away behind the scenes, so that the skin looked identical but the framework was cheaper. At Uppark, where the National Trust were luxuriating in the position of not having to pay, the argument had been made – and carried – that if a room were plastered on to the expanded metal sheets which are standard in modern construction, there would be a danger that they might look right but would *sound* different to the original, where the plaster would have been laid on riven oak laths. Riven oak laths were used at Uppark; expanded metal was to be used at Windsor. Equivalent Restoration also has the advantage that where you can't see it, all the best modern practice in terms of fire compartmentation, service ducting, hygienic materials and strengthened floors can be used without quibble.

Equivalent Restoration, as the Options Report argued, is also central to the tradition at Windsor of what the architect Sir William Whitfield calls 'a certain fictive quality, a sense that a theatrical performance is being put on here'. Whatever the stage flats look like, they are only the outer face. Behind the scenes you can abandon the illusionism and attend to less historical questions: do they stand up, will they last and will they not cost too much?

There was a third option costed for Windsor room by room, which the report called Contemporary Redesign. This was thought to be the cheapest at £29 million, a figure that rose to £31 million if the opportunity was taken to add a new Private Chapel and accommodation in the Kitchen Court. The report offered no overt opinions on whether redesigning the burnt area would be a good idea or not. From noises coming out of the DNH at the time, it was clear that the Department liked the look of the savings. The Options Report, at least superficially, held back from commitment, suggesting only that 'a contemporary design approach would include replanning previously unsatisfactory staff and ancillary accommodation'.

That, of course, is precisely what the Duke's December memorandum had envisaged. Meanwhile, the Royal Collection was deeply concerned that the treasures at Windsor should be returned not to rooms that had been subject to a Contemporary Redesign but to the restored or replicated rooms which George IV and his team of advisers had created for them in the 1820s. Hugh Roberts, then Deputy Surveyor of the Queen's Works of Art, had the task within the Options Report of describing the historical background to the burnt rooms and at the same time, at least subliminally, of making the case for restoration rather than redesign.

In a few pages, Roberts puts on a bravura performance. The context for his own argument is the sneering contempt with which Wyatville's remodelling of Windsor was generally being treated in the press. Roberts slams back: 'The area that Wyatville remodelled presented, before the fire, a superb and unrivalled sequence of rooms widely regarded as the finest and most complete expression of later Georgian taste. The three styles of architecture selected by Wyatville and King George IV – Classical, Gothic and Rococo – were deliberately and carefully orchestrated throughout the building to emphasize the function of the different rooms and to harmonize with the furniture chosen or designed for them.'

With those sentences in mind, any argument for a comprehensive redesign of the rooms in question becomes impossible. But the point is driven home: 'Each room on the principal floor, whether considered separately or as part of a sequence, was intended to embody the union between architecture and the fine and applied arts to the extent that, in very nearly every case, the furnishings originally selected for these rooms have remained for the most part where they were placed in the 1820s.' Were the 1990s, the buried question asked, going to do the damage to this unique ensemble from which even the Victorians had drawn back?

Throughout the body of the report, room by room and detail by detail, the same point was made: the rooms might look or be dreadfully damaged but the walls, floors and ceilings were no more than the decorated shell within which the room existed. A room was effectively made by its furnishings and they had survived.

There were four possible exceptions: the State and Octagon Dining Rooms, savaged by intense heat during the fire, had no element of decoration remaining on walls or ceiling. They were candidates for redesign. The rather ugly Private Chapel, reshaped in the 1840s and then redecorated in the 1970s when it was painted a peachy cream colour with some gilding, was in planning terms unsatisfactory anyway as an awkward dog-leg knuckle between the Private and State Apartments. No one would be sorry to see that changed. And there was St George's Hall. Its Authentic Restoration was estimated at £4.5 million. Equivalent Restoration would shave £800,000 off that, but few people had loved the room in the past – it was too long, too boxy and too flat. Perhaps there was a chance to do something there.

Through the Options Report, the Household had shown that its own requirements for Windsor and its own way of working dictated a whole string of design decisions. It could scarcely have been clearer: architecture cannot be conceived in abstract but only in relation to the people and institutions that will one day use it. If anyone really thought that the Royal Household would commission a radical and comprehensive redesign of this part of the Castle, they had not understood the client.

The Options Report gave few steers on St George's Hall, but in every other way it was an extraordinarily effective document: a closing down of choices is portrayed as a laying out of options. A covert recommendation of the one route to follow is disguised as a comprehensive map of the entire terrain.

The framework was now ready to take the project on to its next phase. Not everything had been settled, but the outline was clear. It was important, though, for the Household to take the other key players along with it and to avoid any imputation that it was acting independently of national opinion.

On 22 April 1993 the first pivotal meeting was held in the White Drawing Room in Windsor Castle. It is a small room, the smallest in the succession of Crimson, Green and White which form Wyatville's enfilade of drawing rooms along the east front of the Castle. The door from the White Drawing Room into the Green, from the undamaged to the devastated area, was boarded up. Here at 9.30 in the morning, at a meeting chaired by the Duke, the Household put the options to key representatives of the outside world. The meeting, and the Restoration Committee of which it was the embryo, would, as an internal memo put it, 'enable external views to be sought across a broad spectrum. It will submit recommendations to the Queen.'

A list of who was there sounds like a catalogue of the two sides drawn up on the field of Crécy, or at least its modern, sober-suited equivalent. For the Household, there was Michael Peat, Director of Finance and Property Services, and his Deputy in the Property Section, John Tiltman. They were accompanied by Sir Geoffrey de Bellaigue, then Director of the Royal Collection, and Lieutenant-Colonel Blair Stewart Wilson, Deputy Master of the Household.

From the outside world came Lord St John of Fawsley, Chairman of the Royal Fine Art Commission, Sir William Whitfield, the architect, Lord Rodgers of Quarry Bank, Director-General of the Royal Institute of British Architects and his President, Richard MacCormac. Jocelyn Stevens, Chairman of English Heritage, came with his Chief Executive, Jennie Page. Hayden Phillips, Permanent Secretary at the Department of National Heritage, had with him the Secretary of State's Architectural Adviser, Brian Jefferson.

There were certainly some people there who had been conducting trenchant public polemic over the months since the fire had occurred, but the April morning in the White Drawing Room passed smoothly and calmly enough. John Tiltman gave an illustrated talk with slides outlining the salient points of the Options Report. He had rehearsed it to Michael Peat the evening before in his office looking on to the Buckingham Palace Quadrangle. As always with such critical presentations, there had been an element of uncertainty over the right approach and Michael Peat suggested a major pruning of the contents.

Nevertheless, the outcome on the day proved that the two men had got it right. The Duke of Edinburgh beset Tiltman with questions and the presentation worked extremely well. After he had finished, the Duke, a brisk and decisive chairman well known for the speed with which he drives questions to a conclusion, took the meeting to a series of highly significant decisions. The Grand Reception Room, the Green Drawing Room and the Crimson Drawing Room were all to be

reinstated, according to the principles of Equivalent rather than Authentic Restoration. The area of the Private Chapel, the ceiling of St George's Hall, the screen at its east end and both the Octagon and State Dining Rooms were to 'be redesigned'. For Sir Geoffrey de Bellaigue, the Director of the Royal Collection, and others who worked with the Royal Collection, this suggestion that the Dining Rooms should be redesigned, when so much of their original furnishings survived, was deeply unwelcome. Over the following weeks, they would work to have that suggestion overturned.

The committee approved a list of five architectural practices which had been drawn up by the project managers and the Household's Property Section. The candidates were from among the country's leading conservation practices. They would be asked to tender for a double job: to act as co-ordinating architects; and to be the architects in direct control of those state rooms which were to be restored as before.

Most significantly of all, however, it was established that a new lead-covered, steel roof 'to the previous profile' would be put on St George's Hall. Although it was recognized that such a roof would limit the scope to design a combined roof and ceiling over St George's Hall, it was

In the summer of 1993 the new steel-beamed roof goes on St George's Hall, to keep the weather out and to put momentum into the project. Its low pitch predetermined the scope of any design to the ceiling below it.

At the same time, a new roof was put back on the Grand Reception Room, a queen-post structure, similar to its timber predecessor, from which the replica ceiling could be easily suspended.

agreed that it would be inappropriate to change the external profile of the building. The argument went that only a small part of the Upper Ward had been damaged and so whatever was inserted here should not disrupt the overall coherence of the Quadrangle as Wyatville had left it. Equally, to wait for an integral solution would seriously delay provision of a weather-tight envelope. Even so, the new roof did give about three feet of additional space underneath it which would later allow any ceiling to be steeper than the Wyatville ceiling that had been there before the fire.

In many ways, this was the most important design decision made over the whole project. Members of the architectural profession would later see it as a failure of nerve. Frank Duffy, successor to Richard Mac-Cormac as President of the RIBA, makes the point quite forcibly: 'There was a possibility here to bring about a frisson between the old and the new, a frisson based on the solidity and strength of the existing architecture and the lightness and transparency of the interventions. Something could have been done here with air and glass to bring out the tremendous beauty of the existing buildings. That is certainly a pattern of which there are many Italian examples, in Milan in particular. But here, in the late twentieth century, crude technology was used which cut off all sorts of possibilities. It was a collective failure of judgement but more than that it was a failure to understand, in a Puginesque way, the importance of architecture in determining the feel and quality of the space. It wasn't a Gothic decision.'

For the Household, the arguments about the external integrity of the Upper Ward and the importance of getting the project moving overrode such considerations – for the Duke of Edinburgh, in particular, this challenge was about rehabilitating a damaged building, not an exercise in demonstrating the state of modern architecture – and work began in June on the new steel roof beams for St George's Hall, the Grand Reception Room and the Chester Tower. They were designed by the engineers Hockley and Dawson. For the Grand Reception Room, they simply replicated the previous timber trusses in steel and in St George's Hall, they designed something that was no more nor less than an efficient structure. They knew it would never be seen; it simply had to do the job. None of the drama of elegant engineering, which architects in this century, as in the later Middle Ages, have made central to their art, was to be allowed a place here. All that was needed was a lid on a box. The requisite structure is called 'a pitched tapering beam'. Like the roof itself, the description is exact and pragmatic. Each of the thirty trusses is made up of a pair of steel beams, pitched at a shallow angle, bolted to each other at the ridge and to concrete pads in the walls at each side. The beams are tapered – fatter in the middle than at the ends – because the maximum turning force is at the ridge and so that is where the deepest section is required. The structure, called a portal by engineers, deliberately has no base to the triangle it creates, giving the maximum amount of room beneath it to accommodate the Household's brief that the new ceiling should have as much clearance as possible at the centre. Its designers also raised it slightly higher than the pre-fire roof for the same reasons.

The installation of the roof was not quite so simple as its conception. The walls of St George's Hall are not quite parallel, and so each truss had to be of a different length. Putting up the new steel roof around the preserved iron trusses installed by Sir Robert Smirke in 1818 was, according to Jim Gillam of Wallis's, the site manager who was running the job, 'a saga in itself'. That was not the only constraint. They were under time pressure to get the roof on as soon as possible but whenever the Private Apartments were occupied they needed to keep disturbance to a minimum. Between Friday and Monday lunchtimes, no deliveries could be made into the Quadrangle nor could forklift trucks be used there.

By the beginning of 1994 the new St George's Hall roof was complete. The brick reinforcement of the upper walls and the concrete padstones on which the steel trusses rest, like the roof itself, show clearly the workings of the philosophy of Equivalent Restoration: no pretence at an antique finish where it would not be seen.

Nevertheless, the work on the roofs developed at speed. A scaffold runway was built over the top of St George's Hall to the Grand Reception Room. Along it the remains of the previous Grand Reception Room roof were taken away. Both rooms were entirely filled with a birdcage scaffold. Gillam had to work to what he calls 'a rolling club-sandwich'. Each layer of the process could be started only as its predecessor came to completion. First English Heritage had to finish their investigations of the floors. In St George's Hall they were still excavating the chalk infill of the supporting vaults. Then the scaffold could go in. Then the bricklayers could create the beds high up in the walls for the pre-formed concrete padstones. Then a hole could be opened up in the temporary roof, through which the crane could lower the concrete padstones, each a metre square, into position. Then the temporary roof could be closed again. Then the steel for the trusses themselves could be brought in, positioned and bolted. Then the carpenters could build the timber framework, the purlins, the rafters and the plyboard sheets between them, on which, finally, the leadworkers could lay the outer skin. When that was complete, the scaffolders could at last dismantle the temporary roof. It was surgery in reverse, the layers of skin being peeled back on. By February 1994 the new roofs were finished, at a cost of £940,000. It was fifteen months since the fire.

The debate about what should be done had, in broad outline, been settled within the Household. On 29 April 1993 the Lord Chamberlain, Lord Airlie, held a press conference in which the conclusions arrived at in the White Drawing Room meeting a week earlier were announced to the world. Some feathers were ruffled. The Replicationists were alarmed at the idea that any new design should interfere with the Wyatville scheme in the State and Octagon Dining Rooms. The Modernists did not like the sound of options being closed down for St George's Hall.

Already in train, however, were two projects which could not have taken into account the Household's rapid decision-making. Both Mark Girouard, the architectural historian, and the magazine *Country Life* had separately invited architects and designers to come up with ideas for what might be done with St George's Hall. Both wanted to widen debate, to articulate some of the currents then moving through the architectural world and to see what happened when the theoretical positions people were taking up were forced into the rather more concrete form of drawings and models.

The results of both invitations were put on show together at the

Above: *The suggestion for St George's Hall made by Mark Fisher and Stuart Hopps had a ceiling with a 1m wide opening running the entire length of the Hall, precisely aligned with Heathrow runway 09/27. It did not meet with the approval of the Royal Household.*

Richard MacCormac's scheme was more serious, being a modern interpretation of the Gothic spirit: the timber, steel and bronze structure was designed to be 'an engineering spectacle'.

Architectural Foundation in London in July and August. The difference from the Household's own carefully modulated position could not have been more distinct. A chaotically and dynamically inventive zoo of solutions and ideas emerged. A spiral hall, like the vastly inflated fossil of a Jurassic tower-shell, skewered its way, in one scheme, across the Upper Ward. In another, a gold-foil-edged slit, one metre wide and perfectly aligned with runway 09/27 at Heathrow, ran the length of St George's Hall. 'We preserve the aristocratic ruin,' the designers stated, 'whilst exploring the free movements of peoples in the flight paths overhead.' Another had a 120-foot-long wave-machine installed along the window wall of St George's Hall. A crown was set bobbing in the fluid; it was, in fact, a royal wave. Ron Herron, who teaches at both the Architectural Association and at the Bartlett School of Architecture, produced a variation on an earlier work entitled 'Sets fit for a Queen', in which he saw the Queen as 'superstar' in a paper-thin temporary stage set which on completion the contractors were to 'lightly spray with dust and into some corners spray latex cobwebs' and where 'the chair cushions to be worn in places, i.e. by use of sandpaper carefully applied and on completion to be heavily dusted with a mixture of soot and talcum powder to simulate dust'.

The romance, but also the revenge, of the ruin, most elegantly expressed in Rowan Moore's idea of a flowery meadow within the charred and broken walls, dominated a whole section of the response, but others were more generous towards the idea that the Sovereign and her Household might actually have a use for the rooms that had been destroyed. Richard MacCormac, until recently President of the RIBA, produced a roof, as others did, whose method, as he now describes it, was 'to abstract the Gothic. The original medieval roof was an engineering spectacle and that was what our roof would have tried to recreate.' His proposal was a light, tensed structure in which steel rigging, drawing on yacht technology, held the forces of the roof in obvious but elegant control. 'We are not talking about a terrifying modernism here,' MacCormac says. 'What's going on now is not blunt, brutal, deliberately non-contextual, but the very opposite of that. Not the hi-tech stuff, but much more about the enjoyment of materials, light and form and a sculptural way of looking at architecture.'

Giles Worsley, who at the time was the Architectural Editor of *Country Life*, saw the MacCormac-type approach as 'a complete misunderstanding of what this building was about. Windsor has always been about tradition, about the monarchy establishing its validity by

new steeply pitched timber roof

GEORGE

walls restored

CROSS SECTION

Roderick Gradidge's High Victorian suggestion (left) of a steeply pitched crown-post roof and uncompromising decorative idiom, to be executed by Christopher Boulter, would have run *foul of the new shallow-pitched roof (below) which was being installed in St George's Hall even at the time Gradidge was drawing up his ideas.*

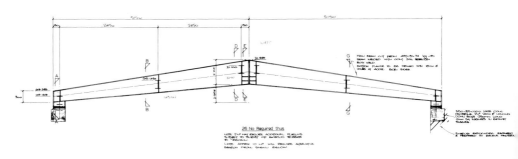

wrapping itself up in the garb of previous monarchs. Were Windsor to cease to be a Royal castle and become just a museum then it would be perfectly appropriate to do a forward-looking scheme which would almost be celebrating the end of monarchy.' But for Worsley, and other traditionalists, many of whom submitted designs for the *Country Life* competition, the monarchy had not come to an end, Windsor was still a Royal castle and those circumstances dictated a traditionalist scheme.

For many of those to whom Windsor was a working, functioning building, the tenor of this discussion was miles wide of the mark. As the Prince of Wales says, 'I have never thought of Windsor as somehow symbolic of the monarchy. Everybody else has these extraordinary ideas that they put into our heads which just don't exist. If you happen to be the Sovereign or whatever, and you are born into this whole exercise, you don't think all the time about how you symbolize monarchical principles. People around you do that,' he says with a smile. 'You have to constantly keep them under control to stop them getting carried away, I find.'

One of the most convincing schemes of all those thrown up by the two outside competitions was by Roderick Gradidge, a leading member of the Art Workers Guild and distinguished country-house architect in the Lutyens tradition. He and the decorator Christopher Boulter submitted a spectacularly full-blooded exercise in the manner of William Burges or Viollet-le-Duc, with a hugely tall crown-post roof to St George's Hall, painted a deep midnight blue and decorated with gilded stars. New murals coated the whole northern side of the Hall, while the East Screen was smothered, as the west end originally had been in the 1820s, with all the plate Windsor could muster, as though that end of the Hall were dressed in golden armour. It was, in its way, a demonstration of how spectacularly courageous, vital and exciting a historical approach could be. 'Gradidge's scheme is entirely practical,' the *Sunday Times* pronounced in July and it was awarded the *Country Life* prize. What neither Gradidge nor the judges had taken into account was the low-pitched steel roof even then being installed over St George's Hall. Gradidge's High Victorian roof was far too steep to be accommodated within it.

Meanwhile, as Windsor was being mentally reconstructed and deconstructed, salvaged and destroyed, taunted and cosseted in all the different corners of the architectural world, the decision-making system which the Royal Household had established was moving imperturbably towards its own solutions. The waves of controversy tended to break on the Castle walls and then ebb away.

At the end of July 1993 the Duke's Restoration Committee met for the first time in the Duke's Library in Buckingham Palace. The meeting lasted less than an hour. Its essential function was for the Household to inform and listen to its advisers in the four key organizations: the Department of National Heritage (Hayden Phillips), the Royal Fine Art Commission (Lord St John of Fawsley), English Heritage (Jennie Page, standing in for her Chairman Jocelyn Stevens) and the Royal Institute of British Architects (Frank Duffy). As these organizations and most of these people had been at the April meeting, where so many of the key decisions had already been taken, there was relatively little to do. The Duke suggested a new chapel might go in the space previously occupied by the Stuart and Holbein Rooms 'leaving the previous chapel area as an ante-room connecting St George's Hall to the Drawing Rooms'. It also considered the suggested membership of the Prince's committee, rejecting some people, adding others, and then handed on the torch.

The Prince of Wales's Design Committee, made up of architects, architectural historians and interior designers, met for the first time in September 1993, again in November and again in April 1994. The three meetings, in turn, established the brief, refined it and then considered the proposals which the chosen architects had made. The Design Committee was to concern itself with only two parts of the Castle: the Octagon and State Dining Rooms; and St George's Hall and the previous Private Chapel area, including the Holbein and Stuart Rooms. Everything else was under the direct supervision of either the Restoration Committee (the Drawing Rooms and the Grand Reception Room) or the Household Property Section (the Kitchen and staff areas). Even in those parts which the Design Committee could attend to, their role was simply to recommend to the Restoration Committee, not to make any final decisions themselves. The Household was clear from the beginning that control should remain with the Queen. The Restoration Committee itself was also only an advisory body. With every aspect, the final decision rested with the Queen, closely advised by the Duke of Edinburgh.

Everyone was anxious to avoid anything that smacked of an architectural competition. Competitions are difficult to administer in themselves and, after the winning design has been chosen, often lead to acrimony, entrenched positions, disintegration of timetables and escalating expense. A designer, not a design was to be chosen, and there was to be no throwing open of the project to all-comers. The exoticism of the Girouard and *Country Life* experiences loomed as an all-too-alarming object lesson in what an open field might produce. Four architectural practices were therefore asked to submit schemes for the Octagon and State Dining Rooms, for which they would be paid £5000 towards costs, and six others to do so for St George's Hall and the previous Private Chapel area, for which the honorarium was £7500. All ten practices were selected to submit ideas by the Design Sub-Committee from the long list drawn up by the Household and the project managers after consultations with English Heritage, the Department of National Heritage, RIBA and the National Trust.

In the Dining Rooms, Hugh Roberts and the Royal Collection were still fighting hard for a reinstatement of the earlier scheme. He suggested a display should be mounted for the members of the Design Committee of the original design drawings made for the firm of Morel and Seddon which had been responsible for most of the finished appearance of the Wyatville rooms. Once the committee had seen those, 'at least if it is decided to do something wholly different, everyone would be really aware of what they are abandoning and what the knock-on effect on the surrounding area will be'.

For the other areas where new designs were suggested, the ceiling and East Screen of St George's Hall and the Private Chapel area, there was far less of a move to defend the old. Wyatville's flat plaster ceiling in St George's Hall had never been liked, least of all by Wyatville himself, who had described the room simply as 'this unsatisfactory apartment'. Two members of the Design Committee, the historian John Martin Robinson and the architect Sir William Whitfield, argued for its reinstatement on the grounds that it represented one of the earliest attempts to re-create the atmosphere of a baronial hall 'of olden time', only preceded and perhaps inspired by Walter Scott's much smaller hall at Abbotsford. But they did not carry the day and both later changed their minds.

As for the Private Chapel, no one had loved that. Once, before the alterations by Hugh Casson in the 1970s, it had a sombre and numinous air, filled with Blore's Victorian gated pews and with a marvellous pulpit, entered from the Vestry, where the Prince of Wales as a boy used to play at giving sermons to the empty Chapel. But that air had been banished with Casson's white-and-gold refurbishment. The pews and pulpit had gone and the space had become a half-effective, inefficient and ungainly elbow between the Private Apartments to the south and the State Apartments to the west. In planning terms alone, it was obvious that something better could be done there. The Prince of Wales was keen on a 'tribune', a top-lit chamber like the one in the Uffizi in Florence. Hugh Roberts spoke of a *Schatzkammer*, an inner jewel box of a space, where 'gems, orders and decorations, miniatures, jewelled and plain silver gilt, early cabinet pictures' could all be displayed.

General parameters of the design were set: the quality was to be appropriate to a historic castle used for state functions at the end of the twentieth century; there should be a sensitivity in any design to archaeology and history; natural materials should be used; St George's Hall was the great secular room – the counterpart of St George's Chapel in the Lower Ward – for the Order of the Garter and that should govern the designers' thinking. The shields of all the Garter Knights there had ever been should form a part of the proposals. Sir William Whitfield suggested that the Chapel space might provide the climax to the Hall 'with a high ceiling allowing shafts of natural light to illuminate the east end of St George's Hall'.

Ballpark budget figures were established: £2 million for the Private Chapel area, £2.5 million for St George's Hall, just over £1 million for

Zoffany's great painting of the Tribune in the Uffizi in Florence had been evacuated from the Castle during the fire. The image it conveys of a richly furnished, top-lit chamber, filled with treasures, was suggested by the Prince of Wales as a model for the space previously occupied by the Private Chapel.

the two Dining Rooms together. The Prince was adamant that the work should be 'a celebration of craftsmanship'.

At the end of November 1993 the instructions went out to the selected architects. They had until April to come up with their ideas. Although the brief was quite explicitly 'intended to elicit outline design proposals rather than detailed drawings', the different architects responded in different ways. Some produced outline design proposals as requested and they didn't get very far. Others presented their ideas in beautiful, expensive and highly detailed drawings, models and samples. They did.

The suggestions for the Dining Rooms turned out to be a disappointment. Robert Kime, the interior designer and member of the Design Committee, thought that one scheme, a ring of columns squeezed in around the table, looked as if the architect 'had spent too long in Saudi'.

This proposal, Kime thought, looked like a London hotel in the twenties. Others were too austere or failed to take into account the Pugin furniture, of whose virtues Hugh Roberts had been such a consistent advocate.

The best ideas were by Roderick Gradidge, who had been co-winner of the *Country Life* prize for St George's Hall. Cooperating again with the painter Christopher Boulter, Gradidge produced something quite different from his High Victorian St George's Hall scheme. Here in the State Dining Room he suggested a zingy, all-singing eclecticism which took in raw medieval masonry, late Edwardian gilt and enamelled decoration and nineteenth-century wrought- and cast-iron structural members exposed in the walls. The Pugin furniture became just another flavour in the mix.

Gradidge is not a man for middle-of-the-road politesse. His fearless proposals contained other, equally uncompromising elements. There was a new blackberry-purple, domed lobby, intended to be a fire memorial between the two Dining Rooms. The Octagon Dining Room was to be covered in a mural depicting the symbolic relationship of England to Heaven. Oriel windows were to break through the walls of Wyatville's Brunswick Tower. Prince Albert might have loved the scheme but it was too much for the Design and Restoration Committees when they came to consider it in the spring of 1994. Sir Geoffrey de Bellaigue, Surveyor of the Queen's Works of Art, expressed the general feeling in 'recommending the retention of the purity of the previous interior'. It was felt that in a straight contest between Gradidge and Wyatville, Wyatville won. The committee decided that the Dining Rooms would be reinstated as before, with improved lighting, and Donald W. Insall Associates, the architects previously taken on to restore the Grand Reception Room and the Crimson and Green Drawing Rooms, were invited to bid for this aspect of the job too.

St George's Hall and the area previously occupied by Blore's Private Chapel was a much more difficult question. The panelling on the north and south walls of the Hall, as well as its western end, had all largely survived the fire and was all going to be retained. The steel lid was going on the box and so the architect had to devise a ceiling which was an improvement on but still coherent with Wyatville's scheme for the room. It was a challenging task, the same but better, concordant with what was there, but an example of the best that could be done now.

With the area previously occupied by Blore's Chapel and the two small passageway rooms beside it, the scope was greater. There was a complex articulation to be made between Private and State Apartments, there was the possibility of completely replanning those rooms, to ease that awkward knuckle in the corner of the Upper Ward, and there was the challenge of relating the huge tunnel-like length of St George's Hall to the much tighter and condensed spaces in the area of the Chapel.

The six architects divided into two groups of three: the radical and the traditionalist. Nearly all the elements of the public debate that had occurred a year earlier found their echoes in the schemes that were submitted. Something approaching a Ruinist position was adopted by the Hungarian architect Imre Makovecz, whose name had been suggested by the Prince of Wales and who had astonished the world with his Hungarian pavilion at the Expo in Seville in 1992. In the pavilion a huge oak tree was embedded in a glass floor so that every root and every branch was visible. An enormous upturned hull in laminated timber acted as the roof. A cluster of bell-towers burst through that roof as though an illuminated drawing of a medieval city were erupting through it.

Makovecz's vision is a profoundly serious one, drawing on deep, archetypal forms and images with which to redeem the fate of modern man, who, as Makovecz sees it, is increasingly divorcing himself from the natural world. The oak tree in the Seville pavilion represented the emergence from deep roots of something that might flower in the present. In this way the poetic and the ever-present possibility of the tragic are equally bound up in the buildings he creates. It was perhaps inevitable that he would produce a scheme for Windsor that stepped beyond the bounds of a comfortable formality.

What emerged were some of the most extraordinary ideas to be suggested for Windsor. A Gothic vault in steel, with glass between the ribs, would cover the area of the Private Chapel and the eastern end of St George's Hall. The Household's steel roof, already installed, would have to be broken open there. Light would flood in from above and plants would grow in the Chapel to give it as much of a natural appearance as possible. The bare masonry of the walls would be gilded, a ruin made precious, 'showing the raw reality and at the same time the glitter of gold'. Statues of angels, some with the appearance of modern overcoated people with wings, deriving their imagery from Wim Wenders's film *Wings of Desire*, would hang above the Chapel space, as though blessing it. The rest of St George's Hall would be restored to its previous appearance, as though emerging from ruin and disaster.

To Sir William Whitfield, and others on the Design Committee, it

The Sunday Times *invited the architect* Will Alsop *to redesign the fire-damaged areas and this was his largely glazed, top-lit version of the Upper Ward. The Queen was to make her Christmas broadcasts from a studio in the alembic-on-legs with which Alsop replaced the Brunswick Tower.*

was clear that the signals given out by the Makovecz scheme were likely to be read not as hopeful but as tragic, celebrating ruination and the ending of things. That message could scarcely be countenanced.

Two of the architects made broadly Modernist or Vitalist suggestions. Sir Colin Stansfield-Smith proposed a tall louvred ventilation tower above the Private Chapel, which, he says, 'seemed to me would be a beacon above the Castle. I fell in love with the idea and it began to design itself. It would be both a practical answer to ventilating the building and a statement of conviction in royalty, symbolic of Windsor and of royalty and of new life.' The uncompromising nature of Stansfield-Smith's new tower, with its louvred panels and external wire bracing, effectively scuppered his idea, while his proposals for the ceiling of St George's Hall were not developed enough for a judgement to be made. His suggestion of an outside staircase in the Quadrangle, giving direct access to the principal floor, which would have solved a series of difficult circulation problems, could not be taken up because of the early decision that the external envelope should show no signs of alteration.

John Outram, the British architect admired in Europe and America for his use of intense colour and elaborate, quasi-metaphorical schemes, proposed the ingenious and beautiful idea of taking a Gothic moulding from a column in St George's Chapel, vastly enlarging it and turning it on its side, so that the form could be used as the new suspended ceiling for St George's Hall. The Garter shields would be a brilliant and con-

The Hungarian architect Imre Makovecz imposed a Gothic vault in steel and glass over the ruined shell of the Private Chapel in which the exposed stonework would be gilded. Angels, some slightly Germanic, some in overcoats, would hang over the transformed space.

John Outram took a moulding from St George's Chapel, turned it through 90 degrees, enlarged it vastly and used it as a suspended ceiling across which the shields of the Garter Knights would spread as a rippled and continuous polychromatic carpet.

tinuous heraldic carpet laid across the ceiling's rippled and shadowed surface. For the Private Chapel area, Outram again took a previous form, this time a Moorish stalactite dome, of the sort to be found in small niches in the Alhambra, and both perforated and enormously enlarged it. An oculus at its head admitted the light to create a 'Rose of Light' above the ante-chamber to St George's Hall. Its surfaces too would have been brilliantly coloured.

Such a strong idea, pushing Windsor into territory which it had never previously entered, was quite simply too risky for the Committees and Outram's ideas were also rejected through their lack of compromise.

Over the site of the Private Chapel, Sir Colin Stansfield-Smith proposed a tall, glass, louvred ventilation tower which contravened the condition that the outer envelope of the Upper Ward should not be disrupted.

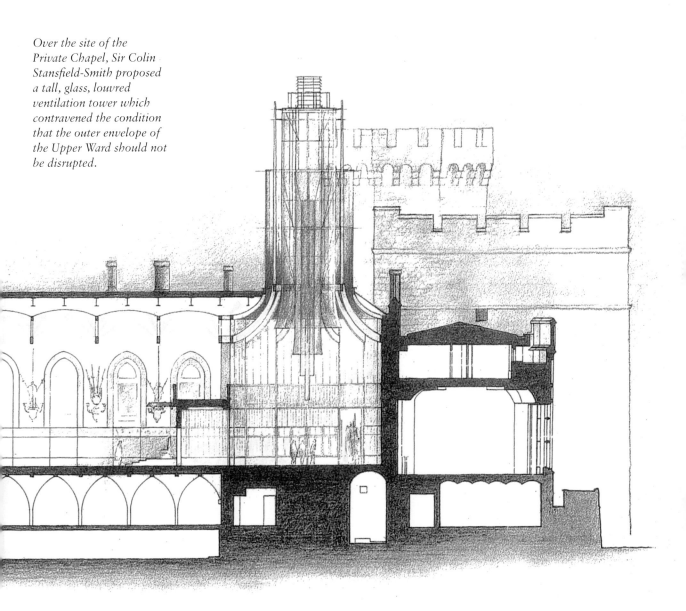

'In Britain as a whole,' Outram now says, 'there has been a rearguard action since the war and the end of empire. The general feeling now is that it was all done better in the past. Anything modern is seen as cheap, tricky and problematic. There is almost an inability to conceive that something done today could actually be done better than it was in the past.' As for the work that was eventually done at Windsor, Outram savages it: 'It's not what you'd expect from an important client. They just don't do things like that in America or the Continent. Or if they do, you know they ought to be an offshoot of Walt Disney.'

It would be surprising, perhaps, if a rejected architect from one tradition were to speak any differently about his successful rival from another. The other three architects headed much more obviously down the track which, in retrospect, the Household was almost bound to follow. This was not an exercise in demonstrating the state of modern British architecture but in rehousing one part of the monarchy and its functions. The Crown is an evolutionary not a revolutionary institution and it is inconceivable that Windsor could have sponsored or accommodated anything which would have undermined its own standing.

Of the traditionalist architects, two, Christopher Smallwood and Giles Downes of Sidell Gibson, were thought most impressive. They were operating in very much the same territory and both produced highly finished drawings and models of their intentions. Smallwood's scheme was a fan-vaulted ceiling to St George's Hall, lit with a glazed clerestory. On the site of the Private Chapel, he proposed a two-storey, classical tempietto, which was strict and austere in the manner of the High Renaissance. Giles Downes also had a medievalist roof to St George's Hall but it was more of a hammerbeam construction, which gave a simpler effect. For the site of the Private Chapel, his idea was an elegant and stripped-down version of a Gothic chapter house, in which the ribs of the columns grew up and out into the vault of the space itself, on the apex of which a glazed lantern admitted the light.

These two proposals were the ones that the Design Committee focused on most closely when they met in the Queen Anne Room of St James's Palace on 27 April 1994. There was a general admiration for what had been produced but various elements came in for criticism. Sir William Whitfield was concerned at Smallwood's mix of styles – High Renaissance was not really a Windsor mode – and preferred the Sidell Gibson. But Sidell Gibson's rose window in the east wall of St George's Hall was thought wrong and Giles Worsley, the architectural writer,

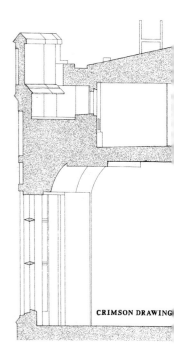

A section through Christopher Smallwood's proposal for a two-storey, Bramante-esque tribune on the site of the Private Chapel. The austerity of the classical vocabulary was not, in the end, thought to be appropriate to Windsor

CRIMSON DRAWING

preferred Smallwood's suggestion of a genealogical tree there. The clerestory was generally thought a mistake in Smallwood's St George's Hall ceiling and Dr Dmitri Porphyrios, the architect, wondered if the Sidell Gibson chapter house would be better in stone.

They were clear, however, that this was a choice of architect not of a design and so the conclusion was easier to arrive at than might have been imagined: that the Prince of Wales's Design Committee would recommend Sidell Gibson as the architects for the Private Chapel area and Christopher Smallwood for St George's Hall.

TRIBUNE

This was, however, far from being the final hurdle. A little less than a month later the Duke of Edinburgh's Restoration Committee met again in the White Drawing Room at Windsor Castle to consider the Design Committee's recommendations. The chosen schemes had something of a gauntlet to run. Here, Smallwood's scheme came in for heavy criticism from Robin Nicholson, Vice-President of the RIBA who in the early days after the fire had been prominent in advocating either a Ruinist or a Vitalist approach. The clerestory was wrong, the side vaulting was unconvincing and 'the overall effect is more suited to a hotel'. Nicholson admitted there was no good contemporary solution but feared the outcome could be regarded as a lost opportunity for a twentieth-century contribution. He suggested that other architects, including Sir Norman Foster, should be invited, but that idea was turned down. It was already too late in the whole process to widen the field. As Michael Peat had said, 'Coming up with radical and stimulating designs for insertion in a relatively small part of a large and historic building is not easy; some excellent architects have been asked for their ideas and there is nothing to suggest that others would do better. Secondly, we are choosing an architect rather than a design. The designs are at this stage only initial concepts which would be developed over the next few months.'

The Duke of Edinburgh then brought this part of the discussion to a decisive end. Giles Downes for Sidell Gibson should be appointed for St George's Hall, he said, and the committee then turned to the Private Chapel area. The Duke of Edinburgh liked Smallwood for its practicality and thought the floor in the Sidell Gibson ante-room, a complex design involving the insignia of the Garter, 'over-fussy'. He also liked the gallery and the new Private Chapel on the site of the Holbein Room, both of which Smallwood had included, where Sidell Gibson had neither.

The Design Committee had recommended Smallwood for St George's Hall and Sidell Gibson for the ante-room. At this point, it looked as though the Restoration Committee was about to make precisely the mirror-image of that decision. As a way out of the impasse, Lord Airlie, the Lord Chamberlain, following up a conversation between Michael Peat and the Duke of Edinburgh before the meeting, suggested they appoint Sidell Gibson for both parts of the job and simply adopt 'preferred features' from other schemes.

It was a convenient and opportune suggestion and the Duke's committee happily took it up. Sidell Gibson was appointed and asked to adapt its designs. A gallery should be incorporated and a new Private

The organo-Gothic style of the submission made by the Sidell Gibson partnership secured them the commission although what was eventually built turned out to be significantly different from these first proposals.

Chapel should be conjured out of the site of the Holbein Room. As Sir Colin Stansfield-Smith, but no other architect, had recommended, the ante-room should be centralized on St George's Hall. The modernists' preferences were left aside, Giles Downes set to work and the long odyssey of choosing a designer, which en route had visited most of the more exotic aspects of modern architecture, had at last come to an end.

PROPOSED LANTERN
ACCESS FROM THE ROOF.

FORMAL ENTRANCE TO ST GEORGE'S HALL

PREVIOUS ALTAR AREA
SUGGESTED MUSEUM OF THE FIRE

4 The Revealed Past

The fire-damaged site at Windsor could be understood only by immersion in it. Real comprehension could not be snatched at here; it could only accrue. The density of detail, the layer on layer of idiosyncrasy in the building, the sheer lack of repetition from one area to another, the number of different, usually conflicting, factors that had to be taken into account, the need to accommodate the various requirements of a many-headed client, and the very public cost of failure: all of that imposed immense strains on those who were trying to bring the job to fruition.

Particularly in the early days, as one of the project managers remembers, 'it was a very, very difficult time. For about the first year, in every important relationship on the job, between contractors, within the Royal Household Property Section, and in the project management team, there were some very, very tense relationships. There was a lot of shouting down phones.'

Michael Peat, the Director of Property Services, reporting directly to the Duke of Edinburgh and the Queen, was adamant that this job was to be a model of its kind. His training was as an accountant in the family firm of Peat Marwick and he was not prepared to accept any hint of the slackness that he saw as endemic in the building business. This was to be a crucible of excellence.

According to a well-established nostrum in the building industry, any one of the three governing criteria – high quality, quickness and cheapness – can only be achieved at the expense of the other two. High quality costs more and takes longer. Rapid completion is also expensive and

Layer on layer and density of detail: the silk damask on the walls of the Crimson Drawing Room is framed by watergilt composition work, laid over the 1820s brickwork of Sir Jeffry Wyatville's re-creation of the Castle. Wyatville used bonding timbers to strengthen his walls but the fire reduced them to charcoal.

yet endangers excellence. Squeezed budgets can threaten schedules and will almost inevitably cut back on the quality of the work that is done. That was the orthodoxy among contractors but the Household would not accept it. There was a determination to impose unprecedentedly tight ways of working.

The restoration of Windsor in the 1990s, as the operation was conceived from the first, was to be comparable in effect, and superior in execution, to the great building campaigns of the past. Edward III's chivalric palace-fortress of the fourteenth century; Charles II's triumphant exercise in English baroque after the Restoration in 1660; George IV's lavish rebuilding of the Upper Ward in the 1820s, which the Chancellor of the Exchequer in 1824 described as exhibiting 'a degree of splendour that was becoming the sovereign who ruled over the country, but also the country over which he ruled . . .': these were the precursors against which this restoration was to be judged and whose effects were to be equalled if not excelled. 'I am not one for looking back to a golden age,' Michael Peat said. 'Look at athletics. It is always said "You couldn't run it faster." But it always turns out that you can and people do. Life is always getting better and the way things are done nowadays should be better than it was in the past.'

If the results of the great historical building campaigns had been good, the means of getting there had not. Every one of those previous transformations had run massively over budget and schedule. Edward III's work at Windsor was the most expensive secular building scheme undertaken anywhere in England in the whole of the Middle Ages. It cost £50,000, at a time when the Crown's annual income was barely more than £30,000. His grandfather Edward I's castle at Caernarvon, for example, built from the ground up, to the most modern and exacting standards, cost less than half what Edward III spent at Windsor. Only Henry III's work at Westminster Abbey could compare in extravagance. A great deal of the funding had come from the revenues of captured lands and ransoms of captured nobles from the King's spectacularly successful French wars. But Edward also borrowed vast amounts of money from bankers on the continent, several of whom he failed to repay and drove into bankruptcy.

The pattern continued in later centuries. Charles II had also run out of money at Windsor, as he did at Greenwich, Whitehall and Winchester, which was originally intended as the English Versailles. George IV burst all known bounds of financial propriety, stretching an original £300,000 budget for his improvements to the Castle to over £1 million.

Wenceslaus Hollar's seventeenth-century view gives an accurate overall picture of the medieval Upper Ward. On the north side of the Quadrangle, the three courtyards around which the royal apartments were based and St George's Hall (17) are all clearly shown.

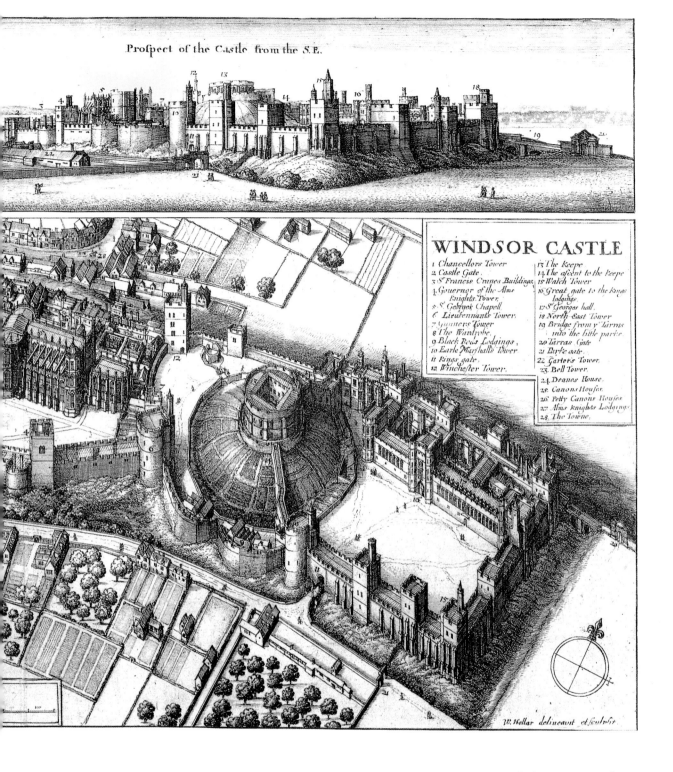

WINDSOR CASTLE

1 Chancellors Tower
2 Castle Gate
3 St Francis Cranes Buildings
4 Gouernor of the Alms Knights Tower
5 St Georges Chapell
6 Lieutennants Tower
7 Gunners Tower
8 The Wardrobe
9 Black Rods Lodgings
10 Earle Marshalls Tower
11 Kings gate
12 Winchester Tower.

13 The Keepe
14 The ascent to the keepe
15 Watch Tower
16 Great gate to the Kings Lodgings
17 St Georges hall
18 North East Tower
19 Bridge from ye Tarras into the litle parke
20 Tarras Gate
21 Parke gate
22 Garters Tower
23 Bell Tower
24 Deanes House
25 Canons House
26 Petty Canons Houses
27 Alms knights Lodgings
28 The Towne.

W. Hollar delineauit et sculpsit

There was a history of extravagance in pursuit of glory at Windsor and there were examples around in contemporary Britain of building projects – the Channel Tunnel, the British Library – ballooning beyond control in both time and money. Neither could be allowed to happen here. The Household, if it was aware of nothing else, knew that the control on this job had to be incomparable in its rigour. It was, Michael

Peat insisted, 'to be efficient, of high quality and to keep to time and budget with lethal precision'.

As the Design and Restoration Committees were considering the conceptual problems that surrounded them, the Royal Household Property Section was devising a system by which the project could be managed with these goals in mind. At first, they thought that the Household could keep the project management in house by employing someone on a short-term contract. John Tiltman, then Deputy Director, had spent most of his career as a project manager on major government contracts. He soon realized that Windsor was too large a gobbet for the relatively young and still small Property Section, which had only been in existence since April 1991, to swallow whole. It was Tiltman, in one of the most enlightened and significant moves on the whole job, who persuaded Michael Peat to employ outside project managers.

A series of interviews was conducted in March and April 1993. A shortlist of five firms was seen by Tiltman and a Treasury adviser in the Chinese Dining Room in Buckingham Palace. It is a dazzlingly glamorous room on the east front, its contents brought there from the Brighton Pavilion in 1846, just before the Pavilion was sold. The courteous formality of the welcome at the Palace, the opulence and elegance of the room they were interviewed in and the sound of the band of the Household Division drifting in from the forecourt outside, so loud that from time to time they had to raise their voices above its clamour: all this only served to remind the applicants, as Tiltman says, 'exactly what they were getting into. This wasn't any ordinary run-of-the-mill job. They were going to embark on a massive and highly prestigious task and we wanted someone who wouldn't be fazed or overawed by it all.'

The firm that was appointed in May 1993, on a combination of cost and the account they gave of themselves at interview, was Gardiner and Theobald Management Services (GTMS). Simon Jones was Managing Director and at the final meeting with the Household he said he would leave aside his role as MD and devote himself to the Windsor job. Alongside him was Chris Watson. Watson had worked in Saudi Arabia, had been part of the team managing the building of the Sainsbury Wing at the National Gallery in London and in mid-1993 was project-managing the works at the Royal Opera House in London. He would join the Windsor project a couple of months later, at a suitable pause in the Royal Opera House programme.

Both men are ex-quantity surveyors and intensely rational organizers. Both became pivotal figures at Windsor, making sure, as Watson puts it, 'that it kept motoring. You have got to keep these things moving. If it doesn't move, it goes wrong.' They were the central nodes around which the whole project, which Watson calculates eventually involved over 4000 people on and off site, was to turn.

Michael Peat, however, still needed convincing that external project managers were necessary. Simon Jones was called to his office in Buckingham Palace. 'He sat me down,' Jones remembers, 'and said "John Tiltman says we need external project managers. I don't know what they do. What are you going to do for us?" I said, because analogies are easier, perhaps there's a piece of music that a composer has written. The composer is the architect. He's actually put it down on paper. You then need some musicians to play it, to create the sound. So you're interpreting what's on the paper into reality for an audience and you have to do it at a certain time, on a certain day, you have a certain number of performances, you have a certain budget, you have a certain venue to be at, you have a certain number of players that are supposed to be on board because you might need percussion, you might need violins – you get the picture. The person who pulls all that together is the conductor, he sits in the middle of all this and he conducts. He provides the client with the day-to-day control of his own destiny. That conductor is the project manager.' Peat gave him the job.

As Jones saw it in mid-1993, Windsor was 'a mind-blowing jigsaw', the most daunting prospect he had ever faced in his professional life. 'I began to look at it and the first thing was that the building was still absolutely dripping. Everything was dripping. You just put your hand on the wall and it came away wet. The environmental specialists were reporting to me and I was getting feedback from them which just said "It's wet, it's wet." I said "Well, when's it going to get dry?"

'"We don't know," they said. "It's wet, it's wet."'

Confronted with this intractable, sodden hulk, boxed into a publicly announced ceiling to the budget of £40 million and a publicly announced completion date of the summer of 1998, this was a period of acute anxiety for the project managers. 'Chris and I were going away each night,' Jones says, 'thinking "What the hell do we do? We don't know how to start this job." There was wet everywhere. I hadn't been sleeping because we didn't know what to do. But the brain is an interesting thing. It keeps working subconsciously and it nibbles away at a problem.'

The question nagged at them. Nothing could be done with a soaking building. Any finish they put on it would blow. The deadline was ticking against them. The scaffolding and other plant costs were being incurred week by week. Not that they were doing nothing. They were involved in helping John Tiltman prepare the briefs for the architects who were asked to submit their ideas for the new designs and in assembling the rest of the design team: the structural engineers, the mechanical and electrical engineers, the quantity surveyors, the main contractors, the environmental consultants, the lighting consultants, the interior designers and the conservators.

All of those were necessary elements but assembling that team wasn't addressing the main problem. As things stood, the appointed team would come up with a design towards the end of 1994 and the building would still not be ready for anyone to begin work. In the meantime, there was a main contractor on site, Wallis's, beginning to put the roofs on St George's Hall and the Grand Reception Room. It was clear both to the architects and to GTMS that some work could be done which did not depend on the drying out of the main structure and Wallis were ready to do it. It was all part of keeping the rhythm going, of keeping the swing in the job.

These 'enabling works', each tendered for by separate subcontractors, were carried out over the autumn and winter of 1993–4. The Crimson Drawing Room bay window, which had been pushed out during the fire by the expanding steel roof above it, was taken down and rebuilt. Large parts of the Kitchen Courtyard were demolished and removed. The kitchen equipment, installed in the Great Kitchen only weeks before the fire, was taken out and stored. Many other small packages of work were carried out and in all more than £1 million was spent in clearing the way for the substantial works to follow.

By the time these works were under way, the project managers had begun to come to grips with the main problem. 'You may think now,' Simon Jones says, 'that it's as obvious as the nose on your face, but it took time to dawn on me that we had to tackle the water first. I could get the design as quick as I liked but I couldn't do anything practically until I'd got the water sorted. We had a very, very wet castle. The water was the main enemy, not the fire. It would actually have been better if the firefighters had just left it. The water they poured in didn't have any real purpose. They were stopping the fire at the firebreaks at each end. If they'd concentrated on that and let the main area burn completely dry, it would have made our job a great deal easier later on.'

As Chris Watson of GTMS says, 'There are three problems in any project: definition, definition and definition. We tried to define what

Damp begins to show through in the vaults of the Undercroft painted as they were before the fire. The machine in operation here is a dehumidifier.

was causing the problems with the drying out, so we got Ridout to do a hot-spot chart of the building, showing where was wet and where was dry. The water had sunk into the robustly thick walls so that, where we had a six-foot-thick wall in the basement that was clad with cement render on either side, the water would sit there for ever.'

The logical route picked through by GTMS, backed up by the architects, was as follows: nothing could be put back until the Castle was dry; nothing would dry until the walls were allowed to breathe; none of the walls could breathe until they were stripped of everything that was lining them: plaster, cupboards, panelling, paint. None of those existing wall-finishes could be removed without a Scheduled Monument Clearance given by the Department of National Heritage. The DNH wouldn't give that clearance until English Heritage advised them to do so. So English Heritage had to be persuaded that this was the way to go.

Jones went to Peat and Tiltman and said to them 'We've got to face English Heritage head-on. We've got no chance of meeting any programme unless we get the water sorted out.' Peat and Tiltman agreed

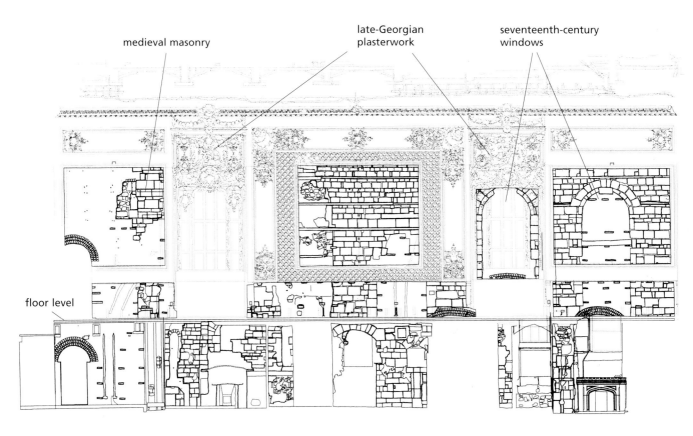

medieval masonry

late-Georgian
plasterwork

seventeenth-century
windows

floor level

and together they went to see John Thorneycroft of English Heritage
for the first of a long and grinding series of meetings that was to last for
four months.

In the late summer and autumn of 1993, there was a danger that a
basic clash of philosophies would emerge between English Heritage on
one side and the Royal Household and its project managers on the
other. The opportunity was rich for conflict and delay. It didn't happen.
As the meetings progressed – and this was a function, at least in part, of
the qualities and characters of the people involved, an openness and
mutual respect developing between them, a desire for this whole business to go well – each side began to acquire some of the attitudes of the
other.

Institutionally, English Heritage is against intervention in historic
fabric. If it can be left, leave it. If it can't, look at it, go carefully and only
touch what needs to be touched. When intervening, only use methods
and materials which are sensitive to the place.

At one early meeting in the Saxon Tower at Windsor between English
Heritage and Donald Insall's, the architects, Steven Brindle, English

Heritage's Inspector of Ancient Monuments, slammed a piece of hard, cement-based render on to the table. It was a shocking moment. In full indignation, he asked them, 'What the hell do you think you are doing using that?' This was an incident he later came to regret – that sort of render had not been used; it came from some of the older works carried out by the Government's old Property Services Agency – but Brindle's outburst is symptomatic of the care and passion with which English Heritage attends to its charges.

On these institutional grounds, Simon Jones's plans to strip the Castle were not easy to stomach. For English Heritage, the wet was surmountable with patience. That was what the environmental consultant, Brian Ridout, who had a long experience of working with English Heritage, was advising. If the Household was prepared to wait, the walls of the Castle would dry in good time and their historic linings would not have to be removed.

That was their theoretical position, but English Heritage archaeologists more often than not find themselves negotiating with a developer who has a budget and a timetable in his hand. It is a situation with which they are deeply familiar. As Brian Kerr, the English Heritage archaeologist, says: 'Most archaeology is rescue archaeology because something has to be destroyed to make room for something else. The English Heritage line was naturally to oppose all the wall-linings coming off. We wanted to minimize the effect of the entire project on the historic fabric. But in the end we had to accept that it had to come off otherwise the building would not have dried out in a reasonable time. Of course "reasonable" is a contentious term, but you have to be reasonable in interpreting "reasonable". You have to give way in unavoidable circumstances.'

There was another element in play here. English Heritage is a protective agency but it is also an investigative one. It wants to find out about the buildings it looks after. The two purposes run in opposite directions: the best way of exploring a building is to take it apart. As Brian Kerr very carefully puts it, 'Any excavation is a sign of failure. It is a failure to protect the archaeology. You expand your understanding of the building at the expense of damage to the fabric which you'd rather have avoided.'

This was the chink of light which the project managers were looking for. 'We began to understand,' Simon Jones says, 'that while their standard philosophy was "Don't mess about with historic buildings", there was a side to them that was itching to get behind the panelling and

The English Heritage photogrammetric survey drawing of the east wall of the Grand Reception Room and the Pastry Kitchens beneath it indicates the level of layered complexity with which the archaeologists had to deal. Here, medieval masonry, punctured with openings of various dates, is overlaid by late-Georgian plasterwork, part of which was modelled on eighteenth-century carved oak panels.

plaster.' English Heritage were already involved in a meticulous survey, using rectified photography and a bank of computers in which the images were digitized, to record the historic fabric that had been revealed by the fire. From late November 1992 the archaeologists had been aware that many of the assumptions made about the history of the Castle before the fire were being thrown into doubt by the notched, patched and scarred masonry which the fire had revealed. Simply from the appearance of the fire-stripped walls it was clear that a great deal more of the medieval fabric had survived the nineteenth-century alterations than anyone had guessed. Fire is the most brutal form of archaeology and everyone recognized that here was a probably unique chance to get to grips with the real history of the most important part of the most important medieval building in England. If more could be revealed, more could be understood.

With this tool in hand, GTMS approached English Heritage. The staff bedrooms in the higher levels weren't that important historically. The wallpaper and plaster could surely be stripped from the walls there. That was agreed. In the basement, the layer on layer of gloss paint was preventing the water from emerging. That could come off. In fact if the gloss paint weren't removed, as Alan Frost, the architect, pointed out, the water would seep out through those parts of the thirteenth-century stone vaulting that weren't painted. Seeping water can destroy stone. As the water comes to the surface, the salts in it crystallize in the surface layers of the stone, expanding as they do so. Effectively, the salts then punch off the outer layers of the stone. As more salt-laden water seeps out, more salts crystallize and more stone is destroyed. The vault would in time blow itself apart. John Thorneycroft agreed that the gloss paint and any tiles, hard-rendering or stone lining from the basement surfaces could be stripped. The bare stone that was revealed was then coated in a sacrificial poultice or render, an outer layer of soft plaster and limewash, into which the salts could safely migrate and crystallize, leaving the stonework behind them intact.

For the project managers, they had 'unplugged' the bottom of the Castle. Extractor fans, open windows, dehumidifiers were all introduced. The heating system was turned on full time and the breeze allowed to blow through and into every possible space. The previously rather dank and static air was now mobile within the building, a vast invisible moisture-conveyor which meant that the water seeping down from above into the eight-foot-thick basement walls could now emerge at those stripped surfaces and evaporate into the Berkshire air.

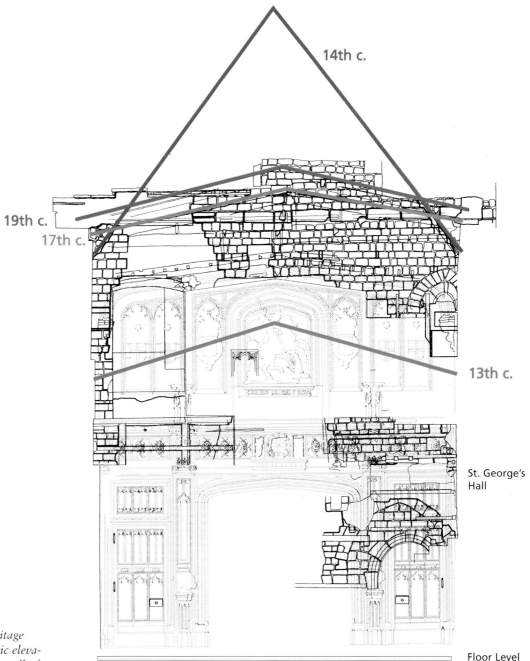

14th c.

19th c.

17th c.

13th c.

St. George's
Hall

Floor Level

The Undercroft

An English Heritage photogrammetric elevation of the west wall of St George's Hall and the Undercroft beneath it. Wall scars showed the archaeologists how Edward III in the fourteenth century had raised the earlier roof, the level to which it had been reduced under Charles II and the slight change in level made by Wyatville in the 1820s.

That still wasn't enough. The architects and the environmental consultants from Hutton + Rostron pushed for more radical stripping of historic wall linings. The greatest challenge was the Green Drawing Room. Over 90 per cent of the wall linings installed in the 1820s were still there. It remained part of what Hugh Roberts, then Deputy Surveyor of the Queen's Works of Art, had called 'the most important sequence of late Georgian interiors in England'. The wall linings had been left virtually unaffected by the fire and now the project managers wanted to take them off, with all the risk of damage that would imply. But to this too, with some reluctance, Thorneycroft agreed. All the elements of the panelling were intensively analysed, minutely labelled and then delicately removed from the wall so that it could, after restoration, be reinstated later. With a mixture of horror and relief – horror that it was there, relief that they had discovered it – a huge patch of dry rot was found in one corner of the room. With the wall linings removed, permanent airflows behind them could be easily established, minimizing the chances of any future fungal growth.

As the way had been opened to a fast-track drying of the fabric, an infectious excitement spread throughout the project team. The exposed masonry revealed, even to untutored eyes, what had scarcely been suspected by earlier historians of the Castle. The great work on the history of Windsor's fabric was by Sir William St John Hope and published in 1913. Unable to poke behind the wall finishes and restricted to interpreting what he could see, Hope had surmised that at least in this part of the Upper Ward, Wyatville had, in the early nineteenth century, largely taken down to principal-floor level anything that had been done before him. It was widely believed that, in this corner, above ground-floor level, Windsor was almost entirely a nineteenth-century castle. The fire, and the subsequent stripping of wall linings, showed that belief to be wrong. The complex physiognomy of the exposed walls, in which medieval masonry, blocked doorways, reshaped windows, re-used stone, seventeenth-century red brick of two kinds and nineteenth-century yellow stock bricks all jostled for space, clearly showed that Hope had been unduly pessimistic. Here, in walls, floors and ceilings, over a large and complicated set of spaces, a palimpsest of overlying, partly erased, partly concordant, partly revealing and partly frustrating marks and meanings were now on view. Windsor retained the material account of its own history.

It was as though they had stumbled on a huge and hidden archive in which past librarians had not stacked and assembled their materials with care but had rummaged through their predecessors' works, tearing out a page or two here, inserting a few of their own there, rearranging the order, pretending the new order was the same as the old, confident in the knowledge that their breezy attitudes to the records of the past would never see the light of day. Now they had.

The Household agreed, as is the legal requirement of any developer in these situations, to pay for a careful survey and investigation by English Heritage's Central Archaeology Service. Wall by wall and stone by stone, using mile after mile of scaffolding erected for the purpose within the rooms, they photographed, analysed, hand-drew and placed on a computer record the revealed fabric of the Castle. The results of the survey were an essential tool for all those in the restoration project: only by knowing precisely what was there could the body of the work begin.

Simon Jones's 'mind-blowing jigsaw' had its counterpart in the evidence unearthed. To take one example from many, simply to give an indication of the complexity of material which it was the historians' task to unravel, this is what appeared in the walls of the Grand Reception Room, once its glamorous neo-rococo skin, created after 1825 to frame a set of Gobelins tapestries depicting the story of the Golden Fleece, had been stripped away. There was a scar on the east side of the room where an internal medieval wall had at some stage been demolished. Why and when? Most of the rest of the east wall, south of the scar, was late-seventeenth-century work, including two huge windows, hidden until now, of precisely the pattern built all over the Upper Ward by Hugh May under Charles II. They must have looked out into an open court, later covered in. North of the scar, though, the medieval masonry remained intact, with huge chalk courses, interrupted by the remains of a small fireplace, probably made before 1259 when the Great Kitchen was built against that east wall. On the west side, there was a large doorway, blocked, and three windows, also blocked. These openings, or ex-openings, were all either mid-fourteenth century or late-fifteenth. No one could tell because, in common with nearly all the equivalent scars and hints, virtually all the mouldings and other details were absent. Downstairs on the ground floor, below the Grand Reception Room, evidence emerged of a thirteenth-century hall, with large windows and window seats set within them. The windows had obviously been cut in two by a new floor being inserted in the earlier hall. No one ever discussed the possibility of restoring that hall to anything like its original condition. To have done so would have destroyed far more than it could possibly have revealed.

One room, a mass of questions. What did the wall scar represent? What was the large door on the west side for? Where did it go? Was there an outside staircase or gallery there? Were the door and the windows of the same date? What was the medieval purpose of the room? How had its function changed when the floor was inserted? Why had such a high-status room been sliced in two with a new floor? Why had there been such large-scale rebuilding of the east wall in the seventeenth century?

This level of rich, fragmentary information and consequent uncertainty was multiplied across the whole of the fire-damaged site. What has been found, measured, recorded and now for the most part covered up again is still open to interpretation. It may seem curious but in this enormously important medieval building, radical questions about form and function in the Middle Ages are still unanswered.

It is not for want of trying. Dr Steven Brindle, the English Heritage Inspector for Windsor, and the archaeological team have meticulously, methodically and dedicatedly struggled to make a coherent picture out of what the evidence is telling them. What follows relies almost entirely on their efforts and what emerges is a fascinating continuity in what might be called 'the Windsor manner'.

Until the fire, the Castle, or at least its Upper Ward, had experienced three moments of radical reconstruction: in the fourteenth century under Edward III; at the end of the seventeenth century under Charles II; and at the beginning of the nineteenth century under George IV. Each one of those builder-kings was moving through something of the same philosophical territory. Each saw Windsor as the place in which to buttress the standing of the monarchy. Each intended the new work to bow towards its ancient surroundings. Each embodied a contemporary spirit in an archaic or retrograde manner. Each intended an efficiently functioning building to be integrated with a symbolically effective castle style. And in the work of each, the essence of Windsor is to be found in a turning over and relayering of its own history. It is a remarkable sequence, a cultural continuum that consists largely of an awareness of exactly how continuous it is.

At the beginning of the fourteenth century, the reign of Edward II had been a disaster for the English Crown: the King was talentless, incompetent, personally weak and corrupt, defeated by the Scots, humiliated by the barons and finally deposed by his wife and her lover. Edward III, who succeeded his father as a boy, looked back a generation further, to the standing and authority of his grandfather, Edward I, the conqueror

Dr Steven Brindle's sketch reconstruction of the St George's Hall range in the late fourteenth century. From the left, it reads: the King's apartments; the Spicerie or Main Gate; the royal chapel (cut away); St George's Hall, with two smoke louvres on the ridge; and the Kitchen Gate, a service route into the Kitchen Courtyard designed to look like a principal entrance to a fortress. Why?

of the Welsh in the 1270s and 1280s and of the Scots in the 1290s, the greatest castle-builder of all English kings, who had allied himself with Parliament against the barons and had established a highly efficient royal administration.

Conquest, castle-building, an adroit manipulation of Parliament and a recognition of the purposes of glamour shaped the grandson's reign as it had the grandfather's. Edward I's Welsh castles were themselves far more than military blockhouses. Caernarvon, the greatest of them, with its bristling, sharp-edged polygonal towers and polychrome banding in the walls, was consciously modelled on the great Roman fortifications at Constantinople. Its silhouette, in which tall staircase towers rise high above the larger bastions, is an exercise in symbolic and sculptural dominance as much as in military effectiveness. There is clear evidence, even in the late thirteenth century, that the cultural idea of the castle and its visual power was already a shaping force in the way castles might actually be built. Medieval builders, it seems, had medievalist ideas.

That provides the key to Edward III's enormously extravagant remaking of the Upper Ward at Windsor. This was to be the most dazzling image of a castle ever made. It was in the charge of William of

Wykeham, a clerk of humble origins who was in such high favour that, according to the chronicler Froissart, 'all things were done by him and without him nothing was done'. Edward had triumphed over France, destroying the French navy at the sea-battle of Sluys in 1340 and the French army at Crécy in 1346. He captured Calais a year later. The Kings of both France and Scotland would be his captives at Windsor. Edward turned down the invitation to become Holy Roman Emperor.

He was the king of chivalric Europe and Windsor was to be a monument to and a setting for the theatre of chivalric greatness. His first attempt at creating it was a failure. In January 1344 he held a triumphant tournament at Windsor, with 'a great supper at which he began his Round Table, and received the oaths of certain earls and barons and knights whom he wished to be of the said Round Table'. There were to be 300 members of the order and a 'most noble house which should be called the Round Table' was at least started. It was to be vast, 200 feet across. Forty thousand tiles were bought to roof it but the project collapsed as the money drained away to finance wars in France.

Not a single piece of evidence for it has ever been found. It may perhaps have been on the site of St George's Chapel, which was founded four years later as the spiritual headquarters of the new, far more exclusive Order of the Garter, whose members were the King, the Black Prince and twenty-four companions.

Soon after the founding of the Order, Edward had splendid, but temporary lodgings built within the Round Tower into which his household could move while the Upper Ward was reshaped. A new gateway, now misleadingly called the Norman Gate, was built at the entrance to the Upper Ward, richly decorated with dramatic machicolations on its outer face, elaborately vaulted within the gateway itself, with lion masks that are still to be seen on the bosses of the vault. This was the dramatic entrance to the Inner Ward, the first signal of how 'castly' Edward III wanted the new buildings to be.

On the north side of the Upper Ward, he entirely recast the royal lodgings he had inherited. Evidence emerged in the post-fire investigations that, as the works continued, their scope increased and the King's ambitions for his new castle expanded. In the final scheme, a new hall, dedicated to St George, whose cross his infantrymen had worn in France, and a new private chapel, were constructed in a range that stretched along the north side of the ward. Unlike the practice in virtually every other medieval palace, there was no break in the roofline to mark the transition from hall to chapel. They formed a continuous range, a pattern William of Wykeham would imitate at his foundations of New College and Winchester. At each end of the hall–chapel range at Windsor, symmetrically placed, stood a giant, multi-storeyed and heavily armoured gatehouse.

Nothing like this self-consciously aesthetic, muscled, martial architecture had appeared before. Battlements were even built around the inside of inner courts, where they could have had no practical use. The two large gatehouses were also a curious anomaly. One, without a gate-passage behind it, could scarcely be called a gate at all – Steven Brindle describes it as 'an incredibly elaborate porch' – and the other opens into the distinctly low-status zone of the Kitchen Courtyard. The role of these symmetrically arranged gatehouses was plainly symbolic, but to what end?

Edward's rebuilding of Windsor was intimately bound up with his founding of the Order of the Garter. Obscurity cloaks the Order's origins but it can be said with some certainty that it was intended to be England's highest order of knighthood, that it was originally divided into two opposing teams and that those teams would confront each other and display the chivalric virtues in tournament. The King himself probably led one team, the Black Prince, his eldest son, the other.

Temporary grandstands, from which the ladies and the distinguished visitors watched, and two opposing gates from which the teams emerged, were already well-established aspects of temporary tournament architecture by the middle of the fourteenth century. Could it perhaps be that the two oversize and functionally inappropriate gateways, fully equipped with all the martial features of arrow slits, portcullises and machicolations, with the long, big-windowed range stretching between them, were in fact parts of the largest, most elaborate, most permanent, most prestigious and most expensive tournament grandstand in England?

The idea that this is theatrical architecture begins to make sense of the medieval shape of the Upper Ward. If it was, the ward itself was the tilt-yard in which the Knights of the Garter could demonstrate their prowess. For many years homage had been paid to the cult of Arthur and his knights. Edward I had held a series of Round Tables after his victories in Wales. Slightly later than the works at Windsor, Louis d'Orléans created a Hall of the Knights of the Round Table at Pierrefonds near Compiègne in France. Edward III's transformation of Windsor was the peak of that cult. He had no fewer than fifty-nine chivalric romances

in his library. He had in his youth dashed on horseback to rescue the beleaguered Countess of Atholl from the castle of a knight who had kidnapped her. In France, he had fought single-handed and incognito a lowly French knight whom he eventually disarmed. At the banquet celebrating the English victory, the King gave him a chaplet of pearls and freed him without ransom.

This is the world the Upper Ward at Windsor was intended to enshrine. Its vast cost, much of it spent not on the rather strict and austere architecture itself but on enormously rich tapestries and furnishings, drained the Exchequer, despite many ingenious new tax and credit-raising mechanisms developed during the reign. It was a pattern which later builder-kings would match.

The medieval Upper Ward was a monument to an ideal of chivalric knighthood which in many ways had been left behind by the practice of war. The fourteenth century had revealed, at Bannockburn, Crécy and Poitiers, the overwhelming effectiveness of a disciplined force of lower-class, unknightly, well-paid foot-soldiers, whether pikemen or archers. But Windsor was to be devoted to the display of a mounted chivalry. This is the repeated Windsor paradox: nothing in the country at the time was more modern but its modernity was consciously antique. It would generate equivalent antiquarian gestures later in the century, such as Bodiam in Sussex, a castle a hundred years out of date the day it was built.

If this is the ideological framework in which Edward III's great recasting of the Upper Ward can be seen, then the details of what he brought about start to make sense. What he found was Henry III's palace disposed around courtyards on the north side of the Upper Ward. The Great Hall was probably on the ground floor on the site of the Grand Reception Room. It was the window seats of this hall that the archaeologists found in the back parts of the pastry kitchen beneath the Grand Reception Room. The focus of that earlier palace was turned in towards its own small courtyards.

A fifteenth-century representation of Richard II presiding at a tournament. What is remarkable is the symmetry: the two gateways, the two teams, the centrally placed royal presence, the framing curtains and the tiltyard in front of it all. Was this, in a vastly grander form, the model on which Edward III reshaped the Upper Ward?

What Edward III did went in two simultaneous, in some ways contradictory and in some ways complementary, directions. He increased the privacy and comfort of his own lodgings, looking on to the Quadrangle, west of the Spicerie Gate, and of his Queen's rooms, on the northern side. There was a withdrawal into the comforts of privacy. For other members of the court, almost equally well-furnished and equally self-sufficient lodgings were built all the way around the east and south sides of the Upper Ward. These were probably reached by staircases, giving on to the Quadrangle. In some ways, the works of Edward III established a collection of individual 'lodges' in the Upper Ward of which his is the most magnificent.

But at the same time as there is that move towards privacy, there is an even more powerful move in the opposite direction, towards communality and an integration of the Upper Ward as an architectural whole. St George's Hall, as the centrepiece of this unprecedented royal building project, was the most magnificent communal hall the country had yet seen. It is raised more prominently than ever before on to the first floor, where previously and much more conveniently it had been on the ground. It is decorated with all the brilliant polychromatic dazzle that heraldry can supply. Its long range fronts a quadrangle on to which the whole emphasis of this castle-as-palace-as-castle is now laid.

This communal hall was a great theatrical gesture. It had an exaggeratedly steep 55 degree pitch to the roof, much steeper than the roof which preceded it, whose scar the archaeologists found on the west wall of St George's Hall. It may or may not have doubled as a grandstand for tournaments but its great row of dignified windows certainly dominated the Upper Ward. Placing the hall here, and not where its predecessor had been on the ground floor below what is now the Grand Reception Room, created appalling problems in the functioning of the medieval palace. For Henry III, the Kitchen had been right next to the hall. Food could travel easily from kitchen to table and remain hot on the short journey. For it to reach the fourteenth-century St George's Hall, no one is sure what route it can have followed. It may well have crossed the Kitchen Courtyard, gone up a spiral staircase, over the top of the Kitchen Gate, which was probably the Council Chamber, and then into the hall at the dais end. The alternative was for the food to have gone in – and the dirty plates come out – via Edward III's Great Chamber, on the site of the Grand Reception Room. Neither would have been a comfortable or an efficient arrangement.

It might also be asked why the Kitchen was not moved to serve the new hall? To move a medieval kitchen was only done with great reluctance. A kitchen, more than any other room, was plugged into the services, even in the Middle Ages. One of the great discoveries of the archaeology was the well in the Kitchen Courtyard, lined with blocks of greensand, probably from the fourteenth century, but perhaps earlier, roofed in with a little seventeenth-century brick dome and then filled with rubble, perhaps during Wyatville's work. Where would the Great Kitchen have gone if it was not to stay where it always had been?

Finally, there is the problem with the main entrance. From the Quadrangle what looks like a beautifully ordered palace can only have been entered by a convoluted twist through unsatisfactory spaces and corridors behind the great new Spicerie Gate at the west end of St George's Hall. Equally, if those symmetrical gateways were indeed the points through which the tournament teams emerged on to the tiltyard, then one of them would have had to wend its way through the Kitchen Court, with all the low-grade mess and hubbub that would inevitably involve.

This sense of grandeur cheek by jowl with the domestic and even the squalid had a reflection in the archaeology after the fire. Buried deep within the building, as part of a lavatory and washroom complex, covered in ceramic tiles and the ubiquitous institutional gloss paint, the archaeologists found the remains of Edward III's Kitchen Gate: the

The medieval stone-lined well and its seventeenth-century brick cap discovered in the Kitchen Courtyard during the course of excavations.

grooves in which the portcullis ran, the pin or pintle on which one of the gates would have hung, the batter or slope at the foot of the walls, even the arrow slits — all there to create an impressive and theatrical backdrop when seen from the Upper Ward, later buried within the building by Wyatville and his Victorian successor Blore.

Any sense of indecorum, though, may not have had as much resonance in the Middle Ages as it does today. A reredos, a place to rest one's back, was certainly constructed in the Great Kitchen at Windsor, for the King to go and sit in warmth and comfort. The so-called Larderie passage – the name means the Meat passage – which runs along the south side of the Kitchen Courtyard, was as finely made, with the royal rose on the bosses of the corridor's vault, as any part that survives of Edward's palace. There was an intimate connection between the important lodgings on several floors along the east range and the Kitchen Court below them. As was revealed by the fire, large windows looked down from, and an important door and stairway connected, what is now called the Prince of Wales Tower and the Kitchen Courtyard. It was then the Board of Green Cloth Tower, in part of which the kitchen accounts were kept and in other parts of which high-grade officers were housed. There was an intimacy between different grades of the Royal Household in the Middle Ages — when the Groom of the Stool, on which the sovereign would go to the loo, was a peer of the realm — from which later ages would turn away.

Nevertheless, the planning and presentation of Edward III's palace only makes good sense in terms of putting on a great show. In medieval Windsor, function came a long way second to performance. As Steven Brindle puts it, 'Although we have this great and apparently architecturally unified palace, built by Edward III and uniform in all sorts of ways, as to roof line, window heights, cornice line, floor and ceiling heights, in planning terms we have barely begun to understand it. It is terribly confusing but it is the essential matrix of the State Apartments since.'

It is confusing if you imagine that efficiency was its purpose. It becomes less confusing if theatricality takes the lead. The need was for privacy, but the money went into communality. The critical military arm had become the infantry, but the emphasis here was on the cavalry. The requirement was for a great palace, but it was dressed up as a castle. It becomes almost inescapable here to think of the Upper Ward of Windsor, as reshaped by Edward III, as a theatre of kingship, chivalric, communal, martial, playing the part for England and the later Middle

Ages that for France and the era of the Sun King would be played by Versailles.

Edward III set the framework for the Upper Ward inside which all later builder-kings and architects have worked. For Charles II, Hugh May, his architect, created a series of great rooms, much of which survives as the State Apartments to the west of the fire-damaged site but which in the north-east corner of the Upper Ward were almost entirely swept away by Wyatville. For this act, the Prince of Wales, among many others, has called Wyatville 'the greatest vandal ever to have worked at Windsor'. May's works, particularly in his adaptation of the Private Chapel and St George's Hall, of which early-nineteenth-century water-colours are the only record, were perhaps the greatest baroque interiors ever created in this country. It was, perhaps facetiously, suggested that the fire offered an opportunity to restore not Wyatville's mechanical

Above: *The Royal Chapel as decorated by Antonio Verrio and Grinling Gibbons for Charles II and as recorded in the early nineteenth century by Charles Wild. The destruction of this room, and of the baroque St George's Hall (right) with which it formed a suite, led the present Prince of Wales to call Wyatville 'the greatest vandal ever to have worked at Windsor'.*

Gothic, but the masterpieces he had destroyed. Needless to say, such a course would have been almost inevitably a disaster: bogus Verrio murals and ceilings, fake Grinling Gibbons carvings, a complete Disneyland vision of late-seventeenth-century England. No one really contemplated it.

In exile in France and Holland, Charles had absorbed the glamour of the new French style. Here, with May as his architect, the Italian Antonio Verrio as his decorator and painter, Grinling Gibbons as his woodcarver and René Cousin as the gilder, he could set about making a baroque palace within the Castle.

Here again, though, the new works took account of the context in which they were placed. The matching suites of King's and Queen's rooms reproduced the medieval arrangement. The integrated baroque scheme for St George's Hall and the Chapel, with its screens of trompe-

A fragment of the Verrio painting discovered underneath Wyatville's nineteenth-century plaster-work and battening. A depiction of these flowery swags can be seen high up on the right-hand wall in the picture on page 126.

l'oeil columns and skies populated with floating goddesses and monarchs, paid court, at least in part, to the medieval inheritance. The Chapel was decorated with the *Resurrection* and *Christ Healing the Sick*, including depictions of both May and Verrio. St George's Hall, however, was decorated with a huge mural the length of its north wall, showing the Black Prince received in triumph by Edward III. In the centre of the ceiling, Charles II wearing the robes of the Order of the Garter sat enthroned surrounded by clouds and angels, while each of the oeil de boeuf windows that ran along the top of the south wall was encircled with a giant blue Garter, bearing the Order's motto in gold.

The vocabulary was classical, the Black Prince and Edward III were in Roman dress, the medieval manner of chapel and hall had been obliterated but even so, at the very end of the seventeenth century, at what might be thought the low-point of any interest in the Middle Ages, the Charles II–May–Verrio scheme was drenched in medievalist allusion. It can even be maintained that May's huge, coved, round-headed windows, with which he regularized most of Windsor's medieval façades, and the austerity of their undecorated setting, were a late-seventeenth-century shot at what Giles Worsley, the architectural historian, calls 'neo-Norman'. As Worsley points out, May's work at Windsor could easily have been as elaborate outside as it was within and not to make more of a conventional baroque show in the façades can only have been a deliberate choice. This was certainly how it was seen by Vanbrugh, who in 1707 wrote about his designs for Kimbolton Castle: 'As to the Outside, I thought 'twas absolutely best, to give it Something of the Castle Air, tho' at the same time to make it regular . . . This method was practic'd at Windsor in King Charles's time, And has been universally Approv'd.'

Charles II redesigned the clothes worn by the Garter Knights, had a giant Garter Star, which his father had introduced to the Order, installed on the northern face of the Castle (it was removed by Wyatville), commissioned a rich and elaborately illustrated history of the Garter by the antiquarian Elias Ashmole and held magnificent feasts in St George's Hall. Even in the seventeenth century, and even as the most modern international style was being imposed on the building, Windsor was the place to record and perpetuate the habits of an ancient national past.

That idea, paradoxically enough, did not rule out utterly radical transformations of the building. As the archaeology after the fire has revealed, rebuilding posing as a form of restoration was not a Victorian invention. Hugh May, in some ways harking back to the Middle Ages, nevertheless obliterated the medieval hall and chapel, rebuilding the roof, rearranging the windows and redecorating the rooms. In the 1820s again, Wyatville, wanting to make Windsor a more appropriately medievalist national symbol, obliterated almost everything May had done, again rearranging the windows, demolishing the wall that had separated hall from chapel, keeping the roof structure, but dressing it in a thin plaster Tudoresque imitation of a medieval ceiling.

Immediately after the fire, one question occurred to those who knew and cared about the Verrio scheme, and deprecated everything done by the vandal Wyatville: Did anything of the Verrio paintings survive? To begin with nothing of the Stuart paintwork was found and it was assumed that Wyatville had got rid of it.

Only in November 1995, deep into the reconstruction works, did a sudden surprise spring itself on the project team. The new roof for St George's Hall, designed by Giles Downes, is intended to enrich the rather stark, box-like space created by Wyatville. One of its means of doing this is to make the roof trusses spring from corbels that are lower down the walls than Wyatville had them. The corbels themselves remain those made for Wyatville in the form of kneeling knights, almost all of which survived the fire.

In November 1995 work began to take the Kneeling Knight corbels off the walls before repositioning them. Near the west end of the hall, where the pre-Wyatville chapel had been, the restorers found small but utterly distinct patches of the Verrio painting. Excitement spread down the telephone. Did the life-size figures of *Christ Healing the Sick* survive further down the wall? Was the greatest baroque interior in England lurking beneath the plasterwork skin? Further trial holes were cut in January 1996 but they revealed the worst. Wyatville's men had given no thought to what they were replacing and the bulk of the mural had been destroyed. Only at high level were parts of columns, capitals, garlands and the heads of three figures anything like intact, and there were nineteenth-century battens interrupting them. The nineteenth-century plaster was cut away, the surviving mural was cleaned but not restored, a high-quality rectified photograph was made, the dry linings closed over it and the whole thing then plastered over again, as had originally been planned. Temporary labels were attached to the new plaster where it hid the seventeenth-century work, as a warning to anyone fixing or drilling there to go carefully. The labels said: 'Caution Verrio Wall Paintings'. One by one, they were neatly altered by the men working on site. 'Caution,' they came to say, 'Very Old Wall Painting'. The past was past.

The most expressive of all the Verrio mural fragments shows an onlooker who had climbed up a column for a better view of the scene of Christ Healing the Sick. *Everything lower down had been destroyed.*

5 Back of House

William of Wykeham, the great fourteenth-century organizational genius, self-promoter and entrepreneur on behalf of the Crown, was widely loathed and distrusted among his contemporaries, at least partly because he was not one of the great aristocratic magnates of the kingdom but a clerk who had risen from poverty. As he was coming to the end of his transforming works in the Upper Ward at Windsor, where in effect he had been the project manager, he is said to have had the words '*Hoc fecit Wykeham*' inscribed on one of the inner walls.

(The story is not unlikely. The inner faces of the fourteenth-century palace were lined in soft, eminently inscribable chalk ashlar. Sadly, though, this particular graffito has not been rediscovered.) When, presumably maliciously, this was pointed out, the King was irritated at the presumption and the arrogance. Credit for the rebuilding of Windsor should reflect on the Sovereign alone. His parvenu Chancellor had to explain himself hurriedly. The words meant not, as Edward imagined, 'Wykeham made this' but the very opposite: the humble, grateful and self-abasing acknowledgement that 'This made Wykeham'.

There are constancies across time. Over four centuries later, the country-house architect Jeffry Wyatt, not in the top rank of his contemporaries but like Wykeham another brilliant self-promoter, was in 1824 invited to suggest changes to the Castle. He was already working on the Royal Lodge in Windsor Great Park, the King liked him as a man – he was straight-speaking and lacked courtly unctuousness – and that connection probably explains why the invitation was made. Wyatt was already fifty-eight and recognized this as the chance of his life. He produced a set of parallel drawings. One showed the existing, over-regular structure largely as it was left by Hugh May, drab and lifeless. The other, in brilliant colour, showed his own proposals sparkling with enrichment and glamour.

His scheme to romanticize the Castle followed almost to the letter the recommendations which Sir Charles Long, the artistic adviser and intimate of George IV, had drawn up: a silhouette with more drama, façades with more incident, interiors with more chic and comfort and a plan of greater efficiency. The high-class drawings, in many ways like Giles Downes's seductive submissions in 1993, presented to an equally distinguished Committee of Taste, played a great part in getting him the job.

Wyatt was anxious to distinguish himself from the large number of his relations who were in the same line of business and who had the same surname. Royal patronage was a well-established route to lasting success and Wyatt knew he had to mark the moment.

As the first stone was laid, on 12 August 1824, he asked the King if he might change his name from the indistinguishable Wyatt to the altogether more exotic, medievalish, perhaps somehow Anglo-Norman Wyat*ville*. George IV's response shows that his enthusiasm for the medieval was not entirely untinged with irony: 'Veal or mutton, Mr Wyatt, it's all one to me. Call yourself what you will.' Veal it was and Jeffry Wyatt became Jeffry Wyatville.

'Let George,' as a verse in the next day's *Morning Chronicle* put it,

Sir Jeffry Wyatville sold his services to George IV on the basis of these drawings: dreary past (below), glittering medievalist future (above).

> whose restlessness leaves nothing quiet,
> Change if he must the good old name of Wyatt;
> But let us hope that their united skill
> Will not make Windsor Castle Wyatt Ville.

But in some ways they did and if Wyatville made Windsor, then Windsor certainly made Wyatville. The King authorized him to add a representation of the new George IV gateway to his coat of arms and to use the one word WINDSOR as his motto. For the duration of the works, the King installed him in the Winchester Tower, the same tower that Wykeham had occupied in the fourteenth century, and knighted him in December 1828, the first architect-knight since Vanbrugh.

Wyatville left his mark on the fabric he had transformed much as Wykeham had. His newly medievalized name was inscribed on a glass plate and set in the foundation stone of the George IV gateway. The

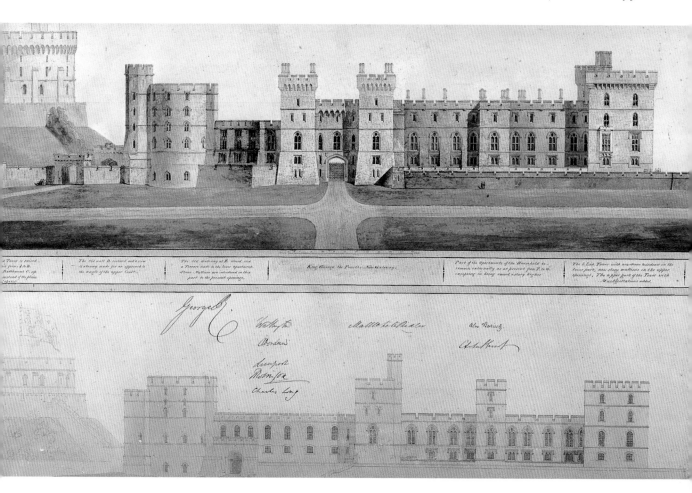

plate doesn't quite say '*Hoc fecit Wyatville*' but the implications are the same: to work at Windsor, whether now, in the nineteenth century, in the seventeenth – Verrio went on to a string of country-house commissions on the back of what he had done here – or in the fourteenth, was to make your reputation. Whoever made Windsor would be made by it in return.

In common with the whole of the building industry in 1993, the Royal Household was supremely aware of this Windsor factor. John Tiltman, as the Royal Household's Project Director, found himself in his Buckingham Palace office receiving an almost unending series of deputations from the great and the good of the building world. People from all the necessary disciplines were clamouring to do the work.

This demand from the industry opened the door for the project's managers to establish systems which would give them unprecedented control and leverage. All work for the Household of any significance is always put out to competitive tender, according to the standing arrangements by the Financial Memorandum of 1991. No consultant, no contractor, no subcontractor or craftsman could be appointed without that tendering process, with at least three competitive bids involved.

The tendering system at least guaranteed that the competitive urge to be involved at Windsor, and to reduce prices accordingly, would work in the Household's favour. The phrase that circulates around the industry is 'buying the job'. If what is called a marketing advantage can be derived from having worked on the restoration – if you can tell people that you have worked there and that helps you get their business – then that marketing advantage has a real if in some ways indefinable value. In other words, it would be to anyone's advantage to work at Windsor, at any level, and make no money. To break even, or actually to make a loss, on Windsor work might, if you could afford it, be a sensible investment.

'It would be very nice to come out of it with a nice fat cheque,' one of the contractors says, 'but under the circumstances, like an awful lot of other people, you wipe your nose on the job and then you rely on the kudos at the end of it.' You wipe your nose on the job? 'You cover your costs and no more.'

There is no doubt that in many disciplines, over the whole length and breadth of the project, companies have 'bought' the Windsor job. The degree to which they have done so of course varies and is a commercial secret. Nevertheless, the quantity surveyors reckon that over the whole five-year project, of about £36.5 million, perhaps 10 per cent has been saved by the Household through what could be called this *Hoc fecit* mechanism. Phil Rowley, the Contracts Manager for the main contractors Higgs and Hill, explains how the 10 per cent might be absorbed at the subcontractor level. 'The subcontractor's supervisor who comes here probably doesn't book his time against it. He books it against another job down the road. Or he takes it on the chin because he goes home and the wife says "Where have you been today?" And he says, "I've been to Windsor Castle and I'm building it for the Queen," and that's something worth paying a bit for, isn't it?'

It should not be said that commercial gain was the only factor in play. As the architect Donald Insall says, 'There is a much deeper factor in operation here, a special challenge and satisfaction to be had from being able, given the chance, to do a near-perfect and truly exemplary job. That chance does not come very often and when it does you will give your all to take it.'

For all that sense of commitment from the professionals involved, the Household was nevertheless deeply concerned that it should have sufficient safeguards against such a complex project dilating out of control. So much was unknown about the building – the fact that the twelfth-century curtain walls of the Castle, for example, have no foundations whatsoever and are simply laid on the chalk of which the Windsor hill is made, was only discovered in the course of the archaeology – that the chance of expensive, complicating discoveries was extremely high. In the Options Report, the quantity surveyors included a massive 20 per cent contingency figure to cover this level of uncertainty.

It was felt within the Household Property Section and by the project managers whom they took on in the spring of 1993 that unprecedentedly rigorous cost- and programme-control systems had to be evolved for the project if the Household was to emerge with its reputation untarnished.

The system did not spring fully formed to life at the beginning of the works but evolved over the course of 1993 and early 1994, principally from discussions between Michael Peat, the Director of Finance and Property Services in the Household, and Simon Jones, the leading project manager.

There were three key elements to the system they put in place: rolling final accounts; project managers' instructions; and the division of the the work into highly defined and discrete packages that would be put out to tender in tightly regulated groups.

The rolling final accounts were in some ways the most important. The building industry has always tended to have something of a confrontational element to its central relationship between client and contractor, hinged perhaps inevitably to the question of money. Although this is disputed by any contractor, it is nevertheless a well-established fact of the industry that contractors tend to quote low so that they get the job and then find, as work progresses, that large numbers of variations to the work add to its value. Often the precise value of those variations is not finally worked out until well after the job is finished and many of the details have either been forgotten or have been covered up so that nothing can be checked. This process of low quote, followed by variations and concluded with a long-delayed final account is known in the business as 'building a claim'. The claim for extras can represent the difference between profit and loss on a contract.

The Household had recently experienced difficulties of this kind and was determined that nothing of the sort should happen at Windsor,

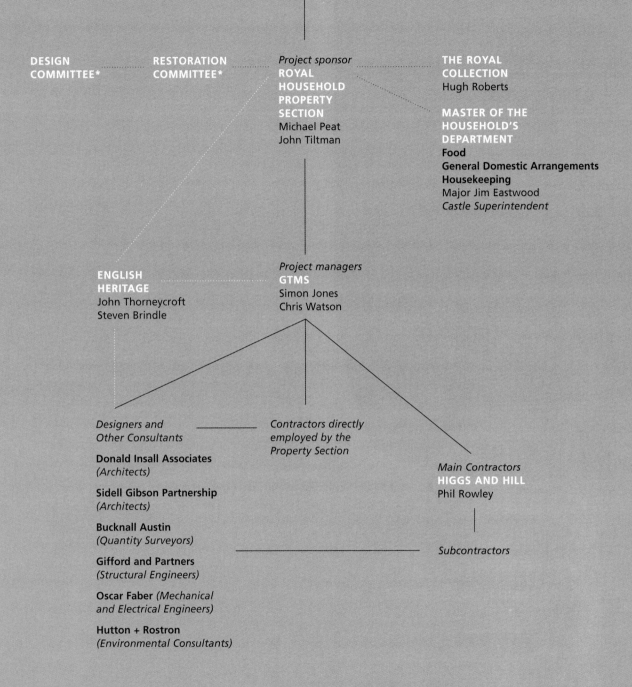

**THE QUEEN
THE DUKE OF EDINBURGH**

**DESIGN
COMMITTEE***

**RESTORATION
COMMITTEE***

Project sponsor
**ROYAL
HOUSEHOLD
PROPERTY
SECTION**
Michael Peat
John Tiltman

**THE ROYAL
COLLECTION**
Hugh Roberts

**MASTER OF THE
HOUSEHOLD'S
DEPARTMENT**
Food
General Domestic Arrangements
Housekeeping
Major Jim Eastwood
Castle Superintendent

**ENGLISH
HERITAGE**
John Thorneycroft
Steven Brindle

Project managers
GTMS
Simon Jones
Chris Watson

*Designers and
Other Consultants*

*Contractors directly
employed by the
Property Section*

Donald Insall Associates
(Architects)

Sidell Gibson Partnership
(Architects)

Main Contractors
HIGGS AND HILL
Phil Rowley

Bucknall Austin
(Quantity Surveyors)

Gifford and Partners
(Structural Engineers)

Subcontractors

Oscar Faber *(Mechanical
and Electrical Engineers)*

Hutton + Rostron
(Environmental Consultants)

*The Royal Household Property Section channelled all the requirements of the
Royal Collection and the Master of the Household's Department, as well as the
recommendations of the Design and Restoration Committees, to GTMS, the
Project Managers.*

——————— Formal liaison
.... Informal liaison

* A list of committee members is given on page 276.

whose scale and complexity brought with it the risk of an enormous claim. If the final account was allowed to run on for five years or more, there was no telling what the total figure would be. It was established early on in Michael Peat's mind that the financial relationship between client and contractor should be held on a far tighter rein. This was the origin of the idea of rolling final accounts. Every three months, all claims would be settled. No issue would be allowed to run beyond those regular and rigorous horizons. It was something unheard-of in the construction world, but the Windsor factor, and the recognition by the Household that it held the whip hand, meant it had to be stomached.

For rolling final accounts to work, there had to be utter clarity at every moment about exactly what had emerged on the job, what had been authorized by the client, what had been estimated and agreed and what had been executed, on whose authority, when and why. If those things weren't known, no account for work done could be settled. This was the origin of the system of Project Manager's Instructions or PMIs under which the restoration of Windsor Castle has been run.

Again, the degree of client control which the PMI system implies was unprecedented. Traditionally, architects, structural engineers and the mechanical and electrical engineers all issue instructions to the contractor. He then does the work he has been asked to and the quantity surveyor only agrees after the work has been done what the costs were. That multi-headed system had to go. The Household had decided to adopt a certain form of government contract known as 'GC Works I' of which the crucial element is to give the key decision-making powers to the project manager rather than to the architect. GTMS were instructed to control the issue of all instructions and, as Simon Jones puts it, 'We said, "Right, we are the project managers. The contractor doesn't act unless we issue instructions."'

This method had the potential of becoming a paper chain. Any of the consultants who wanted work done had to put in a request for a PMI. The request then went to the quantity surveyors. The cost of the work was discovered by putting it out to tender, and its implications for the rest of the programme were then assessed. If the cost was relatively small, a few thousand pounds, the project managers themselves would take responsibility for it and sign it off. An instruction would be issued to the main contractors to appoint the chosen subcontractor. If it was more than £10,000, John Tiltman, Deputy Director of Property Services, had to sign it off. If it was over £100,000, the request had to travel from consultant to project manager to the quantity surveyor, back to the project manager, to Tiltman and then to Michael Peat, the Director of Property Services. If he liked the look of it, in terms of cost and programme, he would then sign it and it would travel back down through Tiltman and Jones and Watson, who would issue the Project Manager's Instruction to the main contractor who would integrate the subcontractor's work with his own programme.

It sounds like a recipe for either chaos or paralysis. Simon Jones says, 'If we are going to be responsible, we've got to have control. And we have dogmatically followed that system all the way through. It has been so time-consuming but we felt we had to do it. We have put thousands of hours into it. If we don't put the effort in, we get a log-jam, a huge log-jam. There have been thousands and thousands of these PMIs. So we have to make the system work. If the paperwork isn't moving, it means the instructions aren't getting down to the builder and the job's not going well enough. The project manager has got to drive. If you've put that system in place, you've got to put energy in to drive it, otherwise the whole thing will just stagnate.' The cost implications for those administering the job were vast, particularly the quantity surveyors, Bucknall Austin, whose workload was several times what they expected it might have been on a conventionally run job.

The third element of that control system, on top of rolling final accounts and PMIs, was the discrete packaging of the work into closely constrained elements which were let out only one at a time. It was a straightforward piece of stick and carrot management: if contractors did well on one section, they could be rewarded with the next. If they were doing badly, they could be threatened with not getting the next package of work. This is where the Windsor factor bit hardest: the project managers knew that everyone involved, particularly the main contractors, wanted to be there at the end of the job when, as Simon Jones says, 'the spotlights would come on'. The threat of absence from the final podium was something that could be kept hanging over the contractors for the entire length of the project. It is a measure of the Household's sternness as a taskmaster that it was prepared to ensure high performance with this exacting and astringent mechanism. 'We're always ready to kick people off site,' Michael Peat says, 'if they're no good.' It had happened on earlier work but, as it turned out on the Fire Restoration site, not a single firm was summarily dismissed.

In some ways, though, the control system softened in practice. The contractors, with men and equipment ready and to hand, did not always wait for the paperwork to emerge before embarking on the work it was intended to authorize. Many decisions were made more on the hoof than the theoretical structure would have allowed. As John Tiltman says, 'the system relies on goodwill. If you had a barrack-room lawyer in the contracting firm who wouldn't move without a written instruction, you'd be in trouble. You really do rely on contractors slightly proceeding at their own risk, without complete authorization, in the real world, because the team can't always get the instructions to them fast enough. At Windsor, there have probably been instances where the contractors have started work in advance of receiving the written instructions. They have been more than fair really. We all want the job to succeed.'

There is a mature and complex psychology at work here. An element of distrust lies at the core of the control system but that system would probably have been unsustainable without a carefully nurtured spirit of cooperation between client and contractor. John Tiltman, the Household's Project Director, and the two project managers from GTMS were the double hinge of that complex and in some ways paradoxical process. They sat at the centre of the system like the waist in an hourglass, transmitting instructions and solutions one way, problems and difficulties the other, all, at least eventually, in written form, thousands upon thousands of Requests for Information, Project Managers' Instructions, suggestions by architects, revisions by members of the Household, a double information stream, four and a half years long, from which a building had somehow to emerge.

But did it work? Certainly at Windsor, it did. The proof of its effectiveness can be seen in the results. Spring 1998 was originally announced as the completion date, although there was some measure of leeway built into that. The schedule was more than met with the reopening of the fire-damaged area for a reception with music on 20 November 1997, the Queen's Golden Wedding anniversary and five years to the day after the fire, with not only the building completed but all the pictures and furniture in place.

As for budget, the Household announced a ceiling of £40 million in early 1993 and at the same time, but privately, the Treasury approved an overall cost limit of £35.5 million for the construction work alone. Contingencies were built into that Treasury figure. At the beginning of the works the projected figure was over £3 million below it but, as things developed, projected expenditure gradually crept towards the Treasury's limit. In April 1994 it was £32.3 million, by July a year later £33.5

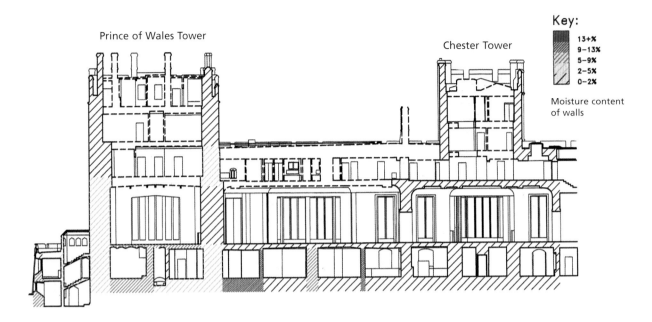

million and in November the same year £33.8 million. In February 1996 it had moved to £34.3 million and by November £35.2 million. In November 1997 the final account was estimated at £35.3 million, to give, with around £1 million spent on picture restoration and furnishings for the Royal Collection, an estimated final total cost of £36.5 million. The increases in expenditure mainly reflected changes to and improvements on the original design. The changes mid-stream to the Kitchen Court building cost a great deal of money but that was largely compensated for by very keen pricing by the contractors. More elaborate carpentry and joinery in St George's Hall, the new Private Chapel and the new Lantern Lobby together added £1.56 million and the reinstatement of the fourteenth-century Undercroft cost an extra £500,000. But, as John Tiltman says, 'The Household had expected something like this to happen and in the end the level of contingency proved to be pretty well judged.'

By 8 July 1993 the full team of consultants was in place for the restoration works. Every part of it had been selected through a combination of competitive tendering and interviews with Tiltman and Simon Jones of GTMS. The successful consultants managed to get an advantage over their competitors by offering stronger teams while still reducing the percentage of the works on which their fees were based. They too, in many cases, were doing no better than breaking even. Each firm or partnership was in the vanguard of their field: Donald Insall Associates, one of the country's leading conservation practices, were to

Hutton + Rostron's electronic moisture sensors sent information down the telephone to their computers near Guildford. This chart, produced in May 1994, shows how the water that had been poured into the Castle during the fire had sunk into the basement, where the wall linings were preventing it from evaporating. The restoration could not proceed until this issue of the damp had been sorted out.

be the co-ordinating architects, the architects for the Kitchen and Kitchen Court as well as for those State Apartments whose pre-fire state was to be replicated. Bucknall Austin were the quantity surveyors, Gifford and Partners of Southampton the structural engineers and Oscar Faber Consulting the mechanical and electrical engineers.

Towards the end of the year, Hutton + Rostron took over as environmental consultants, pursuing a far more aggressive strategy towards banishing the wetness from the building. Tim Hutton, ex-soldier, ex-vet and a man with an intense and crusading enthusiasm for the need to treat a building as an organism, brought a sudden new dynamism to the problem of damp. 'You must think,' he says, 'about the way a building breathes to understand its health in the way a vet might understand an animal. This is something that has suffered intense trauma. Nurse it back to wholeness. Think how it might heal itself. If someone had fallen into a river and freezing cold water and was suffering from hypothermia and shock, you wouldn't just stand there and say, "There, there, never mind." You'd do something about it, wouldn't you? What would you do? You'd take their wet cold clothes off, wouldn't you, and start to dry them out.'

If that was medical talk, there was a military air to Hutton's operations. A system of electronic wetness monitors was pushed into the walls all over the fire-damaged site and then linked by telephone to the H + R headquarters near Guildford. Electronically and telephonically produced sections, colour-coded for different levels of humidity, were printed out for all members of the project team and the Royal Family to get a visual fix on the problem. Specially trained rot-hounds, a labrador and a spaniel, were sent sniffing for dry rot all over the site.

As the first anniversary of the fire approached, Windsor began, as Chris Watson puts it, 'to motor'. In the project manager's office, first in the Saxon Tower and then in the Lord Chamberlain's Upper Stores in the Middle Ward, the dynamic of the project started to accelerate. 'We have a discipline here,' he said to me one day in his office, surrounded by the rank on rank of lever-arch files in which the immense volume of paperwork generated by the works was arranged package by package, consultant by consultant, subcontractor by subcontractor. 'If I get twenty problems across my desk per day, then I can answer nineteen of them myself. One per day will have to go to John Tiltman, so that's five a week. If he gets five questions a week, he can deal with four of them. One would have to go to Michael Peat. Michael Peat will get four queries a month and he might be able to deal with three of them. One per month would have to go to the Duke of Edinburgh. And he usually gives a pretty prompt answer. That's been a very valuable part of the job, the knowledge that answers are going to come back down the line pretty well pronto. But we can't let it rest at that. I don't just sit back and say "Well, I've done my bit, I've done my nineteen, and these difficult ones have gone to John. That's on his plate now." I chase answers. These things go wrong when they start going slow. And everything gets written down and sent to anyone who needs to know. My job, or part of it anyway, is to keep people informed.'

The wettest parts of the basement, it was clear, had to be left until late in the project. Only then would they be dry enough to work on. The State Apartments, as the most subtle and important of the rooms, were still years away from being ready for reconstruction. That left the staff rooms in the upper levels of the Chester, Prince of Wales and Brunswick Towers, the Great Kitchen and the area next to the Kitchen known broadly as the Kitchen Court. This, at last, was where the heart of the job could begin.

Before reconstruction, however, both removal of debris and any associated archaeology had to be carried out. There was one overriding reason why this back of house, these areas that were not part of the theatrical front of Windsor, could be tackled first. Everyone was agreed that large parts of what had existed here before the fire could be taken away and dumped. The Kitchen Court was, initially anyway, thought to be an undistinguished mess of nineteenth- and early-twentieth-century buildings which were inefficient and in need of replanning. The walls here did not need to be dried out; they could simply be removed. Every brick took an ounce of water with it.

English Heritage monitored the demolitions carefully. In the Kitchen Courtyard, they made an important discovery. Buried in the mass of later work, they found a wall which, from its brickwork and the huge round-headed windows it contained, turned out to be from the early eighteenth century. It was the outer wall of the Privy Kitchen, where the Royal Family's own food was prepared, built in the reign of Queen Anne, relatively soon after Hugh May had baroqued the Castle for Charles II and using the large, round-headed window form that May would have used. The architects had to adapt their first ideas to take account of this historically important wall and for the engineers it proved a headache. The wall they were asked to retain was far weaker than the walls they were asked to demolish on either side of it. Demolition had to be by hand. Some electric hammers were used but otherwise the bricks were picked away one by one. The fourteenth-century well, whose presence had been predicted from documentary sources, but whose precise location in what had been the open courtyard was only now discovered, contributed further to the delicacy of the operation. The initial design of the building that was to be erected there had one of its steel legs landing right on top of where the well was discovered. Gifford's, the engineers, had to rejig their scheme with great rapidity, putting the contractors on hold while the leg in the design was moved and all the other steel beams that fed into it were recalculated and repositioned.

At the same time, another, in many ways more important, integration of the historic and the modern was in progress next door in the Great Kitchen. It had always been thought that the roof of the Great Kitchen was a Wyatville design. Although it was a form of hammer-beam construction, the roof was covered in the sort of finicky softwood and cast-iron detail that was typical of the early-nineteenth-century idea of what a medieval roof should look like. George IV, whose badge decorates one wall of the Kitchen, liked to take his guests on a tour of the Kitchen areas – that had also been his habit at Brighton – and Wyatville had obviously created a space which would gratify those rather touristic ideas of the Roast Beef of England. At Carlton House, the Prince Regent's great London palace which was demolished when he became king and whose furnishings were distributed between the new works at Windsor and at Buckingham Palace, parties had been held on precisely that theme. It was part of the vision of 'The Mansions of England in the Olden Time', to use Joseph Nash's slightly later phrase, which was so prominent a part of English Romanticism.

But the fire, here more than anywhere else in the Castle, brought an extraordinary revelation. Wyatville had not built a new roof to the Great Kitchen; he had medievalized the existing one, bolting softwood braces and panels to an earlier oak structure. The irony of it was, as the fire revealed, that the oak structure, a complex arrangement of hammerbeam, lantern and tie-beam truss, was itself a wonderful medieval roof. The architects, historians and archaeologists suddenly realized they had on their hands the oldest, substantially unchanged and still working kitchen in the country and one of the oldest in the world.

Before the fire, there were thought to be no medieval royal kitchens in existence. It was now clear that the Great Kitchen at Windsor, sited here, from documentary evidence, in 1259, had never moved. The documents describe how that thirteenth-century kitchen was heavily remodelled in the great building campaign of Edward III. Dendro-chronological analysis, by which the pattern of rings in timber can identify the moment at which the tree containing them was felled, suggested a date for the earliest timber of some time quite soon after 1337. It was the lower wall plate and the likelihood is that the Kitchen roof of which it formed a major structural element was built between 1361 and 1363. There are references to the roof being lathed and plastered, in other words the final finishes being applied, in 1363. The medieval Kitchen had four huge fireplaces and possibly open hearths in the centre, with the smoke going out through the roof louvre or lantern, which was as much to allow light in as smoke out.

But the bulk of the roof which the fire revealed was later than that. The lower wall plate, embedded in the masonry surrounding it, was the only element not replaced when the whole of the Kitchen roof was rebuilt in 1489. No one knows why that work was done. It might be that in the fifteenth century the Castle had been relatively neglected and the roofs had decayed. It was repaired again in 1577 and in the early eighteenth century, before Wyatville's hyper-medievalization of an almost perfectly medieval quasi-hammerbeam roof.

This obscuring of the medieval with a neo-Gothic skin was practised by Wyatville elsewhere in the Castle. In the Round Tower, for example, he concealed virtually all the medieval timberwork, boxing it in and hiding it behind false ceilings. In the Great Kitchen, it was part of a comprehensive scheme of redecoration, with new kitchen braziers and work tables, of heroic proportions, which have survived.

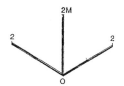

It may be that Wyatville thought the roof was far later than it was. At various times, decay, particularly at the joints and those places where the timbers were inserted into damp masonry, had been repaired with iron forelock bolts, which would have given the roof something of a seventeenth-century appearance when Wyatville found it.

Those iron bolts had, ironically, wrought havoc during the fire. When oak burns, its outer layer chars to a depth of about an inch and that charred skin, which burns very slowly, actually insulates the heart of the timber. Where the iron forelock bolts were fixed to the timbers, and iron pins were drilled right through them, the iron acted as an extraordinarily effective conductor of the heat. Because of those iron bolts, inserted as strengtheners, most of the joints in the roof were burnt out, removing some of the most important technical evidence for the date of the carpentry and leaving the whole structure in a teetering and precariously balanced condition.

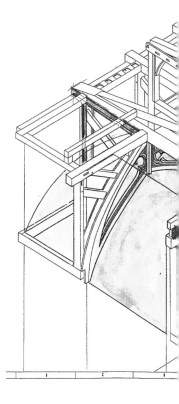

Richard Swift of Gifford and Partners, the engineers, devised an ingenious solution with which to re-use the timbers of the late-medieval Great Kitchen roof. His diagram, below, based on a drawing by John Pidgeon for English Heritage, shows how behind the plaster coving (orange), hidden steelwork (blue) clasps the timber structure (white) which the fire left in an unstable condition. The timber left was bolted on to galvanized steel frames that were securely embedded in the top of the medieval Kitchen walls.

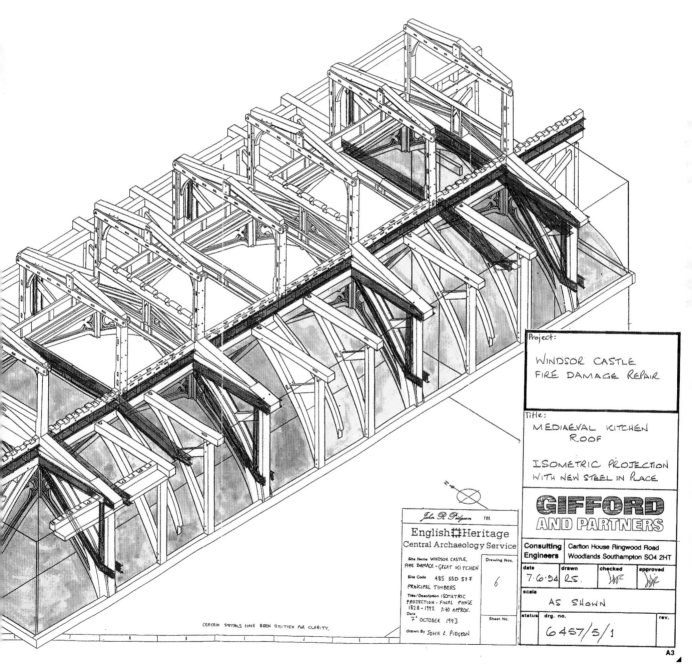

CERTAIN DETAILS HAVE BEEN OMITTED FOR CLARITY.

John R Pidgeon

English Heritage
Central Archaeology Service

Site Name WINDSOR CASTLE.
FIRE DAMAGE - GREAT KITCHEN

Site Code 485 SSD 51 F
PRINCIPAL TIMBERS

Title/Description ISOMETRIC
PROJECTION - FINAL PHASE
1828 - 1992 1:40 APPROX.

Date
7ᵗ OCTOBER 1993

Drawn By JOHN L. PIDGEON

Drawing Nos.
6

Sheet No.

Project:

WINDSOR CASTLE
FIRE DAMAGE REPAIR

Title:

MEDIAEVAL KITCHEN
ROOF

ISOMETRIC PROJECTION
WITH NEW STEEL IN PLACE

GIFFORD
AND PARTNERS

Consulting Engineers	Carlton House Ringwood Road Woodlands Southampton SO4 2HT

date	drawn	checked	approved
7·6·94	R.S.		

scale
AS SHOWN

status	drg. no.	rev.
	6457/5/1	

A3

A birdcage scaffold was erected to fill the whole body of the Great Kitchen to hold the roof up, to let John Pidgeon of English Heritage survey, measure and draw it and the architects and engineers first to inspect it and then come up with an idea of what to do. Richard Swift, leading member of Gifford's, the engineers, was confronted with the problem.

He was faced with the charred collapsing wreck of a huge 500-year old structure, 80 feet long and 30 feet wide. 'There were four options,' he explains. 'Should the remains of the old roof be swept away and a new steel roof put on? We felt that was probably what Michael Peat wanted. It was the cheapest option. Should we put a new green oak roof up there? That would have been more expensive, but you would have lost the historic fabric, even though you could have replicated it quite closely. Should we use a glue-laminated structure, which is much more predictable in what it does – the wood doesn't move as green oak does when it is drying out – but is more expensive again and is a relatively modern method. Or should we try and salvage what was there? That was the most expensive of the lot. But it was the answer that, apart from cost, was going to satisfy most people, including both the historians and the engineers.'

Gifford's produced six reports on this one roof over the autumn and winter of 1993–4, juggling the conflicting requirements. Soon, a consensus was moving towards salvage, but the actual way of doing that was not immediately obvious. What remained had been seriously weakened by the fire or by rot and death-watch beetle before it. One of Swift's ingenious schemes proposed a complete but relatively narrow steel frame alongside the medieval timber one, with the narrow modern steel elements being hidden behind new softwood mouldings to match those that Wyatville had added for his Gothic effect. The medieval timbers would have remained there for appearance's sake only, effectively bolted to a modern steel roof.

Richard Swift calls this answer, which would have been utterly secure, 'not very brave. There was probably something more we could do.' The walls of the Great Kitchen are enormously thick, six or seven feet in places, and capable even at the top of carrying large horizontal loads. It would take an enormous force, in other words, to pull them in or push them out. Equally, some of the big medieval tie-beams that continued to span the roof had, even in their superficially charred state, some strength in them which the engineers could use.

This combination prompted Richard Swift's final solution. Big triangular frames made of galvanized steel were built into the top of the

The mass-produced, cast-iron cusps in the Kitchen lantern windows, the softwood strips nailed on to the oak tie-beams and the little softwood crenellations at the far end are all signs of Wyatville's hyper-medievalization of a medieval roof, all faithfully salvaged or reproduced in the 1990s restoration.

Kitchen walls alongside the medieval trusses. These corbel frames, which are now hidden behind the restored plaster coving, effectively reach in towards each other from either side of the Kitchen and are held *apart* by the big surviving tie-beams that continue to bridge the space. What could be saved has been and the roof is now a combination of modern steelwork, both medieval and modern oak, and modern softwood mouldings which replicate Wyatville's decorative additions from the 1820s which were burned in the fire.

Although the steelwork carries most of the weight of the roof, and any snow load it will have to bear, the medieval timber that survives, with its charred skin chiselled and then sand-blasted off it, does play a structural role. It is not merely window dressing, and the architects and engineers derive some satisfaction from that.

The lantern which surmounts the roof had almost entirely disappeared in the fire except for a few charred oak members and some softwood window frames. These were fitted with cast-iron cusps, easier to mass-produce in that material, even in the 1820s, than to cut and carve each one by hand. Many of them were reinstated. Its central section

The Kitchen Courtyard
after the fire, seen from
the roof of the Grand
Reception Room, with the
wall of St George's Hall
on the right, the Prince of
Wales Tower in the back-

ground and the wall of the Great Kitchen on the left. Before the fire, the medieval courtyard had acquired a clutter of buildings which the fire almost totally destroyed.

had been medieval and its outer wings added by Wyatville. The 1990s restoration has installed concealed plant rooms in those outer elements, with large air-handling units with which to ventilate the Kitchen, and reproduced the central section in green oak as a glazed source of light. Work was begun on stabilizing the walls of the Great Kitchen in June 1994 and the roof was structurally complete fourteen months later in August 1995.

The green-oak elements in the lantern, by Carpenter Oak and Woodland, arrived on site and were installed with a moisture content of 50 per cent or more. They were allowed to dry and move for another year before the huge curved surface of the cove, rising inward and upward from wall to lantern, was plastered in. For that year, as the Great Kitchen rested in its cleared and semi-finished state, it was obvious to anyone who walked in there what a beautiful room it was, in many ways, to a modern eye, the most beautiful at Windsor. With the new rafters installed in the great cove, arcing towards the lantern from all four walls, and the fresh clean look of the green oak in the lantern, it had the air, strangely enough, of one of the organic buildings designed by Imre Makovecz, the great Hungarian architect whom the Prince of Wales had invited to submit proposals for the restoration at Windsor. The Great Kitchen roof was a ribbed and seed-shaped hull upturned on a giant stone box. During that year, as the works were proceeding elsewhere on the many levels and half-levels of the complex site, the Kitchen stood quiet and empty, an abandoned place, with something about it of a great kitchen in an old country house, whose establishment has shrunk since the time it was built.

Alongside the Great Kitchen, in the building that was to occupy the Kitchen Courtyard, the team of architects at Donald Insall's, led by Alan Frost, was grappling with the same spectrum of problems as the roof of the Great Kitchen itself had presented. How to build something new, good, economical and efficient which nevertheless took account of its important historical circumstances? The old arrangement in this area of preparation spaces and staff rooms, of staircases and stores, had accumulated haphazardly over time. It was recognized from the day of the fire that a rationalization of the Kitchen Court and its communication corridors to the rest of the Castle was required. 'To take one simple example,' Alan Frost says, 'there was only one way into the kitchen area. It was from the North Terrace. Fresh food used to come in through the same opening that dustbins went out. That was neither hygienic nor in tune with the Health and Safety Regulations.' There were potentially useful corridors which had access at one end but no way out at the other. There was nothing resembling the number or siting of emergency exits that might comply with modern fire regulations.

The first element tackled by John Dangerfield and Alan Frost at Donald Insall's was the circulation system but, as a practice specializing in the restoration of important historic buildings, they had made a thorough investigation of the historical layering of the Castle. Towards the end of 1993, those two factors – historical awareness and efficiency of plan – came together. The architects realized that the Kitchen Courtyard had originally been open, and that a passage through the Kitchen Gate had originally led into that court from the main Quadrangle of the Upper Ward.

A beautifully vaulted fourteenth-century corridor, the Larderie Corridor, led along the south side of what had been the open court and the Victorian architect Edward Blore had made an elegant, if small, arcaded and top-lit cloister to the north-east of it.

The architects were keen to make use of these high-quality spaces and to lift the overall feeling from what had been the rather grey paint and chipped enamel atmosphere down here before the fire. In late autumn 1993 the possibilities for a beautiful ground floor were enhanced by the newly discovered medieval Kitchen Gateway, whose portcullis groove and arrow slits had, during the enabling works that preceded the main building campaign, been stumbled on, hidden partly in a gents' lavatory and partly in a heavily ducted plant room.

Alan Frost and the team saw the possibility of opening out the whole Kitchen Corridor from medieval gateway to Blore's cloister. Michael Peat at first proved difficult to persuade – there was another parallel corridor, he told Frost, 'Why do you want two corridors side by side?' Frost told him: 'This is an architectural space, a historical space, a worthwhile space. It is also a more direct route out in case of fire.' On all these grounds Michael Peat acceded to the idea and, in time, was to become one of its most enthusiastic advocates.

Other pieces of rationalization were gradually slotted into the plan. The State Dining Room and St George's Hall, to one of which dinner is delivered on the Queen's dine and sleep evenings and to the other during state banquets, are on different levels. Those levels could not be changed and so the behind-the-scenes service areas on the principal floor, along with the hoists that brought the food up from the Kitchen, had to be replanned. The architects built in a lift that could stop at either level. Previously all the food for St George's Hall had to be

The Larderie Corridor, one of the high-quality medieval spaces around the Kitchen Courtyard which Alan Frost and the team of architects at Insall's were keen to rehabilitate.

walked up stairs, with the occasional but inevitable disaster. Partly for this reason, the royal chefs have always cooked an extra twenty plates of each course when preparing dinner for the 161 people who sit down to a state banquet in St George's Hall. Because state banquets are served from both ends of the Hall, another new lift was installed at the west end, rising from the Kitchen to the Queen's Guard Chamber. That lift was also designed to take disabled people up to principal floor level.

The big question confronting the architects was what to do in the Kitchen Courtyard. As the Options Report had identified, an entirely new building was both possible and required there. Its parameters began to set themselves. A new staircase was needed, both for safety and efficiency, at the west end. Food-preparation areas were needed on the ground floor, connecting directly with the Great Kitchen. There were to be staff dining rooms on the first floor, for the Household's F branch (F stands for Food) and offices for the Master and Deputy Master of the Household on the floor above it.

Those were the essential planning needs. Aesthetically, it seemed important to Alan Frost and the team around him that the new building should articulate three things: the Queen Anne wall with its large round-headed windows should remain an overt part of the design; the building should nevertheless be unashamedly of its time, a modern building in a historic setting; and finally it should reflect the fact that this was originally an open courtyard and that the new building had been dropped into it. Here was a chance, as the architects saw it, to bring out something of the frisson between old and new which, for example, Sir Norman Foster's Sackler Galleries in the Royal Academy had so intriguingly expressed. It was also an effect which the Household's Property Section had triumphantly achieved in the recent development of new accommodation for the Royal Archives in the top of the Round Tower at Windsor.

It was an exciting opportunity. The huge façades of the buildings on three sides of what had been the open court – the south wall of the Great Kitchen, the east wall of the Grand Reception Room and the north wall of St George's Hall – were all still there. It was clearly possible, with an element of sleight of hand, to make use of these once-external walls within the new scheme to suggest the sequence of events that had actually occurred there: the box came first; its contents, the Kitchen Court building, was put in later.

The key visual mechanism for this came to be known – as one of the most contentious elements on the entire project – as 'The Slot'. For

practical reasons the Kitchen Court building had to be physically related to the older structures around it, but for aesthetic reasons a visual
separation was necessary. This combination of joined but separate was
what the Slot was designed to achieve. Along the whole outer length of
the south wall of the Great Kitchen and along the east wall of the Grand
Reception Room where it gave on to the old Kitchen Courtyard, a narrow band of glazed roofing would allow light to wash down the faces of
those ancient façades. The floors of the new Kitchen Court building
would be stopped short of those façades so that the natural top-light
would penetrate though the layers of the building, picking up every
notch and knobble of the ancient walls' brick and heathstone surface.
On the outer wall of the Grand Reception Room, the giant Hugh May
windows, blocked by Wyatville, would remain visible in the stair and
corridors alongside them.

The Slot was to run along two sides of the new building. On the third,
the south side, giving on to St George's Hall, the vestigial remains of the
Kitchen Courtyard were allowed to remain open to the sky in a narrow
enclosed court, with, at first-floor level, the Queen Anne windows to
the north and the windows of St George's Hall to the south. The effect
within the rooms of the Kitchen Court building was to be a wash of natural light, reflected on both sides off historic stonework.

Having bowed to the historical circumstances in this way, which is
very much in the Windsor tradition, the building itself, according to
another part of that same tradition, was intended, in its initial drafts, to
go for a modern design and finish. According to a whole series of drawings produced by Donald Insall's over the autumn and winter of 1993,
presented by them and discussed with John Tiltman, then Deputy
Director of the Royal Household's Property Section, an uncompromisingly non-historical building was to be inserted in the Kitchen Courtyard. Its upper floor was to be a lead-covered mansard roof, with large
sections of glazing to light the offices. There were to be steel columns in
the new western stairway and a tensioned steel-wire balustrade leading
down from floor to floor. There was to be no pretence that this was anything but something put up in the 1990s.

In the early part of 1994 the architects moved on to the working drawings. Over 300 were produced, to cover all parts of this phase of the project, received the approval of English Heritage, and then went out to
tender on 21 February 1994. The tenders were back in by 28 March and
on 11 April Higgs and Hill Special Contracts, who had bid very low (the
Windsor factor working hard) and after a very searching interview by

The demolition men took the courtyard down to ground level and archae-ologists (opposite left) then excavated the complex remains of drainage systems and building foun-dations there. The steel frame of the new Kitchen Courtyard building was then erected (opposite right) leaving a clear slot for top-lighting between its back wall and the wall of the Great Kitchen on the right of the picture.

Tiltman and his consultant team, were appointed as main contractors for this phase of the works, worth an estimated £8.5 million.

Phil Rowley, Contracts Manager for Higgs and Hill, emphasizes how much of a task it is to quote for a job like this. 'We had fourteen different people come to visit the site: planners, other site managers, estimators, quantity surveyors, directors. We had received a cold set of drawings, a set of documents and we had six weeks to try and catch up with people who had been living with the site for twelve to eighteen months.' Higgs and Hill weren't to know this, but Wallis's, the contractors on the Kingsbury works – the rewiring programme in the Upper Ward over the previous six years – and on Phases 1–3A of the restoration, had decided not to come in with a cut-throat price for the remaining parts of the restoration works. They reckoned that any marketing advantage there was to be gained from working at Windsor they already had from their long experience there.

The complexity of Windsor impressed itself on Rowley. 'We had to put in a phenomenal amount of spadework in that tender period, getting in amongst the job and really understanding how it was going to be

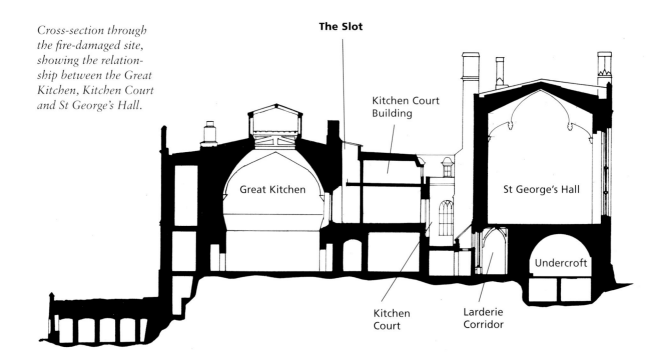

Cross-section through the fire-damaged site, showing the relationship between the Great Kitchen, Kitchen Court and St George's Hall.

The Slot

Kitchen Court Building

Great Kitchen

St George's Hall

Undercroft

Kitchen Court

Larderie Corridor

The roof light for the Slot as originally conceived by the Donald Insall's architects (left), the partly traditional form (centre) that was eventually built and the view of it from beneath (below).

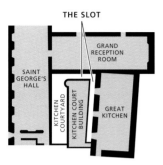

THE SLOT

GRAND
RECEPTION
ROOM

SAINT
GEORGE'S
HALL

KITCHEN
COURTYARD

KITCHEN COURT
BUILDING

GREAT
KITCHEN

put back together. When I first walked round the site, it just looked like a burnt-out wreck of a castle and you think, "Where on earth do you start?"'

On 3 May they started work on the site, focusing largely on the structural elements in the three fire-damaged towers, stiffening the insecure masonry, inserting floors and steelwork. By August they were laying the foundations for the Kitchen Court building. In September the steelwork for the building arrived and in an agonizingly difficult piece of planning and agility, the huge columns were threaded into their tightly constrained site. Higgs and Hill, because there was a limit to the number and weight of cranes that could come on to the site, brought most materials in by hoist and wheeled bogeys. The big steel columns were seven metres long and too big for that method. They were dropped in by giant cranes through holes in the temporary roof that were one metre wide by two metres long, down through the depth of the building and then, when inside the labyrinth of scaffolding and masonry walls, had to be hauled sideways by hand into positions which needed to be millimetre perfect. Each column, of which there were fourteen, took more than an hour to insert, a process compared by Phil Rowley, the Higgs and Hill site manager, to 'sewing with one-ton needles'. Drainage systems were going in, fireproofing to the steels was going in. In Phil Rowley's phrase, 'we were flying'. And then, in October 1994, the works on the Kitchen Courtyard building were brought to a sudden and unexpected stop.

The architects had been pursuing in their design work the details for the Kitchen Court building: sinks, taps, lights, tiles, hinges, handles, catches, switches – everything, in short, with which the bones of a building is dressed. In every one of these areas, their thinking had been guided by the design philosophy which had shaped the architecture: the unashamedly modern in look and feel.

By October 1994 Donald Insall's were ready to present their scheme in detail to the Royal Household. It was, in many ways, the most difficult moment of the entire project. Donald Insall's thought they were moving along an agreed path, with the apparent approval of the Royal Household in the form of John Tiltman, the Deputy Director of its Property Section. Only now, as the building was actually being built, did Michael Peat, Tiltman's boss, the central figure in the chain running from building to client, come to look closely at the proposed finishes. He did not like what he saw. It didn't look to him like something that belonged at Windsor. It was too modern. It didn't take circumstances into account. It wasn't 'castly' enough and their intention to make a sharp difference between old and new did not, as far as Michael Peat was concerned, seem to come off.

Michael Peat, Alan Frost and John Tiltman went to inspect work that Donald Insall's had done elsewhere in London so that the Household could see the effect in the round, but it did nothing to allay the fears that had been raised. The Kitchen Court building, even then proceeding, to use the phrase the project manager Chris Watson habitually returns to, 'like a supertanker' on the programme both GTMS and Higgs and Hill had worked out, had to be brought to a halt and turned in another direction. Rowley was grateful for the way it was handled. 'The worst thing you can do is muddle on, which impacts on everybody. The best thing to do is to stop it at an agreed point. Those people who were up and running were allowed to carry on to an agreed point.'

The overall job was big enough, there were plenty of other tasks the contractor's workforce could attend to, the Kitchen Court building did not have to be finished for another two years or more and so the overall programme was not disrupted by the change, but the Household's decision, crisply and even brusquely made, sent ripples through the project team.

Robert Kime, a member of the Prince of Wales's Design Committee and one of the country's leading interior designers, had worked at Highgrove and at both St James's and Kensington Palaces. The Prince of Wales was a great admirer and included him on his Design Committee. He felt that Kime really understood buildings, with real feeling rather than an academic approach. For the Prince of Wales this was particularly important at Windsor, a building, after all, that was going to be lived in, as well as used for official purposes. Kime was approached by Michael Peat. Could he advise Donald Insall's and steer them in a direction which was less resolutely modernist in tone? He agreed.

Alan Frost of Donald Insall's takes it all quite calmly now. 'It was all very gentlemanly,' he said. 'I went to Michael Peat's office and he said "Look, we have an unease about the details of this. We think that some guidance is needed and we have decided to appoint Robert Kime to help with the embodiment of this part of the Castle." But I'm a born optimist and so there are moments when one has to say to oneself you either get out altogether or you just resign yourself to it.'

Nevertheless, and in the very limited time available at this point in the exercise, everything had to be gone over again at a series of fairly fraught meetings between Donald Insall's and Robert Kime. It was, in a sense, a re-running of much of the debate that had gone on outside the

The architects' drawing of part of the Kitchen Court building façade after the original, more modernist scheme had been rejected.

Castle in the days after the fire: modernism or reproductionism, something that concurred with and repeated existing elements at Windsor or something that was clearly and deliberately set apart from the existing fabric?

In many ways, the famous Slot symbolized this debate. Even as the Kime–Insall meetings were taking place, the framework for the Slot was being built. Robert Kime, and his associate the architect Mary-Lou Arscott, did not like the roof light over it, and that, for a while anyway, was removed from the design, to be replaced by roof lanterns modelled on examples already at Windsor. But that was only the beginning of a comprehensive re-direction of this part of the project. In the Great Kitchen, Kime suggested a stone floor with a fairly rough and not over-polished finish. The Property Section had asked Insall's for 'a non-slip floor covering which would meet up-to-date environmental health standards'. He also suggested original ceilings in the Pastry Kitchen be exposed and not hidden behind a modern suspended ceiling. He felt that a lighting system that in many ways resembled what had been there in the nineteenth century would be best. As he puts it, 'I had to ask myself, "Who is going to speak up for the defence of the room?" The client is understandably removed from it all and in many ways, equally understandably, the client's officers do not see it as their house. There is no blame here. It is simply a very difficult position. I was trying to speak up, in the case of the Kitchen, for a wonderful room – all its bones were intact – and for bits of the building that were being treated in a very much more commercial way than I think they deserved.'

The Donald Insall schemes, which Robert Kime felt to be more modernist than modern, or in his words 'rather seventies, if not fifties, in feeling', were changed at five meetings through October and November. By the beginning of December 1994 the new ideas had reached a stage where they could be collected in a booklet to be shown to the Queen and the Duke of Edinburgh for their comments and approval. What had been the lead and glass mansard roof to the Kitchen Court building had become a lead roof with three rather rounded dormer windows, perhaps a little Viennese in feeling. The steel banisters and columns had gone and, at least in the stairwell alongside the outside of the Grand Reception Room wall, the roof-light over the Slot had been banished and replaced with roof-lanterns, replicated from earlier examples. In the Kitchen Cloister, the glazed roof had been raised to make more of an atrium. In a hundred small details of coving, skirting, vaulting, panelling, cornicing and flooring , the Kime touch appeared throughout

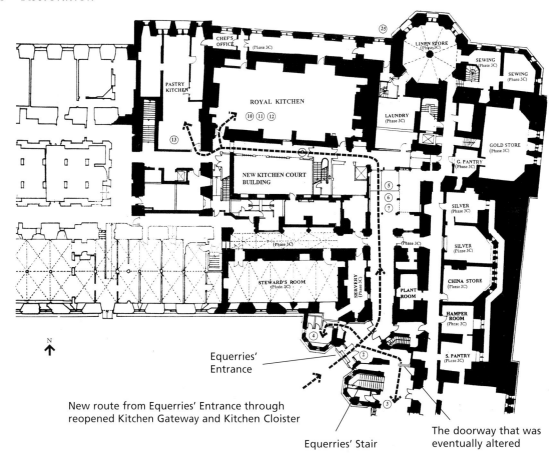

Equerries'
Entrance

New route from Equerries' Entrance through
reopened Kitchen Gateway and Kitchen Cloister

Equerries' Stair

The doorway that was
eventually altered

the Kitchen and staff areas. Floors were to be of York and Purbeck stone
and of slip-resistant Burlington slate. Balustrades were to be of wrought
iron and modelled on Wyatville precedents. For the Great Kitchen, the
Queen chose the chequerboard pattern on the floor. It was made with
two sorts of stone, both from the Isle of Purbeck in Dorset: the creamy
brown Purbeck Thornback and the darker Purbeck marble.

There were to be sixty staff bedrooms and associated areas in the
three towers and above the Crimson Drawing Room. The arrangement
of furniture and lighting, and of radiators and washstands, even the
choice of furniture, was all subject to the Kime touch. So that people
could know where they were in the slightly complicated geography,
appropriate emblems were to decorate the staff areas: the three feathers
and 'Ich Dien' for the Prince of Wales Tower, the Wheatsheaf of the
Earls of Chester for the Chester Tower and the two lions of the House
of Brunswick for the Brunswick Tower. It was all part of an extraordinarily rapid and comprehensive redesign of the entire back of house.

As a footnote to the process, and characteristic of the tough

The doorway (right) between the Equerries' Entrance and Equerries' Stair which had to be widened, at a cost, as it eventually turned out, of over £100,000. Left, the architects' plan of the ground floor to show some of the improvements to circulation at that level.

financial management that was present throughout this decision-making process, Michael Peat wrote as follows to his deputy John Tiltman: 'The budget presently includes an allowance of £282,000 for decorating the sixty staff bedrooms and related areas. We agreed that Robert Kime would be offered a budget of £157,000 and if he said this was too little to top it up by £50,000.' As it turned out, Kime was never offered a budget nor made directly responsible for the work. Nevertheless, this is a classic instance of the Peat method: get someone in because his eye is going to deliver the good taste that is required, but once he is in make sure that bit and bridle are applied to the costs. It is this combination of qualities that is admired by members of the Royal Family and colleagues. As Sir Robert Fellowes, the Queen's Private Secretary, puts it, 'He's a man with that very rare mixture: taste, financial expertise and a determination to get things done.'

Some aspects, but far from everything that went into the booklet submitted to the Queen that December, ended up being built. On one point in particular, Alan Frost, the leading architect at Donald Insall's,

resisted the Kime avalanche of change. 'It came to the point,' he says, 'where I wrote to John Tiltman and said, "Look, John, these lanterns are simply not going to work. We must go back. I will take responsibility for what it will look like, but do allow us to do it."' The Household agreed and the top-light above the Slot that ran along the outside of the Great Kitchen was re-incorporated in the scheme.

The complicated route that design decisions had taken over the Kitchen and staff areas meant that this part of the job was going to run late and over budget. As a result, much of this phase, known as 3B, was deferred to a later date and included with Phase 3C, those parts of the ground floor and basement which were still, in late 1994, too wet to work on. With this sleight of hand, it could safely be said at the end of 1995 that 3B was completed on time and within budget.

The final aspect of the staff areas was in many ways the most exciting of all. This enlarged 3C Phase carried on seamlessly from the completion of 3B at the beginning of 1996 and continued until the summer of 1997. Windsor persisted with its characteristic complexity. The services designed by Oscar Faber had to be threaded though spaces and corridors that could scarcely accommodate them. The need to adjust the route from the Equerries' Entrance to the first floor, involving what seemed at first like little more than the widening of a couple of doorways and the lobby between, turned out to be a major engineering problem.

This piece of work, connecting the Equerries' Entrance and the Equerries' Stair, will be forgotten in the future. Its implications for the efficient operation of the building are important, not least in introducing the Sovereign's guests to Windsor in a way that is graceful and elegant. But the route thus created is not something that anyone in future will stand back from and admire, or even notice. It is something which, if done badly or left unchanged, would have been apparent. It will have succeeded if it is ignored.

This is what it involved. The Duke of Edinburgh was unhappy with the previous access to the principal floor by this route and so Insall's were asked to come up with a solution. They produced plans and perspective drawings for a series of alternatives: a second stairway, rising straight from the Kitchen Corridor to the new Lantern Lobby on the site of the old Private Chapel next to St George's Hall; making a new doorway into the so-called Star Chamber next to the Equerries' Entrance, or reshaping the existing route and widening the openings. The Prince of Wales was consulted and thought a second stairway would be a mistake. As he wrote to Michael Peat at the time, 'I have doubts that a new staircase could be made to work satisfactorily. First of all, it would have to be done *very* well to be credible. Secondly, the whole point, it seems to me, of the Kitchen Court Passage is that you should be able to see all the way down it – a fascinating vista. But if you had to interrupt it with an opaque screen, I can't help feeling it might spoil the effect. Thirdly, the Equerries' Stairs would become redundant and are two staircases really needed?'

It was settled that the openings on the existing route should be widened. English Heritage kept a close watch. Roger Davies of Gifford and Partners, the structural engineers, wrestled with the complexity of jacking up the inside of the tower while rebuilding the doorways. It turned out that the walls through which the doorways in question actually passed were supporting the vast bulk of that corner of the Chester Tower. Gifford's realized that they would be fiddling with a rather tender structure. The upper parts of a small spiral stair in the tower were resting on the doorway wall, and the stair structure was not well supported higher up. There was an acute danger that the upper parts of Chester Tower would collapse.

The more dangerous the condition of the building, the more secure any works to it have to be and the more expensive it becomes. Roger

The insertion of modern services into a medieval castle was one of the greatest challenges ever faced by Oscar Faber, the mechanical and electrical engineers.

Davies says quite clearly 'We were more than reluctant to do this. We were petrified and we did express the view repeatedly to the client that quite a significant cost would be involved.' The Household and the architects were adamant that they wanted the access to the Equerries' Stair improved and the door widened. A temporary goalpost frame of large steel beams was designed by Gifford's and Higgs and Hill Technical Services. The package of works then went out to tender. English Heritage checked it for minimal intrusion. The quotes came back to Higgs and Hill. Bucknall Austin, the quantity surveyors, then awarded the job on price grounds to Keltbray Civil Engineering and the goalpost was erected to hold up the building while the inner of the two doorways was re-formed within it. A proprietary jacking system had to be used and special Strongback props hired for the purpose. Modifications had to be made to the method as hidden voids were revealed within the walls. Each of these changes had to wind its way through the complex system of Project Managers' Instructions.

It was revealed that the top 20 per cent of the spiral stair in the tower, which had cracked in the fire, had to be taken down and rebuilt. It would have been cheaper to demolish and rebuild more of it, rather than holding it all up from underneath, but English Heritage refused clearance for that. It then became obvious that the wall holding up the spiral stair was much thinner than had been expected and the whole thing had to be set in a concrete case to prevent it collapsing eastwards out of the building.

The cost for widening the main doorway and opening up the lobby beyond came to over £100,000. It had an impact on everything around it. Sidell Gibson was working on the new lantern lobby to the west, Donald Insall's were working on the Green Drawing Room to the east, and also on the staff bedrooms above, while Oscar Faber were attempting to insert services in the basement below. All those programmes were affected by the widening of a single door.

The escalating costs made the Household very reluctant to get involved in the same sort of operation with the second doorway. It was felt that the main improvement had already been achieved and what had been done had made the necessary difference. The second doorway, apart from its frame which was removed, remained the width it always had been. The whole saga had been a powerful if in some ways highly coloured epitome of what the Windsor job involved. It is precisely these sorts of factors that make it all the more remarkable that the project has come in anywhere near that impossible formula: high quality, under budget, earlier than expected. That is the measure in some ways

The fourteenth-century Undercroft beneath St George's Hall, previously divided up and drowned in institutional gloss paint, became one of the revelations of the project. 'This is where you have found the building,' a visitor commented, 'this is Windsor.'

of the strictness and in others the flexibility of the project management.

West from the Equerries' Entrance, along the south front of the building under St George's Hall, ran a succession of medieval vaulted spaces, unaffected by the fire but seriously affected by the water which the Fire Brigade had poured in. Taking them from the east in turn, there was the Steward's Room, one of the few recognizable parts of Henry III's palace to survive Edward III's radical rebuilding. The Larderie passage ran along the north side of the Steward's Room. West of it, in what had originally been the great open Undercroft beneath Edward III's St George's Hall and Chapel, were a series of small offices, divided by seventeenth-century partitions and occupied by the Castle Superintendent's staff, the Footmen, the Travelling Yeoman, the Sergeant Footman and the Yeoman of the Royal Cellars, as ringingly medievalist a sequence of men and titles as you could hope to find. Beyond that was a small passage and the servants' hall, where the fourteenth-century stone vaulting of the Undercroft remained open to view as it was originally.

Dr Steven Brindle, the English Heritage Inspector at Windsor, wrote a short paragraph in the historical notes that accompanied Donald Insall's proposals for this area. 'It would be marvellous,' it said, 'if the great vista of the thirteen-bay Undercroft, with its central columns could be re-opened and suitable uses allocated to this premium space.' It would be, as Brindle later described it, 'comparable in effect to the great monastic undercrofts of Fountains and Rievaulx Abbeys.'

The notion of making something more of the Steward's Room anyway had been raised by the Prince of Wales earlier in the year: 'At the risk of interfering!,' he wrote to Michael Peat, 'I do feel that the old Steward's Room could be restored to something very beautiful, if done carefully. It is a magical room. Likewise the passages round the side of the Great Kitchen (the ones with the vaulted ceilings) could be greatly improved if left as natural tone with the ribs picked out in a suitable colour.'

Steven Brindle's suggestion took this enhancement of the ancient ground floor even further, even though, to reinstate the whole Undercroft, a great deal of historic fabric, including the seventeenth-century partitions, would have to be removed. Donald Insall's did not incorporate Brindle's suggestion in their design proposals and Brindle did not pursue the matter. Michael Peat, however, immediately he saw the reference, decided he would ask the Queen and the Duke of Edinburgh whether the Undercroft could be reinstated.

There are many surprising parts to this. One might have expected the Royal Household's Director of Finance to have objected on grounds of cost, rather than to initiate the proposal, and one might have expected English Heritage to object to such an intrusive scheme on preservationist grounds. No one was making any demand for these spaces to be opened up. To remove the little offices which currently occupied them would create difficulties for the rest of the Household. All sides of the project had been subject to financial trimming: no rosettes on new vaulted ceilings, no unnecessary widening of doors. But now, late in the process, in December 1995, here was a sudden and major extension of the scope of works. It took the entire project team by surprise and was one of the best decisions made in the whole course of the restoration.

But complexity seeps back in. A little staircase from the time of Hugh May at the north-west corner of the Undercroft had to be removed and the half-vault reinstated. The floor levels of the different parts of the range varied and many different voices were raised to keep them, to change them or to change some of them. The easternmost section, the Steward's Hall, a century earlier than the rest and quite distinct from it, was at the highest level and floored in huge and beautiful flagstones, eight feet by six. The part of the fourteenth-century Undercroft just west of the Steward's Hall had a nineteenth-century brick wine cellar inserted into it, and so the floor there was at the same level as the Steward's Hall. An original stone floor, discovered in August 1996 under rotten floorboards, remained under part of the west end. The architects and the Property Section would have liked to remove the cellar and in particular to reinstate the original floor level at the west end but there were problems. The stone of the floor at that end was shaling and its slight slope with a central drain – it might originally have been stabling – would make human use of it awkward. More importantly, there were were some real problems for F Branch in moving the cellar.

Utility won out over beauty. Scheme after scheme was produced with the result that a wooden floor at a higher, more convenient level now covers the Undercroft's original flags and the wine cellar remains, for the time being at least. Despite that, the vaulted Undercroft, stripped of its clutter and returned at least in part to its original clarity, is a strikingly beautiful space, giving some hint of what Edward III's palace might have looked like. An Austrian visitor, a government architect, being taken around the site by John Thorneycroft of English Heritage, arrived at the end of his tour down here. 'Ah,' he said, looking around him at the clean stone vaulting and the medieval arcade running down the centre of the room, 'this is where you have found the building, this is Windsor.'

6 Gilt &
Gorgeousness

'Something rustles,' Benjamin Haydon, the history painter, wrote in his journal for 19 July 1821, the day of George IV's coronation, 'and a being buried in satin, feathers and diamonds rolls gracefully into his seat. The room rises with a sort of feathered, silken thunder. Plumes wave, eyes sparkle, glasses are out, mouths smile and one man becomes the prime object of attention to thousands. As he looked towards the peeresses and foreign ambassadors, he showed like some gorgeous bird of the East.'

The figure of this peacock King continues to haunt the great State Apartments at Windsor Castle. They are, in a sense, a setting for his presence. His character and taste were the guiding force behind their creation and these large, fine but in some ways exaggerated and melo-dramatic rooms share some of the complexities and subtleties of his own character. He was an enormous, overscaled man (by 1795, he already weighed nearly seventeen stone in his boots and his prospective wife's first remark on seeing him was the uncompromising 'Je le trouve trop gros') but at the same time strangely delicate; he spent money as though it didn't matter, but his taste was perfect; there was an ab-surdity about him – his first act as Regent was to appoint himself Field Marshal, in which uniform he drove through London in a yellow berlin with purple blinds – but also a deeply held and passionately felt love of his country; debt stalked him all his life, but he was the greatest patron England has ever seen, who enriched the Royal Collection more than any other monarch and created the nucleus of both the National Gallery and the British Library; he was a dandy who nevertheless was often seen to be 'glittering with incessant perspiration' and who in old age asked the young Victoria to kiss him, but for her, as she later confided to a friend, 'it was too disgusting because his face was covered in grease paint'.

This amalgam of contradictory qualities, carried off by the brio with which they were displayed, was transmitted to the interiors that the King created, and nowhere more so than at Windsor. The theatricality, the grandeur and the opulence, the immoderate love, in Mark Girouard's words, of 'gilt-and-gorgeousness' and the sheer lack of restraint are all more fully and uncompromisingly realized in the State Apartments in the north-east corner of the Upper Ward at Windsor than any other surviving rooms that he made.

As Prince of Wales, Regent and King, he had been addicted to building and interior design for decades. These rooms, created between 1826 and 1828, can only be understood as the culmination of a process that had begun more than forty years earlier. In 1783 the Prince had come of age and for his own establishment was given Carlton House, a seventeenth-century building once occupied by Frederick, Prince of Wales, set in a garden laid out by William Kent between the Mall and Pall Mall in the West End of London.

His father, George III, had implored him to try and behave 'like a rational being' when it came to money. There was little hope of that. Within months, the Prince's Secretary and Treasurer was writing to him: 'It is with equal grief and vexation that I now see your Royal Highness totally in the hand, and at the mercy of your builder, your upholsterer, your jeweller and your tailor.' By 1795 his debts stood at £630,000.

The appetite for the gorgeous and gilded was more than sheer lust for glamour. The Prince's almost obsessive decoration and redecoration, extension and improvement of Carlton House, even after he had also begun the huge building works at his 'marine pavilion' in Brighton, was, in its way, a political programme, a demonstration of the strength and glory of the English Crown in a Europe where one throne after another had been knocked aside in the onrush of French revolutionary fervour.

George III, both at Windsor and at his new mock-castle at Kew, had turned to Gothic for the safety and confirmation of what was conceived of as the national style in a world threatened by revolution, first in America and then in France. His son, while equally fervent in his opposition to the republican frenzy abroad, turned, for the most part, in

another direction. It is true to say that the Prince was a great admirer of the French court style before the revolution, but there can be little doubt that the seismic events of 1789 confirmed and enriched a taste that had already formed. Where the first changes at Carlton House had been austerely elegant in a strict, neoclassical idiom, after the turn of the century the Prince moved deeper and deeper into an ever more sumptuous and luxurious vein, drawing its inspiration from the great age of the French monarchy, at the end of the seventeenth and beginning of the eighteenth century. Spectacular chandeliers, gilt and velvet sofas, immensely rich silk velvet and damask hangings, gilt-bronze candelabra, clocks and porcelain, with fleurs-de-lis rampant on carpets, curtains and cushions all poured into his palace off Pall Mall. Carlton House became a shrine to francophilia.

Charles Wild's record of the Blue Velvet Room in Carlton House, showing curtains and sofas in blue fleur-de-lis satin, gold-coloured silk rope for hanging the pictures and on the doors carved gilt-wood trophies, which were later transferred to Windsor Castle.

The final flowering of his taste, late in the day and only when the country had returned to prosperity after the slump that followed Napoleon's defeat at Waterloo in 1815, came in the State Apartments at Windsor. From 1826 onwards Carlton House, which for all its spectacular decoration had been poorly built and scarcely maintained, was demolished and its parts distributed: some to the new Buckingham Palace, some to moulder in St James's Park until they were reused a few years later in the new National Gallery and some to Windsor, including fireplaces, carved giltwood door trophies, perhaps some plaster overdoor panels and masses of the furniture and paintings.

The new rooms at Windsor were to be Carlton House but more so: luxurious, royal, gilded, comfortable, packed with masterpieces. English monarchs had never been able to create a palace with which the Crown could be supremely identified. One after another, for 200 years, royal building projects had been left incomplete. Whitehall, Winchester, Greenwich, Hampton Court: none had become the English Versailles. George IV set about creating two: Windsor Castle and Buckingham Palace were to become the embodiments of the British monarchy itself.

At Windsor, there were essentially two vocabularies available and George IV made use of both of them. Wyatville's work on the exterior gave the Castle a much more martial air than it had before, carrying on from the gothicizing changes made by his uncle, James Wyatt, for George III. Internally, St George's Hall and the Octagon Dining Room

One of the fireplaces by the Vulliamys brought to Windsor from Carlton House. Each of the bronze satyrs presents two naked infants to the comforts of the fire. See p. 251 for its finished condition.

were also to be decorated in a version of Gothic and the State Dining Room in a sort of Tudorbethan.

There had been a Gothic dining room and an incredible fan-vaulted conservatory, in cast-iron and stained glass, at Carlton House but its other rooms, consisting of a series of long, narrow apartments with bow windows to one side, had been in the rich French manner. That is exactly what was re-created here. Over the years, George had assembled at Carlton House an unrivalled team with which to create rich interiors. Plasterers, carvers, decorators, upholsterers, agents skilled in the buying of Dutch Old Masters and French furniture and ornaments, architects and artistic advisers had all been clustered around him for years. The firm of decorators Morel and Seddon, with the Crace family as subcontractors, and Francis Bernasconi as plasterer, working closely with Wyatville, probably formulated the ideas of what was needed here. Wyatville disclaimed responsibility for these rooms but he certainly ordered chimney-pieces, mirrors and panelling to come to Windsor from Carlton House. Morel and Seddon had coloured drawings made of the decorative schemes for the rooms and many of those are signed off or annotated by the King. But, as Hugh Roberts, Director of the Royal Collection, says, 'This was obviously a collaborative effort. The important thing is that this team knew their man. They knew precisely what he liked and they knew he would take a minute interest in every single thing that was done. A very careful pictorial inventory of furniture and so on was made at Carlton House and you can be certain they would have been absolutely sure about what they were doing here.'

Along the east side of the castle, a White Drawing Room led into a green library (now the Green Drawing Room) and on into a Crimson Drawing Room. That gave on to the State Dining Room and then the Octagon Dining Room. From there a new corridor, in which some of George IV's collection of arms and armour was displayed, led to the greatest room of all, which had no precedent at Carlton House and is in many ways the crowning monument of George IV's lifelong commitment to re-creating if not outdoing the spectacular interiors of the *ancien régime*: the Grand Reception Room. This huge apartment, forty feet tall, thirty wide and 100 long, was decorated in a rich and spectacular reinterpretation of Régence style, the filigree-rococo that held sway in France from 1715 to 1723, but executed here on a scale and lavishness which no one from early eighteenth-century France would have recognized.

There was one symptom here, in particular, which indicates more

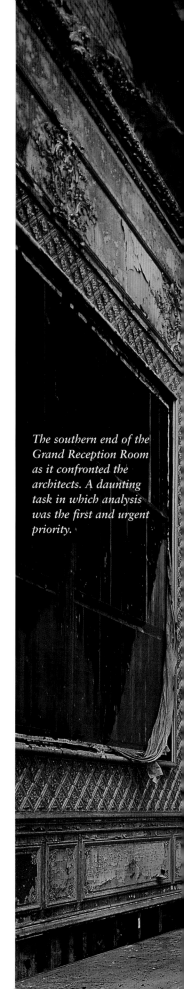

The southern end of the Grand Reception Room as it confronted the architects. A daunting task in which analysis was the first and urgent priority.

than anything else the precise nature of this late-Georgian transformation of Windsor. During investigations after the fire, it was found that the tall, highly decorated walls of the Grand Reception Room are not at all what they seem. Immediately surrounding the Gobelins tapestries, which were their main form of decoration, was a border of rosettes or paterae. These were of gilded 'composition', a paste, made out of ground chalk, linseed oil and rabbit glue. When new, composition can be pushed into moulds but it then sets immensely hard. It is cheaper than carving out of wood but much harder and less friable than plaster.

Outside them, however, the architects discovered something very strange indeed. Up to about twenty-one feet above floor level, the richly carved dado and broad pilasters were in very finely carved wood. They had originally been gilded in the subtle, expensive and labour-intensive form of the art known as water-gilding, which is usually reserved for furniture or picture-frames and involves the application of a coloured clay or bole beneath the gold leaf. When the gilding is burnished the bole is allowed to 'grin through', so that the finish includes that colour as well as the colour of the gold itself.

These carved panels, so expensively treated, had then, curiously, been coated in gesso, a fine white plaster which provides a smooth surface, and then overgilt with a relatively crude coat of oil-gilding. This form of gilding is quicker, simpler and cheaper (at current prices £200–£300 a linear metre, as against £800–£900 for water-gilding). It cannot be burnished to a high shine and doesn't have the same subtlety of effect.

As a further conundrum, the wood panelling stopped at twenty-one feet above the floor. From there on upwards, the same design was continued up to the cove of the ceiling, not in wood but in oil-gilt plaster. What can explain this extraordinary combination of materials and treatments? As the architects soon realized, it is all deeply symptomatic of George IV's methods at Windsor. The lower part of the room is decorated with panels of genuine French eighteenth-century *boiseries*, brought back from Paris for the King in the 1820s. They were beautiful, but not big enough for the huge walls the King was intent on embellishing. The only thing to do was to extend them upwards in plaster and then, to make an integrated whole of new and old, apply the same coat of oil-gilding throughout.

The suite of rooms he had created at Windsor persisted, mostly but far from entirely unchanged, through all the vagaries of nineteenth- and twentieth-century changes of taste until the fire in November 1992. The Options Report prepared by the Steering Group in early 1993 had rec-

Part of a diagram drawn by the architects from Donald Insall Associates analysing, for the first time, the elements in the wall decoration of the Grand Reception Room. What the analysis revealed was an ingenious extension of eighteenth-century panelling to an early nineteenth-century decorative scheme.

Oil gilt on gesso, on timber

Oil gilt on timber

Oil gilt on composition

Paint on gesso

Paint on timber

Paint on plaster

Oil gilt on plaster

English 19th-century plaster →

← French 18th-century boiseries

ommended that the French rooms that had been damaged – the Crimson and Green Drawing Rooms and the Grand Reception Room – should be reinstated as they had been. In the early days after the fire, the fate of the two dining rooms was less certain, but in the spring of 1994 it was decided that they too should be put back largely as they had been before.

Donald Insall Associates, who were the co-ordinating architects, were selected for this part of the project too. From the practice, Peter Riddington was put in charge of the two drawing rooms and the Grand Reception Room, Michael Shippobottom and Peter Cooke the two dining rooms. They were all faced with a vast and daunting challenge.

Each embarked on a massive year-long analysis of exactly what was needed and how they were going to achieve it. The areas allotted to the two architects were very different. The fire had been particularly savage in the dining rooms and very little indeed was left beyond the naked masonry. The instruction from the Household to reinstate the rooms as they had been was all very well, but where did you begin? Although surveys had been made both before and after the fire, it was not even clear, particularly in the State Dining Room, exactly where the wall line of the finished room should run in relation to the stone shell, which was all that room now was. 'We had a plan and spot heights,' Peter Cooke remembers, 'but very few indications of wall lines. In the Crimson Drawing Room, Peter Riddington at least had the line of the skirting and could see the end of the floor. But at the west end of the State Dining Room it was so bad that you couldn't actually know where the room stopped and started. The survey had only measured up to the apparent surfaces with no relation to the masonry behind those surfaces. And we had no real reason to suppose the room was square.'

Virtually no clues offered themselves until the architects found the burnt remains of a single electric wall socket, something that might easily have been pulled out during the clearing process after the fire. But this one hadn't been and was still there sticking out at skirting-board level. Its fire-wrinkled surface was the only sure indication of where the outer face of the panelling had been. The outlet of an air duct in the ceiling – although not entirely reliable: it had probably distorted in the heat – gave another point to which the visible surface of the re-created room could be accurately positioned.

In the Octagon Dining Room next door, at the foot of the Brunswick Tower, the roaring climax of the fire had deposited a twelve-foot-deep mound of debris on the floor, particularly on the west side around the

The State Dining Room in the 1840s, recorded by Joseph Nash, part of the evidence which both the architects and the curtain-designers had to rely on to reconstruct this room, of which nothing survived the fire but a bare stone shell.

door to the China Corridor. This, paradoxically, protected those parts of the room on which it fell. That insulation of part of the room from the destructive heat around it meant, for example, that Peter Cooke was able to copy mouldings from the overdoor tracery panel and from the base and edge of a pier, showing the architrave and skirting cap. From the rest of the room those details had completely disappeared. In the State Dining Room, by pure chance, one of the jib doors within the panelling, leading to a service area behind, had been put in store during the Kingsbury rewiring works that had preceded the fire. That one surviving door leaf gave the mouldings for the State Dining room skirting cap and panel mould.

One or two other fragments were picked from the ashy debris in the dining rooms: a pendant boss from the State Dining Room, 'but', says Cooke, 'it was so badly charred that the only possible thing you got from that was scale'; one or two fragments of the ceiling; and a charred spandrel panel from above the north window in the State Dining Room, which had amazingly remained in situ. Otherwise, the architects had,

essentially, to reinvent the rooms from whatever pictorial documentation they could find.

Luckily, the photographic record was excellent, at least at first glance. A set of rectified photographs, in which the images had been corrected so that the scale remained constant over the whole picture, had been produced as part of the Kingsbury works. These photographs had been taken either straight on to the walls to make a photographic elevation, or lying flat on the floor to give a plan of the ceiling. 'That seems a great idea,' Peter Cooke says, 'but it wasn't, particularly in the Octagon Dining Room.' In the State Dining Room, next door, which is basically a square room, the ceiling rises slightly to a central ridge, no more than one foot higher in the centre than at the edges. In the Octagon, however, there is a tall ribbed plaster vault rising to a central boss twenty-five feet above the floor. Neither the straight-on photographs of the walls nor the pictures taken lying flat on the floor could give any indication whatsoever of the curve of the vault. The architects could have no idea, either from the evidence on the ground or from the main photographic record, of the basic shape of the great rooms they were

A corner of the cove in the Grand Reception Room gives some idea of the richness of effect to which these apartments are dedicated and of the delicacy required in sewing the new into the old.

charged with reinstating. Some anecdotal drawings existed, but they could not be relied on and there were no detailed drawings of ceilings from the 1820s. It was only when some photographs were discovered, taken by an amateur photographer in about 1900 and which had ended up in Birmingham City Library, that the architects had anything to go on. These photographs, taken on the oblique, showed at least something of the curve of the vault which wasn't apparent in the straight-on photos. Without those Birmingham photographs, the architects could have done no more than guess. With them, they could begin painstakingly to map out the task of reinstatement. A segment of the ceiling was made as a trial.

For Peter Riddington, responsible for the two great drawing rooms and the Grand Reception Room, a rather different set of problems confronted him, at least initially. These were the apartments in which the decorators of the 1820s had created the richest and most layered of effects. Looking at photographs of the rooms as they had been before the fire, the impression was of almost overwhelming complexity. What he saw in October 1993 was almost as distant from that image of integrated completeness as it was possible to be: stark, empty rooms, the Crimson Drawing Room and the Grand Reception Room roofless, a few shreds of silk on the walls of the Crimson Drawing Room, large areas of gilt plaster still on the walls of the Grand Reception Room but scorched and water-damaged, the ceiling of the Green Drawing Room still largely there but with a scaffold beneath it, ready to catch it in case of collapse. In short, it was a bedraggled, broken building. Nowhere in Windsor can the hill have seemed steeper to climb. But Riddington, who has inspired confidence in everyone who has worked with him for his pragmatic and straightforward approach to problems and their solution, applied that frame of mind from the start. 'With all of this kind of work,' he says, 'it's a question of breaking it down into its component parts. Things look terribly complicated when you see them as a whole. But when you break them down, you've got to remember they were only built by people. OK, the people then were very skilled, but there is nothing superhuman about it. This is something we could do.'

Before moving towards 'reinstatement', the architects had to know from the client precisely what it was they were being asked to do. The Restoration Committee had decided that these rooms were to be subject to what was called 'Equivalent Restoration'. One definition of that phrase comes from Ian Constantinides of the repair and conservation company St Blaise: 'As long as it looks like what it looked like, it don't

matter if it ain't like what it was like.' In other words, there would be no pedantry behind the scenes. Modern electrical and mechanical services, with dimmer switches for chandeliers and sophisticated air-conditioning systems, modern methods of fixing and supporting, modern methods of heating, plumbing, fire preventing and fire detecting were all going to be legitimate here, because they were likely to be both more efficient and, on the whole, cheaper.

But what about the front of house? These rooms are, in a sense, ambassadors for the nation. They are used during State Visits and the two or three 'dine and sleep' evenings held by The Queen every April. There is no place here for the sort of effect the National Trust, say, might look for in one of its houses, where an air of faded elegance and an ever-thickening patina of age is the greatest service that can be done to a historic interior. That can never be the manner of a royal palace. Working palaces need a certain air of perfection for which a high standard of maintenance is necessary.

It was clear to Hugh Roberts, at that time the Deputy Surveyor of the Queen's Works of Art, that the fire had created a supremely rare oppor-

At work consolidating what remained of the Grand Reception Room cove. The fire had left the gilded plaster in a condition which looked better than it was. The gilded skin was often the strongest part, holding together a core of broken and bobbled plaster.

Regilding the interiors, at a cost of about £40 a square foot, eventually absorbed just under half a million leaves of gold, a total of about 11,000 square feet of gilding.

tunity to return these rooms not, as the National Trust had decided at Uppark, to their condition on the day before the fire, but, more than that, to something approaching their condition when they were first made. Over the years there had been a diminution of the richness with which they had first been decorated, particularly in the curtains and the soft furnishings. What had been full and opulent had gradually become rather thin and formalistic. In the State Dining Room, the continuous oak-leaf plaster decoration running up the pilasters on all the walls had been removed. The 1820s gilding scheme, which to a modern eye was extraordinarily dense with almost every part of the ceilings in the Crimson Drawing Room and the walls in the Grand Reception Room being gilded, had been diluted. The trimmings, or *passementerie*, of the curtains had shrunk from a series of deeply enriched and highly theatrical schemes to something rather more mean, feeble and dead. The silks on the walls had dropped in quality and altered in pattern for the worse. The paint colours on the walls, fragments of which were analysed under a microscope, were found to have changed from the original 'warm stone' throughout to a series of less attractive and less enriching colours: 'a sludgy pink' in the Crimson Drawing Room and 'a dingy green' in the Grand Reception Room, according to Peter Riddington.

An exciting prospect beckoned, even as the rooms were roofless and desolate, of reversing some of these changes and restoring some of the vitality, beauty and frank enjoyment of the visual enrichment to which these great apartments had once been dedicated.

Nevertheless, a narrow path had to be trod. The rooms, while not looking dowdy, should not look new when they were finished. They had to accommodate the furniture that had always been in them and nearly all of which had been in store on the day of the fire. The new oil-gilding, for example – and the job would in the end take a little under 20,000 books of gold, 25 leaves a book, each leaf 3¼ inches square, making 11,000 square feet of gilding – would need toning down to match the furniture, if not quite as much as it had been toned before the fire. The 1820s gilding scheme would probably be thought too much today. The Royal Family does not like large acreages of gold and any-thing over-brash in that way was to be avoided.

The formula they ended up with, in Peter Riddington's words, was 'to bring the rooms as close to their original appearance as possible, while always being tempered by modern taste'. And, needless to say, modern budgets. Although just under £6.3 million was to be spent on these five large rooms, that would still not have covered the cost of doing everything in the way it had first been done here in the 1820s. Even so, these are stupendously expensive rooms. Architectural gilding, for example, costs about £400 a square metre. As Bill Bladon, the quantity surveyor, explains, 'You would normally expect the mechanical and electrical services to be about 30 per cent of the cost of a room. In these rooms it comes to about 2 per cent.'

With the sophisticated target developed by Hugh Roberts in mind – an enhancement of the idea of Equivalent Restoration – the architects could begin. The main structural works to re-create the spaces within which these apartments existed were already in hand. As part of Phase 3A, beginning in the spring of 1993, a new steel roof was installed over the Grand Reception Room and by mid-1994 presented the strange spectacle of an uncompromisingly modern steel structure bridging a space that was still lined with the torn and broken fragments of gilded and painted plaster finishes. Above the dining rooms, in the Prince of Wales and Brunswick Towers, new steel and concrete floors had been inserted as part of Phase 3B, replacing the nineteenth-century iron joists that had expanded, shrunk and buckled during the fire, pulling huge flakes of brickwork away from the inside of the towers as they did so. In the second half of 1994 that was all made good. Above the Crimson Drawing Room another new floor and steel roof went in and the upper part of Wyatville's great bay window, which had split away from the rest of the building during the fire, was taken down and replaced. Finally, above the Green Drawing Room, working with great delicacy over the almost intact plaster ceiling below them, the engineers installed huge braced steel trusses from which the floors and ceiling were eventually suspended.

These vital works were the necessary precursor of anything the architects could create in the rooms below them. But, again, before any serious work of reinstatement could occur, they were faced with the task, both literally and conceptually, of dismantling the rooms they had to re-create. First, there was the plasterwork, on walls and ceilings. It turned out to be evidence of a fascinatingly transitional moment in English plasterwork, in part looking back to the eighteenth century and in part looking forward, in their bulbous heaviness, particularly in the Green and Crimson Drawing Rooms, to the way in which the Victorians would leave no surface unelaborated, no form of decoration unexplored, no hollow undeepened and no form unextended. When these rooms were first made, the eighteenth-century clarity and chastity were in the process of being abandoned for something which, in Peter Riddington's words, was to become 'pretty wild'.

But this transitional quality goes beyond mere appearance. As Riddington discovered in his analysis of those many fragments that had been salvaged from the ceilings, the actual material of which the ceiling was made also bridged the two eras. The huge plaster enrichments that mark out the major patterns of the Grand Reception Room ceiling, and form an almost uninterrupted net over the ceilings of both the Crimson Drawing Room and the Green Drawing Room, were made from the light, quick-setting, gypsum-based plaster. 'Those fragments', Riddington says, 'were our vocabulary. Without them we would have been completely snookered. We needed those elements, either to put back, the best ones, or at least to copy, to use as patterns.'

'It is', he says, 'a curious moment in history where the eighteenth-century traditions of creative plasterwork were being superseded, because this casting plaster, plaster of Paris, had been invented and all of a sudden if you wanted enrichments, you got enrichments. Robert Adam had started using it but by the 1820s they were into an almost industrial process. Casting plaster goes hard in about twenty-four

A detail from one of the meticulous drawings of the Grand Reception Room ceiling made by John Wallace, of Donald Insall Associates. The elegance of Wallace's work belies the complexity of what went into it: sorting through salvaged fragments, examining pre-fire photographs and applying a geometrical rigour to the task. John Wallace died, of an unrelated illness, during the course of the restoration.

hours and so you can cast something in a mould very easily. Previously they had used lime plaster or lime putty which is much heavier and takes many weeks to go off. With lime plaster you have to model it in situ. It wouldn't have been practical to take a mould and replicate large areas of plaster.'

The plasterwork in these rooms, particularly the Grand Reception Room, was a mélange of the two techniques. Around the large number of cast elements, the ceiling was laced with a far more delicate, rococo-esque 'briar work', leaves and tendrils, which had been laid in situ by hand in a soft lime plaster: an eighteenth-century dance around the heavily cast *ronds-points* of quasi-Victorian enrichments.

The result in the Grand Reception Room is a French rococo ceiling, but a little strange: obviously deriving its inspiration from the countless free-form Louis XV plaster ceilings in France but in its scale and heaviness unlike any of them. It was the sort of French rococo ceiling which, as Peter Riddington says, 'if you had a Frenchman go into the room, he would say "My goodness, this is wonderful but we have nothing like it in France." The cast plasterwork is so big, definite and ponderous, that just to add the frills around the edge to free it up doesn't actually work. It looks splendid when it is all done but it doesn't look like a French rococo ceiling.'

The plasterers, from St Blaise, a company which was to end up doing almost two million pounds' worth of various building and conservation works at Windsor, spent a year on the Grand Reception Room ceiling alone. The system they adopted, after a period of two months familiarizing themselves with the complexities of an enormous job, was to lay out all the salvaged fragments – 'bread baskets full of frazzled plaster', according to Ian Constantinides of St Blaise – on the floor in the Mushroom Farm and decide on what needed remaking, remodelling or recasting. The new flat plaster was then laid in three successive coats. The plasterers described the mix as 'bog-standard 1 of lime putty to 3 of sharp washed sand, British Standard 890'. They then had to prepare full-scale working drawings of the decorative elements in the ceiling, using the beautifully precise and elegant drawings of John Wallace from Donald Insall's to do so. Those full-scale drawings were then transferred to the new flat plaster. The big cast enrichments were then applied in the correct position, a mixture of old and new, and the handwork, in a combination of lime, gypsum plaster and glue size, could begin.

When John Thorneycroft of English Heritage first saw the briar work going on, its rather stiff and angular quality made him wonder anxiously if this really was an accurate copy of the original. 'Its sense of freedom was being held back by the cast work around it,' he says. 'These massive and elaborate confections inevitably imposed constraints on the craftsmen which simply wouldn't have been there if it was all freehand work in the eighteenth-century manner.' But the photographs of the ceiling before the fire showed just the same lack of spontaneity in the original, and the St Blaise plasterers, with a great deal of self-discipline, were precisely following the historical model, warts and all.

The St Blaise people, some of whom had previously worked under Cliveden Conservation on the exceptionally fine plaster ceilings at Uppark and with St Blaise at Prior Park in Bath, were not daunted by the prospect. Ian Constantinides, the guiding light of the company, is particularly sanguine about the ability of modern people to do work of the highest craftsmanship. He sees it, in some ways, as an innate ability which the modern world taps all too rarely. 'Many people could do it. You could probably if you were willing to give up twelve weeks of your life. Try it and fail, try it and fail, try it and fail, try it and, hey, am I getting the knack of this? Try it again and yes I am but I have taken five times too long. Let's try and cut the time down. On the eighth week you can produce a result that is acceptable for quality and by the twelfth week you can begin to produce a result that is acceptable for time as well.'

His mixed team of artists, sculptors and trade-trained plasterers were faced here with a knotty problem: how to imagine their way into doing work that, at least when seen close up, was fairly crude and not of the quality of which many of these people were capable. Constantinides sees the necessary approach almost as a moral duty towards the damaged building. 'I have no time', he stresses, 'for those who say there is only one way to do it and that's the right way. That is not on. Or similarly if they start saying, "You know a sculptor should be allowed to sculpt, to produce his art. I can see that this form is awful." To that I say, you are not here to express your ego. You are here to reproduce work of the past. This whole thing is about us getting rid of our egos and working as an egoless team, to a common end, welded together. And the success will be measured in coming up to programme, budget and quality. And with work done in a way that you can't see that piece was done by so-and-so.'

This disciplined rejection of the Ruskinian view of the artist-

Taking the salvaged fragments of the ceilings as a model, the plasterers recast the necessary elements (above left), conserved and restored what remained of their setting on the ceilings (above centre) and then instated the replacement piece (above right). Many of the Windsor ceilings combine freehand work (right) with these cast enrichments. Combining the relative stiffness with the fluidity of the freehand work was one of the most difficult aspects of the job.

craftsman – Ruskin had famously thought that 'the question to ask, respecting all ornament, is this: was it done with enjoyment – was the carver happy while he was about it?' – acted, as far as Constantinides was concerned, as a stimulus. 'The first reaction to Windsor', he says, 'might be "Eugh, I don't like it." But that is because one is privileged enough to have worked on the incredible sophistication of Prior Park and at Uppark. The work is bolder. The stems between flowers and leaves on the Grand Reception Room ceiling work from a distance but are quite crude close up. And you ask yourself, "What are we doing re-interpreting an early nineteenth-century reinterpretation of some French form of decoration?" And then you start working on it. And when you start working on anything that anybody else has spent a lot of time doing, you cannot help but admire it, if for no better reason than you begin to see, feel and breathe the time and effort that went into the making of it. If there is a coarseness of form and crudeness of hand, it is completely overshadowed by the sheer spectacular effect when you are at a distance. And what does it matter, the coarseness of form, if you are not going to be within inches of it? The Sagrada Familia, Gaudi's great cathedral in Barcelona, looks distinctly tacky from close up but is spectacular from a distance and I'm sure, if you went to the top of the Chrysler Building, it wouldn't stand serious scrutiny. I admire and feel thoroughly proud of the work our team has done at Windsor.'

At first, for the plasterers, there was some difficulty over morale, but as they got into the swing of it and started admiring the workmanlike attitude of the people who had made the original ceilings, they adopted something of that frame of mind too. As one of them said, 'We know exactly what we're doing. Don't ponce about, don't prat about, just do it, get it right and bang, you've got the curves. As long as the tension in the curves is right, the rest largely dictates itself.'

And certainly, if you look at the ceiling of the Grand Reception Room now, unified with the massively enriched and gilded panels in the cove and on the walls, alongside the sparklingly cleaned and restored Gobelins tapestries which came from Paris in 1826, nothing could better embody the idea of regal grandeur. Even if you know that behind those huge gilt-plaster enrichments in the ceiling there are the hidden mouths of a modern smoke-detector system, analysing particles in the air as they are drawn past a laser beam; even if you know that beneath the floor, which is largely the old floor but turned upside down and sanded to remove water-staining, is a new sealed-pipe heating system; and even if you know that the 1820s bell-pulls beside the fireplaces are now attached to a panic-alarm system: even with all that, this room, crowned by its great new–old ceiling, remains the apotheosis of George IV's vision for Windsor. It bridges two quite distinct approaches to interior design: one based on a minimal, fluid delicacy; the other on an uncompromising hugeness of effect. But that is its triumph, not its failure. The idea of a vastly inflated rococo style, precisely because the essence of rococo is its lightness of touch, is almost a contradiction in terms. But this ceiling ignores that, takes the model, enormously extends it and produces something which is wonderful because it conveys simply the overwhelming sense of joie de vivre with which it was made.

In the two dining rooms the challenge of the ceilings was rather different. Nothing of any substance had survived the heat here. There were virtually no fragments to be sorted or moulds to be taken. Michael Shippobottom and Peter Cooke, the architects responsible for these rooms, had only photographs to go on. It was clear from the first, though, that these rooms, even if originally run in lime plaster in situ, would most economically be reinstated using a modern casting plaster. The basic strategy for the octagon vault, 8.5 metres across, was to repeat a single segment eight times around the room, cover the joins between them with plaster ribs and cover those awkward places where the ribs met with bosses which would conceal any slight mismatch in the interlocking shapes. The ceiling in the State Dining Room consisted of a grid of heavy plaster beams, with a secondary grid of ligher ribs set on the diagonal within it. At the meeting points of these ribs, large, ornately carved and gilded bosses, some of them crowning small pendant points, provided the glittering enrichment, a whole, raised landscape of exotic and complex forms which would give the room a glamour which its otherwise rather strict appearance might have lacked.

From examining old photographs, it became clear to the architects that the room, as originally conceived, was richer than the condition it had reached immediately before the fire. Before the 1920s the gilded oak-leaf enrichments to the pilasters, set at intervals along each wall, had tied the whole scheme firmly together, attaching, so to speak, the brilliant ceiling to the rest of the room. It was clear to the architects that those cast-plaster enrichments to the pilasters had to go back in.

For the creation of the detail in the running ornament, the decorated spandrel panels above the windows and in the bosses of the State and Octagon Dining Rooms, the architects turned to their photographs. Again, what looked at first like an immensely satisfactory record came, under minute examination, to seem much more difficult as a source for replication. Masses of curling leaves and acorns, with spiralled and twisting stalks, were there to be remade. But if the photographs were enlarged to the point where the details of bosses or other ornament could be seen, those very details started to break up in the grain. The task of making the various decorative elements had been split between the plasterers, Hayles and Howe of Bristol, who were also responsible for the large structural plaster panels of the dining-room ceilings, and the carvers at Herbert Read in Tiverton. Hayles and Howe made in plaster anything in which the pattern repeated: the cornice (as well as the corbels which were almost a part of it), the pendant bosses, of which there were five types, and the enrichments to the pilasters. Herbert Read's carved everything else: the rib bosses, the carved mouldings on the window mullions and the spandrel panels above the windows.

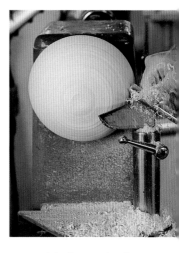

One of the bosses for the State Dining Room ceiling emerges from its pine blank into something approaching its finished form at Herbert Read's workshop in Tiverton. The carvers had to learn to push themselves towards crude vigour. The one thing these bosses had to avoid was politeness.

Philippa Kain, the clay modeller from Hayles and Howe, went down to visit Laurence Beckford, the master carver at Herbert Read's. Both, in their different media, were struggling with the realization of the same problem: how to translate these blurry images into three-dimensional objects that would, when they were installed in the rooms, painted and gilded, read as though they had been put there in the nineteenth century?

'We received a set of photos,' Philippa Kain explains, 'which thank God they had. If we hadn't had those, I don't know what we would have done. And the brief said something along the lines of "We do not require the modellers to reproduce the photograph slavishly but request that they remain within the spirit ..." and so on.'

That phrasing was an act of generosity on Peter Cooke's part, not wanting to box the craftsmen into a hole but, when it came to it, the requirements on the job were indeed reinstatement. When the clients looked at the new apartments, they wanted them to seem like the apartments that had been there before. In these circumstances, the photographs were in some ways a boon and in others a burden to the carvers and modellers. 'If you have a 3D object,' Philippa Kain explains, 'and it is photographed from two angles, the story that those two images tell can be completely different. I spent a year modelling those bosses and corbels and I can tell you, a lot of it was spent in hard agonizing over these pictures.' The large black folder in which the architect had sent her the photographs is now a dusty, battered and clay-daubed object, a case of maps at the end of a long campaign.

Laurence Beckford – and Windsor has some special significance for

him; he is a member of the Wyatt dynasty and his full name is Laurence John Wyatt Beckford – was drawing his way out of the problem, going again and again to the photographs, wrestling with their confusing images – these were pictures, remember, of gilded objects, in which the highly reflective surfaces play havoc with one's ability to interpret three-dimensional form – and each time redrawing what he thought he saw there. 'After a visit to Laurence,' Philippa says, 'I was inspired to go back to basics to try the drawing again but it didn't work for me so I just got a lump of clay and started bashing it. It wasn't easy. One started to get blinded and you knew all the time that the architects would be saying, "We want that; we don't want an interpretation of that." The photo was a mass of information, but it was also a test, a measure of how well you'd done. In the end, they weren't pedantic about it. I know there were situations where mine didn't look like a photocopy of that, but Peter was OK about it.'

For Beckford and his team, who between them carved forty-eight bosses in the State Dining Room and another forty-nine for the Octagon, most of them ten inches across and eight inches deep, but some bigger, this huge task carried a mixed message. Sometimes it seemed like 'yet another lump of bloody wood'. At others, there was an absorbing and stimulating challenge here. 'You just drew what you could see,' he says. 'Some pictures were at an angle which made it easier, and you had to get the callipers on the drawing to make it all equal. What you can't see you have to create.' And what would guide him in that creation? 'I had to feel my way towards what I thought it was meant to be,' he said. In other words, it was an act of the imagination.

He made a couple of trials – each piece took sixty-four hours from pine blank to finished boss – which were gilded and put up in position on the State Dining Room ceiling, six metres above the floor. The mistake he'd made was not being crude enough. 'I'd liked what I'd seen in the pictures, crisp, a lot of depth and vigour, boldness in the design and those spirals or the way some of them grow out and down, with very deep undercuts. But when the trial was up there it looked too polite. I realized then what I had to say to myself: don't hold back, get it deep, you must be aggressive, you mustn't be timid with these things. It's got to be vigorous.'

These wonderful bosses and the other plaster-cast enrichments of the two dining rooms are a triumph. Now gilded, but only on the outside, leaving in recessive shadow those parts where Beckford and Kain cut deep into their Quebec pine or modelling clay, each boss now has its own intriguing inner and outer landscape. If some, as Peter Cooke says, 'look like ladies' Ascot hats', the overall effect of the ceilings, with their gilded highlights and shadow-darkened hollows, is, as was surely intended, a glorious sculpture park hanging twenty feet above your head.

In the Crimson Drawing Room next door, where at least 85 per cent of the wall linings had been destroyed by the fire, a huge effort was needed to replace the vast lengths of water-gilded composition frame that had surrounded the mirrors and silk panels on the walls. George Jackson and Sons in south London have made 'compo' continuously since the time of Robert Adam and in their workshop still have a large number of moulds which they have kept since the eighteenth century. Peter Riddington asked them to take a piece of one of the Crimson Drawing Room frames and try to replicate it. 'One of the problems at Windsor', as Riddington says, 'is that the composition work, so that the form stands out from the background, is so heavily undercut. It has to be carved by hand into the compo itself after the thing has been pressed out of the mould. Then the piece is dressed on to a timber backing, in this case oak, some of whose profiles are like broom handles. It was a hell of a process.'

The trial piece, fully finished and including a very complex corner but still only a couple of feet long, was not quite as good as the original, nor as crisp and, at £8700, fabulously expensive. This was one of the rare cases where the Restoration project tried for authenticity, in an area where authenticity is extraordinarily difficult to achieve, but pulled back, largely on grounds of cost and the time it would take. Nevertheless, if time and budget had allowed, Riddington would with-

One of the composition corners to the wall frames in the Green Drawing Room, repaired by George Jackson and Sons and watergilded by W. Thomas's. An epitome of the George IV effect and extraordinarily expensive. To re-create what you see in this photograph – and three of these corners, badly damaged in the fire, were remade – cost a little over £4000. For Peter Riddington, the architect, this work is 'one of the real triumphs of the project'.

out question have had faith that Jackson's could have done what he was asking of them. They have ended up doing all the repairs to the composition work in the Green Drawing Room, where the frames were far less badly damaged, all the paterae – small flat pieces of ornament, named after the Latin for 'saucer' – for the Grand Reception Room walls and the immensely elaborate corners for the Crimson Drawing Room frames. These corners are a work of art in themselves according to Riddington, with eleven separate pieces going into each of them. Overall, the composition work is, Riddington says, 'one of the real triumphs of the project and the quality of the work is indistinguishable from the best of its type made in its heyday'.

All other damaged composition work has been replaced in the quicker and cheaper if much less authentic fibrous plaster and then water-gilded at W. Thomas's in west London, where Ray Dudman is in control of the workshop. 'We have gilded 85 metres of these frames for the Crimson Drawing Room and another 130 metres repairing what is mostly water damage to the ones from the Green Drawing Room,' he says. 'It has driven everyone up the wall. There has just been so much of it.' The gilding that Thomas's has done has been a £370,000 job, but it is as richly and subtly beautiful an effect as could be achieved by anyone in the world. 'It will last', Ray Dudman says, 'two hundred years.'

One final and outstanding element in the drawing rooms lifts their quality to the highest level. Both sides of all doors in the White, Green and Crimson Drawing Rooms were decorated in the 1820s scheme with giltwood carvings, three per door: a large one in the upper panel, a small decorative band in the centre and a third, halfway between the other two in size, on the lower panel. In the fire-damaged area, that is in the Green and Crimson Drawing Rooms, there were originally sixty-two of these uniquely fine pieces. They were among the treasures transferred here from Carlton House in 1826 and, because they take as their inspiration the Roman practice of hanging arms and the spoils of war from temporary monuments or 'trophies', they are now known as the Carlton House Trophies and are considered to be the finest wood-carvings of their kind in England. Some, principally those in the White Drawing Room, are almost certainly French; others, mostly those in the other two Drawing Rooms, were carved by Edward Wyatt for the Prince Regent's great reception rooms at Carlton House.

They have always been among the things most appreciated by the Royal family. Immediately after the fire, the first question asked by the Queen Mother was 'What happened to the trophies?' and, when it came to the question of their restoration, the Prince of Wales made an impassioned plea to Michael Peat, the Director of Property Services, that only the very best craftsmen should be allowed on the job and hoped that the lowest tender would not necessarily have to be accepted. He asked what the situation was. It was, in fact, a hybrid. Dick Reid, one of the nation's leading carvers, was retained, without having to compete for the role, to supervise the carving of the Carlton House Trophies project. Individual carvers, overseen by him in detail, would compete with each other as usual.

The trophies had been fixed to the doors with small steel pins and, even though they are immensely valuable – to carve and gild a single large replacement trophy today is a year's work at a cost of about £50,000 – they could not be saved during the fire. Those at the north end of the Crimson Drawing Room had been incinerated. Some, at the south end of the Green Drawing Room, were damaged by water from the firemen's hoses but by nothing else. Other damage filled the whole spectrum in between. Some had large chunks burnt away. Others were heavily charred but with the carving still visible. In the luckiest cases, the water-gilding was still there, if battered and flaking, the gesso showing through. In the worst, no more than a single spearpoint or half an acanthus frond remained. On the morning after, Hugh Roberts went through the drawing rooms, picking a few of the savaged fragments from the ash. Others emerged later, from beneath the debris of ceilings, rooms and roofs that had fallen from above.

The trophies are miraculous objects, carved from limewood boards usually no more than ¾ of an inch thick but with a vitality, precision and three-dimensional quality that totally belies their actual depth. A whole series of interlocking motifs appear in trophy after trophy, as though they were part of some arcane iconographic programme: spears, shields, draped flags and fasces; elephants, camels, toothed snakes, monkeys and other exotic beasts; shipping and the instruments of navigation; fragments of Greek, Roman and Egyptian architecture; the fruits and implements of farm and garden, including sunhats, wheelbarrows, rakes, shears, watering cans, wheatsheaves, shotguns, cartridges and dead game. All this complexity might, just possibly, have a masonic context. By 1800 almost all the male members of the Royal Family were masons and the Prince of Wales was Grand Master from 1790 to 1813, precisely the period over which these trophies were bought or commissioned. The research into whatever symbolic system underlies these extraordinary objects has not yet been done. They might

just as well be a celebration, with an undeniably imperialist, tri-
umphalist air about them, of virtuoso carving for its own sake. They
have, according to Paul Ferguson, one of the carvers who has replaced
the damaged parts, 'an astonishing quality of design. All of them have
a basic structure and a basic underlying rhythm – a formalized core
which loosens towards the edge, as though that neo-classical strictness
evolves imperceptibly into something with a beautifully relaxed and
natural quality. The stylized leaves you find in the centre become
hawthorns and honeysuckle as you move to the outer edges.'

The carvers, under the supervision of the master carver Dick Reid,
have naturally pored over every surface of the trophies they have had to
restore. For those which had to be replaced, they have had excellent
close-up photographs which the Royal Collection, by pure chance, had
taken a year or so before the fire for an exhibition on Carlton House.
That intimacy of examination is revelatory. As Ferguson says, 'This is
sculpture within a membrane.' To work on them he sees as the highpoint of his career. 'Whoever drew these up understood what he was
doing. He knew enough to be able to relax in his knowledge. It is so
controlled, so held back but at the same time so easy in itself. That's
what makes these great things. When, in the future, you look at them on
a door, you can never see them as we saw them, here on our bench, in
front of us, in our hands. It's not something you can turn on and off.
You have to think yourself into it. You are involved in the preparation,
cutting a flat – the shape in outline with no moulding yet carved into it
– jointing the new pieces into the old, you get absorbed in it, totally
engaged in the thing in front of you. Looking at a picture, you don't see
half of it.'

Dick Reid did a trial piece to estimate costs. His two square inches
came to £3370. Multiplying up for the job – it took Bill Bladon, the
quantity surveyor, two full days to work it out – the total for all the trophies came out at £511,576. Each of the carvers then tendered against
the others for the work, and eventually the shallow boxes arrived at
their workshops with the remains of the trophies inside. The boxes were
like neat miniature coffins. A full-scale photograph of the piece as it was
before the fire was stuck to the lid and in the box itself was an annotated version of the picture, coloured red where the trophy survived intact;
purple where it survived but was charred; orange where a piece was
missing, either burnt or lost before the fire, perhaps when the trophies
were transferred from France to England or from Carlton House to
Windsor; green where a piece had fallen off in the past and been

replaced wrongly, a hawthorn leaf on an oak bough, a swan's neck not curving gracefully towards the head but making an awkward angle.

Hardly ever can a set of wood-carvings have had so much attention given to them. Certainly in the past, there was evidence of their being taken for granted: crude Victorian repairs with clumsy oil-gilding laid over the original water-gilt surface, even gold paint 'toshed' into the gilding, whole pieces knocked off and, presumably, thrown away.

When the first of the trophies – not all would be complete by the time the building was reopened in November 1997 – were returned to the Green Drawing Room in June that year, repositioned in the door panels precisely where the photographs had shown they had been before, the marks of charring were still on the backs of some of the old ones. White strips of new limewood, a millimetre across, filled the narrow trenches cut by the carvers in the back of the trophies. After the firemen had soaked them, the wood had warped and bowed. The tiny grooves and fillets were there to flatten them out again. The trophies were fixed again to the doors with tiny stainless steel needles fired into them with a compression gun, the heads of the needles then concealed with an almost invisible plug of gold paste.

'Gold is such a chameleon,' Drummond Cuthbert, one of the gilders, says. 'It will always absorb colour from its surroundings.' And when the trophies were up on the doors, the subtle chromatic landscapes of the water-gilding did indeed take up the colour of the new green silk damask on the walls, particularly in the polished highlights on the tips of the spears and the fruits of the snaking leaves. It was impossible to tell new from old or to realize they had ever been away.

In the first days of 1997 the five great State Apartments were moving seamlessly towards completion. Phil Rowley, the coolly sardonic manager for the main contractors, Higgs and Hill, had chivvied and needled the subcontractors, shuffling their requests, disbelieving their excuses and, just occasionally, exploding in anger at their incompetence or slowness. 'Phil knows how to do this,' one of them says. 'He understands what's required. He's calm, he doesn't panic. There's an air of confidence there and, what's probably more important than anything else, an undying passion for the Royal Family. One day he came up to me and said, "What you've got to get in your head is that you're working in Her Majesty's home and I hope you're going to act accordingly."'

In the Green Drawing Room, which had been the least damaged and so was ahead of the rest, the floor had been restored and the ceiling had been painted its original warm stone-colour – a mixture of white with

The marked-up reference photograph for one of the trophies in the Green Drawing Room (left) that was given to the carvers along with the fire-damaged remains of the trophy itself. Those parts in orange had been lost during the fire; those parts circled in red survived only in fragments. (Right) The repaired trophy, regilded and reinstated on its door in the Green Drawing Room.

One of the restored and regilded plaster panels above the doors in the Crimson Drawing Room. The pinkness in the photograph is the correct colour. Both the gilding and the lead paint around it take up the redness of the crimson silk panels which give the room its name.

raw sienna, raw umber, signwriter's red and Oxford ochre – and gilded. The walls were receiving their top coat of lead paint, the decorators carefully stippling away the marks left by their brushes. Next door, in the Crimson Drawing Room, the ceiling was being painted and gilded, parchment size tinted with black and burnt-umber pigments being laid on top of the gold to cool it down. The walls would not be finished until April. The previous autumn, the new and spectacular replica of the mid-nineteenth-century floor had been laid by David Gunton, using laser-cut hardwoods. Another replaced floor was going back into the Grand Reception Room where the ceiling was being painted. Here too there was a return to the original 'warm stone' colour. This historically correct attitude to the painting scheme had, when first proposed, slightly troubled the Duke of Edinburgh. On 30 January 1995 he had written: 'I am a bit concerned about the slavish reproduction of the original Morel and Seddon colour schemes. I accept that the background colour for the Green and Crimson Rooms should be similar, but there is no need for the "warm stone-colour" to be identical in both rooms. I do hope it does not become that much-favoured "Ministry of Works off-white", which is found on all back corridors and stairs of public buildings.'

By seeing samples and through discussion, he was persuaded otherwise. In the Grand Reception Room in particular, Peter Riddington and Hugh Roberts evolved a painting scheme in which there are five distinct tones of the same warm stone-colour: on the ceiling bed, the cove, the walls themselves, the dado and the skirting. The five colours do not read as such but give a subliminal contour to the room, underlying the mass of gilding. Without that subtlety, the Grand Reception Room, which is in some ways a huge tunnel lit by a vast north-light window at one end, might be in danger of having its gaiety and vitality turning a little cold.

'I notice', the Duke of Edinburgh had written to Michael Peat early in the process, 'that the Royal Collection is to be the arbiter for the redecoration of the rooms. Whoever (person rather than a committee) is to be responsible must keep in very close touch with The Queen and it must be quite clear that the final decision rests with her.' Hugh Roberts, Deputy Surveyor of the Queen's Works of Art at the time of the fire, has been that figure, keeping The Queen informed, and in many ways has been the governing influence on the way the State Apartments have been restored. According to the architect Peter Riddington, 'Hugh is extremely knowledgeable, approachable, clear-thinking and decisive, he knows the rooms very well and he knows what exactly they should look like. He always made it clear that this was not an archaeological exercise and that the rooms should read as a suite.'

Roberts himself says, typically, 'The only contribution that I'm at all proud of in those rooms is saying at a very early stage, in mid-1993, to Michael Peat that we must concentrate very hard on the soft-furnishing side. I knew he would think this was getting miles ahead. We had this vast, burnt-out, empty shell and all the rest of it. But I said to him, "We must make sure the curtains and the wall coverings are *really* good and actually better than they were before the fire." Michael understood exactly. And that's where Pam Lewis came in.'

Pamela Lewis is one of the country's leading designers and conservators. Her specialized area is historically correct curtains, upholstery and the exotic menagerie of braids, gimps – a gimp is essentially a cord or wire wrapped in thread – hangers and tassels, collectively called *passementerie*, with which both curtains and furniture are enriched and decorated. Having worked in the theatre, in the government department that later became English Heritage, in several royal palaces and, with Hugh Roberts, in Frogmore House in Windsor Home Park, where she had designed some spectacular early-nineteenth-century schemes, she could not have been more suited to the task that he was to set her.

A process of what Hugh Roberts calls 'Chinese whispers' had occurred with the fabrics and designs both of the wall-silks and of the curtains in the great Georgian apartments. Over the decades since they were first installed, with each new replacement, the exuberance had

Pam Lewis's drawing for the valance in the enormous north window of the Grand Reception Room. Her experience as a theatre designer, combined with an unrivalled knowledge of historical precedent, made her uniquely qualified for this work.

weakened and the glamour had diminished. Hugh Roberts realized that rooms so dependent on brilliance and fullness of effect would never be a success unless this aspect of them went back at least to the spirit of the original. He understood that what looked like the final flourish of these theatrical sets was in fact somewhere near their core.

Pam Lewis arrived in October 1993. She went to the fire-damaged site. 'First of all you think, "Gulp, how am I going to do this?" It was devastating, still very much no floors, you had to look where you were going. The thing that is quite daunting is that everything is very, very big.' She and Roberts were clear that there was no point in repeating what had been there before the fire. 'The scale had shrunk away,' Pam

Detailed working drawing for the passementerie *– gimps, rosettes, hangers and bullion fringe – of the Grand Reception Room valance.*

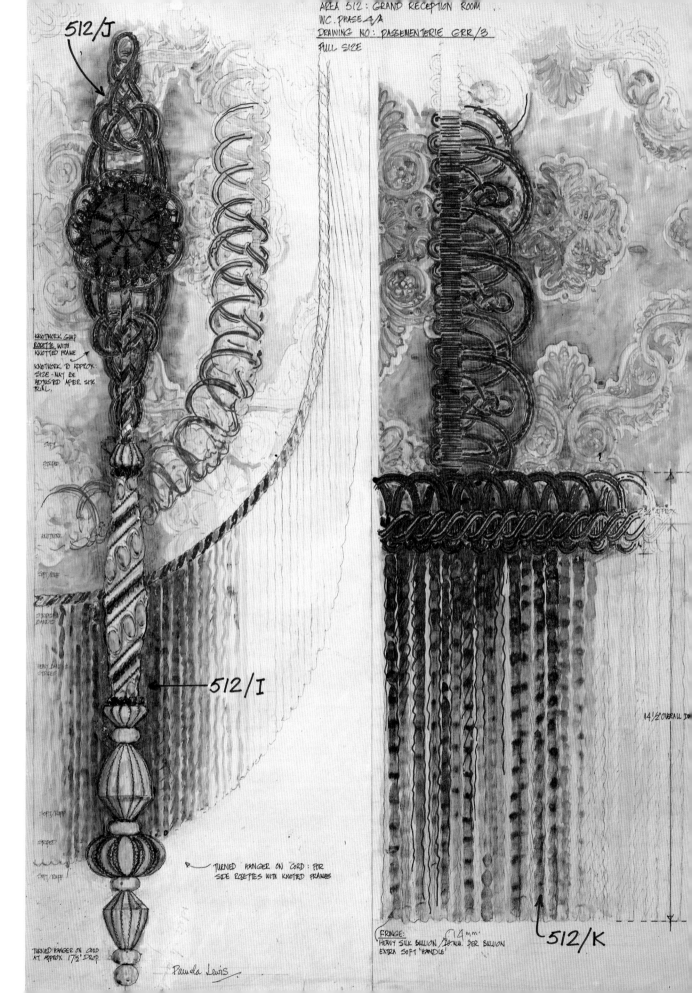

512/J

KNOTWORK GIMP
ROSETTE WITH
KNOTTED FRAME

KNOTWORK TO APPROX:
SIZE - MAY BE
ADJUSTED AFTER SITE
TRIAL.

SOFT
STRIPED

KNOTWORK

SOFT /RUFF

STRIPED/
RUFFLED

HEAVY BAND 2
STRIPES

512/I

SOFT/RUFF

STRIPED

SOFT/RUFF

TURNED HANGER ON CORD: FOR
SIDE ROSETTES WITH KNOTTED FRAMES

TURNED HANGER ON CORD
AT APPROX 17½" DROP

Pamela Lewis.

2¾" APPROX.

14½" OVERALL D

512/K

FRINGE: 14mm
HEAVY SILK BULLION, 140mm PER BULLION
EXTRA SOFT 'HANDLE'

Lewis says. 'Baby little tassels, everything scrimped.' There was an opportunity to regain the scale of the original, 'a new confidence', as she says, 'an unashamed theatricality, in tune with the verve of the originals'.

They turned to the archive of materials and *passementerie* samples at Windsor; to the coloured drawings made by Morel and Seddon and presented to the King in the 1820s; to the paintings by Joseph Nash from the 1840s; to a set of photographs taken of the rooms in 1867. Particularly in the shadowy upper parts of those photographs you could see, in the Green Drawing Room for example, a shaped valance in silk damask, with masses of gold thread over underpadding, garlands with oak leaves, one writhing mass of frogged and over-embroidered sunbursts and roundels, like the coat-front of an officer in the Légion d'Honneur, and below it all a bullion fringe punctuated with giant tassels and overlaid with heavily gimped, twisted and silk-wrapped hangers.

There was, though, the question of cost. Although a tiny element of over-embroidery was eventually incorporated in the new Green Drawing Room tabard valance – some curved brackets embroidered by the Royal School of Needlework – the sheer volume of the nineteenth-century work would be unthinkable today, simply on the grounds of the money and the time it would take. There were also other elements in the original scheme which, as Hugh Roberts and Pam Lewis knew from the start, could not possibly be accommodated in a modern budget. In the 1820s, for example, the walls of the Crimson Drawing Room had been lined in about 400 metres of figured, that is to say patterned, silk velvet. Today one metre of that material would cost about £1500. To have relined the Crimson Drawing Room in figured velvet would have added £600,000 to the restoration budget. 'You couldn't have gone back to that,' Hugh Roberts says. 'It would have been ludicrous, out-of-all-recognition expensive.'

Both in labour and materials, then, there was some holding back. Nevertheless, this is not a cheap route to go. The silk damask for the Green and Crimson Drawing Rooms, reproducing what had been there in the 1867 photographs, for example, cost over £78,000 in itself. Making some of it up into curtains for the Crimson Drawing Room, whose bay window is needless to say enormous, cost £33,000, and the *passementerie* to go on them another £36,000. While it would have been quite possible to spend ten times that amount, for an effect which would perhaps in the end have been too much for modern taste, there is no doubt that, when these rooms are seen – and they are now for the first time going to be open to the public who come to Windsor – the extraordinary fullness and beauty of the new silk damasks on the wall, the new curtains and their *passementerie*, immeasurably more luxuriant than anything that has been there for the last hundred years, and designed to last at least for the next hundred, will be the pre-eminent memory that people will carry away with them.

That effect will largely be due to the efforts, anxiety and perfectionist attention to detail, over four years, of Pamela Lewis. 'You have to be obsessive to do this kind of work,' she says. 'I can't remember the number of times I have woken up in the middle of the night and thought, "Have I left a wall panel out? Are those hangers the right length? Are they hanging in the right place? Is it full enough?"'

A thousand metres of these cloths, for which the order was placed in January 1995, were hand-woven by Humphries Weaving in Essex, all on Jacquard looms that came originally from Spitalfields. Test pieces were woven, dyed and sent for approval. Choices were made and the bulk of the order then completed. The fabric arrived, dyed in batches, and the very best of it was chosen for the flat valances and drapery, which would draw most attention, and the walls opposite the windows, where, particularly in these very bright rooms, the most intense and searching light will fall. Those lengths destined for the curtains themselves, whose folds can hide more colour variations than the silk laid flat on the walls, were cut to size, avoiding the natural flaws in the cloth – 'the first cut makes you twitchy', according to Jim Hill, the project manager at the curtain makers Chapman's – lined in soft-brushed cotton cloth for pliancy and then backlined for heaviness in the hang: 'They wanted 100 per cent fullness here,' Hill says. The means of holding up these enormously heavy curtains, some of them five metres in length, is a very solid heading tape, with big, plastic, clip-in hooks. 'There's more of a call for that sort of hook on a stage curtain,' Jim Hill says. 'It's a non-domestic type hook.' Once made, the curtains are allowed to hang in the works, shrouded from dust, to allow the fabric to settle.

The world of *passementerie* is an obscure and private universe of strange forms and strict relationships between them. In the Crimson Drawing Room, the curtain makers had trouble with the overswags and bells of the valance, because the sheer weight of *passementerie*, including a heavy Hungarian gimp, drop-hangers, whose oval drops were overlaid with cottage gimp, and a bullion fringe, were all disrupting the natural hanging form of the cloth, even though there was a shorter bullion fringe on the over-drapery. Five attempts were made to get it right before the designer was happy. For the gimp-work, she was usually able to refer to historic pieces and the Windsor archive provided the models for the large gimps edging the curtains. Even so, every piece of *passementerie* was painted out on a full-size cartoon and trials made. With many examples of the complex early-Victorian work, two or three trial pieces had to be made before a satisfactory result was achieved and for those the expertise of Brian Turner of G. J. Turner Ltd was always, as Pam Lewis says, 'invaluable'. For the Green Drawing Room, however, she and Hugh Roberts both travelled to Chatsworth to check on the form of a particular hanger and some other details. Those in the Grand Reception Room, taken from a Frogmore precedent, with spiral twisting facets in the shaft, were very difficult for a turner to make. A retired ICI chemist in Preston managed to make them in the end. 'There's been a lot of trial and tribulation here,' Pam Lewis says. 'Tears have been involved.'

Jane Brighty, one of the *passementerie* makers, has a factory in Portugal. The Windsor connection, she says, is important for the people working there because it was the Treaty of Windsor in 1386 between the English and Portuguese crowns which established both countries' oldest surviving alliance and 'that is something which every Portuguese schoolboy knows. If there was one job which they would like to have done, this would be it.' But what about the actual designs Pam Lewis was asking them to execute? 'What we are involved with here', Jane Brighty says, 'is a visual crescendo, an enormous explosion of grandeur. Sometimes I think of those rooms as architecture on steroids and that is what this mass of incredible *passementerie* that Pam has designed is intended to match and to bring out. This is the sort of job that everyone dreams of doing.'

Shell gimps, arched gimps, rosettes – which are called macaroons by the Portuguese – cabled gimps, cottage gimps, stiff-whipped gimps, nine-piece hangers, with some pieces smooth-wrapped, some in corded silk, some with twisted, some with plain, bands, silk-bullion overskirts to the tassels, with inner skirts of wool, the tassels suspended from what is called a four-legged, double soufflé – that is a sort of rope: George IV would undoubtedly have loved it all.

The finished effect in the Green Drawing Room, with tabard valance, gimps, cords, embroidered brackets, bullion fringe, hangers and tassels all re-establishing the verve and spirit of the Georgian original.

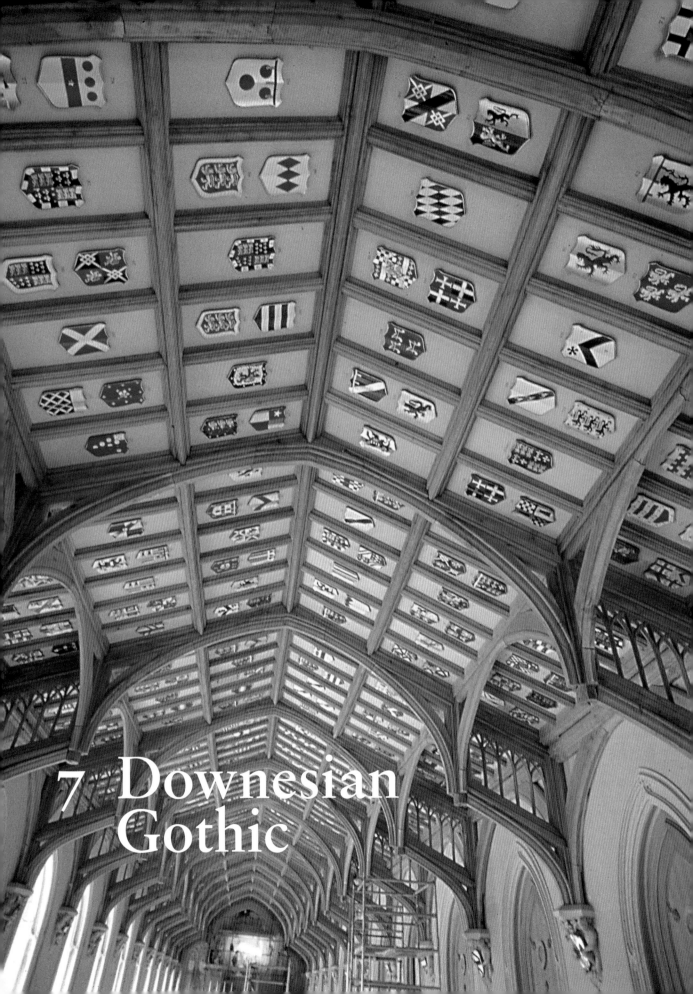

7 Downesian Gothic

Until the middle of March 1995 the vast new oak ceiling that now graces St George's Hall, 180 feet long, thirty feet wide and its ridge almost forty feet above the floor, with its 1800 feet of rafters, its 1400 feet of purlins, its raking struts, arch struts, pendant posts and top-chords, was still growing as 350 oak trees in a wood near the village of Sarnesfield in Herefordshire.

The wood is marked on the map as Whiterails Wood but is known simply to the people who work there as 'the Big Wood', part of the Sarnesfield Estate. It is that rare and beautiful thing, a piece of woodland maintained over generations in the best possible traditions of woodmanship, growing oaks the like of which could hardly be found anywhere else in the country. This clay loam over an Old Red Sandstone foundation is the best oak-growing land in England: fertile, relatively warm, plenty of rainfall, poorly drained and so never dry – nothing slows the growth of a tree like drought – and as a result 'sticky all year round', as Steve Potter, the woodland manager, describes it. This is the place for fast-grown hardwoods. Trees that elsewhere might take 100 years to achieve a metre diameter at chest height can reach that in 75 years at Sarnesfield. And quick-grown timber has a clarity of grain that slower-growing trees can never match.

The oaks in the Big Wood do not conform to any usual image you might have of great trees. They are not the stubby, gnarled and knobbly things you see on pub signs or in the illustrations of Arthur Rackham. The Sarnesfield oaks, through intensive management by people who have known over many years what they were about, are growing beams, straight for sixty feet or more from the ground up. If you find yourself in this wet wood, at least in those parts from which the 350 Windsor oaks have been extracted – and it is a measure of the excellence of the place that even with so many trees gone it does not feel in any way denuded – the oaks still make an almost continuous canopy high above you, sustained by colonnades of slender grey trunks: a shadowy, temperate rainforest, perhaps the most beautiful crop England can grow. Stand here and it is not difficult to understand why, until the Renaissance, most English buildings were made of wood. The growing trees look like architecture waiting to happen.

It was an eighteenth-century idea, wrong but immensely powerful, that Gothic architecture was somehow a reflection of those growing trees, an emanation of the soil. 'The Goths', as one speculator wrote, 'having been accustomed to worship the Deity in groves, when their religion required covered edifices, they ingeniously projected to make them resemble groves as nearly as the distance of architecture would permit; at once indulging their old prejudices, and providing for their present conveniences, by a cool receptacle in a sultry climate.' The pointed arch, according to this theory, was the distilled form of nodding boughs.

Medieval builders and architects would not have recognized the theory. In the Platonic civilization of the Middle Ages, where, it has been said, 'architecture was the gateway to ineffable truths', the heart of any beauty in buildings was always thought to lie in their geometry and the harmonious concordance of parts which geometry, and geometry alone, could bring about.

Gothic architecture, as the surviving examples from the Middle Ages so clearly show, was above all, a *linear* art. The clustered shafts, the ribbed vaults, the fine but richly shadowed mouldings that delineated any windows or archways, and the whole hierarchy of forms on which the great Gothic buildings depend, all served one purpose: to impose the beauty of geometry, and the cosmic order of which that was an image, on the mind's eye.

The outstanding achievement of the new work at Windsor by the architect Giles Downes has been to meld these two readings of Gothic into a single vision. He has created an architectural language that both mirrors the natural world and abstracts it, aspiring towards a condition of geometrical purity. What turned out in the end to be a late twentieth-century Downesian Gothic was not done simply for propriety's sake. As Maria Tindall, who works at the Sidell Gibson Partnership with Downes, explains: 'We looked at Windsor as a whole, as a castle, its medieval origins and its successive overlays of Gothic architecture, and it seemed clear that over the ages everyone has had their own idea of

The Gothic inheritance: Wyatville's 1820s hypermedievalization of the medieval fabric – this is his statue of Edward III above the State Entrance – was one pointer for the 1990s architects. They realized that Gothic was an architectural system that could be adapted to any age.

what Gothic means, what it is about. We were thinking about Gothic because Gothic fits well here, but moving it forward, producing our own interpretation rather than a pastiche. Gothic is actually a very, very effective structural system. It was the idea of using that which was exciting: a logical, careful, clever way to build the thing. We could see a way of making it work like that. It wasn't just thinking, "Gosh, it's Windsor, so it had better be Gothic."'

The heart of the commission, as they saw it, was St George's Hall. Wyatville's room – Sir William Hope, the great historian of the Castle, had called it 'this preposterous apartment' – had the proportions of a railway carriage. Downes looked at it and saw, essentially, a failure. 'It was trying to be, or is intended to be, a Gothic national space, an idealized version of a king's banqueting hall. So, if we did something very alien with the ceiling, which was a major element of it, it would no longer be any sort of idealized medieval king's banqueting hall. It would be something else and we didn't think that was right.'

Steven Brindle of English Heritage guided them to the great surviving royal halls: Eltham, Westminster, Hampton Court. They also visited a large number of medieval churches.

Received opinion had it that the disastrous quality of Wyatville's St George's Hall was its length. That was, in fact, Wyatville's own verdict on the room and he only created it because George IV, perhaps under the influence of Sir Walter Scott, asked for it. The two baroque apartments it replaced should have remained separate. It was generally agreed that no room that long could be visually satisfying. But Downes soon realized that it was not the length that was the problem. There were any number of churches equally long whose interiors were beautiful and sculptural spaces. It wasn't the length, it was the proportions. 'St George's Hall', Downes says, 'wasn't tall enough. At 11.5 metres high and 9.5 metres wide, it is only just over its width in height. That's why you see a railway carriage.'

Wyatville had been forced to make his oak-grained plaster ceiling within the shallow-pitched roof put up there by Hugh May at the end of the seventeenth century and reinforced at some expense by Smirke in 1819. Downes was faced with the same sort of problem: he had to fit his ceiling in under the new, steel-beamed roof installed here over the autumn and winter of 1993–4. The straightforward option of improving the proportions of the room by raising the roof, to the sort of 45–55° pitch a medieval roof might normally have had, was not there for Downes, as it hadn't been for Wyatville. As it turned out, the installation of a heavy oak ceiling beneath that roof, at times with no more than four inches' clearance, was to be one of the most difficult parts of the whole job.

The proportions of a room whose walls, floor, roof and windows are fixed can only be changed by some kind of illusionism. Downes adopted two techniques. He decided to make each truss of the new ceiling a stepped arch: from the top of the walls on each side a broad sloping panel, filled with Gothic tracery, would move in towards the centre of the room, culminating in a pendant post. Only from those pendant posts would the main arch of the truss spring towards the ridge line. In this way, he would, as he puts it, 'bring in the effective visual line of the wall and so the effective visual height of the room would also rise.' By this sleight of hand, St George's Hall would look narrower and taller; its proportions would have been squeezed into something more like those of a great Gothic hall. To help the effect, the kneeling-knight corbels from which those trusses spring would be brought lower down the walls and the ridge would also be raised, about four feet higher than Wyatville's ceiling, squeezing it in under the new roof. With a lower starting-point, a steeper pitch and the much stronger rhythm which these fourteen trusses would give to the room, the new ceiling would add a richness to the hall on which the pre-fire plaster ceiling had been little more than a structurally featureless lid.

But what material to make it in? There were essentially two choices. Green oak is newly felled and shaped timber, still very wet, with a 50 per cent moisture content. It is the authentic material of medieval roofs and would be cheaper, it was thought, by about £50,000 on a ceiling that might cost over £1 million. But its behaviour as it dries is not entirely predictable. Splits, or shakes, develop in drying wood, which also contracts. Alternatively, there was the option of glue-laminated oak. This material was heavily favoured by the engineer Richard Swift at Gifford's, naturally drawn to something whose performance was highly predictable. 'Glu-lam', as they call it, is a modern technique, in which sections of very dry wood, which will not move over time, are glued together with very reliable modern glues, whose precise behaviour is also scientifically known. Glu-lam had been used in replacing the roof of York Minster after the fire there in 1984.

Swift is now quite explicit about it: he didn't want the liability for any failure of the roof to land at his door. He had worked with green oak previously, at New College in Oxford and elsewhere, but the scale of St George's Hall was quite different. 'Whenever you use green oak,' Swift

At George IV's coronation banquet the King's Champion, in full armour, processes into Westminster Hall through a temporary Gothic screen that was put up for the occasion. This suit of armour now decorates the east end of the restored St George's Hall at Windsor. Lithograph by M. Ganci after G. Wennhap.

says, 'there is the problem of timber shrinkage and in that setting, which is used for major events, you can just imagine those joints shrinking down and large shakes opening and defects appearing in the timber. I wrote and said, "The only way to ensure that those defects do not occur is to use glue-laminated timber." He was horrified at the prospect of a rafter pulling out of its purlin or a plaster panel bearing the shields of the Knights of the Garter coming adrift during a State Banquet. 'Knowing Michael Peat's reputation, and our being held accountable for the performance of the structure as a whole, I felt we had to safeguard our own position.' Swift made sure that a letter was on file detailing precisely the risks of going down the green-oak route.

Despite his warnings, green oak was the option taken. The Design

Ridge purlin

Third purlins:
position varies

TOP CHORD

Pendant
post purlin

MAIN ARCHED
STRUT

Seasoned
oak framed
spandrel

Wall purlin

Upper arched
longitudinal brace

Wall
plate

Pendant
post

Lower
arched
longitudinal
brace

WALL
POST

Seasoned
oak boss
at base of
pendant
post

Raking
Strut

LOWER
ARCHED STRUT

Oak
blocking
to brick
wall face

Open spandrel

Wall post bearing on
stone corbel supported
by steel structural bracket

Moulded
plaster
kneeling
knights

Roger Capps and the director in charge of the job, Bob
Goodman, were adamant
that the methods used to
make the St George's Hall
ceiling should be as true to
medieval precedent as possible, aiming to achieve the
richness and visual warmth
of a hand-made finish even
on such a large scale. Here
scratch-stocks, the correct
medieval tools, are used to
cut the mouldings in the
green-oak members.

Committee had been in favour of it, there was an excitement to it, a sense of adventure and an aesthetic advantage in the masculine vigour of the material. No one had made such a large and finely detailed green-oak roof for centuries. And, although there was an element of theatre here – this was after all a ceiling beneath a modern steel roof – 'Glu-lam' would have been even further away from the medieval examples they were hoping to emulate. Green oak, in Downes's words, 'would be more straightforward.'

He was then faced with the challenge of designing it in detail. The joints with which large-scale architectural carpentry has always been pegged together are one of the great examples of vernacular engineering. By the fourteenth century, joints had emerged through centuries of trial and error which were of baffling complexity but proved effectiveness. Later building techniques, using metal fastenings and glues, had dispensed with these complicated joints but they are integral to green-oak architecture. After consulting with many companies, including Capps and Capps, specialists in the repair of old buildings from Llowes near Hay-on-Wye, these were the joints that Downes decided to go for. No one had any practical experience of anything like this in green oak and so his designs were based on theoretical knowledge and historical examples. As a result, the trusses of his roof were immensely complicated structures. The two halves of each truss were symmetrical about the ridge line and each half was itself divided in two parts: the main centre arch, springing towards the ridge, and the lower arch coming down to the corbel on the wall. At the junction between the two was a pendant post, from the bottom of which a large boss hung down into the hall. At the top of the pendant post, the point around which the whole structure worked, four different timbers had to be accommodated: the top chord coming up from the wall plate and then going on up to the ridge; the pendant-post purlin coming in from the west; and another pendant-post purlin going out to the east; and of course the pendant post itself. Four large pieces of timber – and green oak is immensely heavy – had to be held within a single joint.

In barn architecture, these elements could, without much ceremony, be slapped one on top of another. But this was not barn architecture. Downes had been up on a scaffold with people from Capps and Capps to look at the mouldings on the timbers in Westminster Hall. What he had seen there had excited him: roll-mouldings as fat as rainwater pipes, others like clustered scaffolding tubes, richly and fully carved by the original carpenters with a roundness and a depth of undercutting

The immensely complex and heavy roof trusses in St George's Hall were designed to reduce the visual width of the room. Integrating its complicated jointing system with the purlins and wall-plates – seen at the top of this diagram in section – proved agonizingly difficult. The photograph (left) shows rafters stacked in Capps and Capps's yard in Herefordshire and reveals how the mouldings control the splits in the drying oak.

from which classical architects would have shied away. The timbers in his St George's Hall must have the same fullness of form and 'vitality of shadow-life'. But if the mouldings were to work they had to run into each other where timbers met. The eye must not hesitate at the joints and so you could not simply put one piece on top of another. Everything had to be integrated, everything had to run together. The timbers, as the technical term goes, had to be 'housed' in each other. The joints that are needed to bring this about are mind-boggling in their intricacy. The basic principle is that each timber that is introduced to the joint helps to create the housing for those that follow. To complicate things still further, Downes was anxious that, as the green oak dried, visible gaps should not appear between the timbers. Each of the joints had to be 'face-housed', cut in such a way that the mouldings would continue to conceal the joint even as the timber opened. The whole joint then had to be pegged with oak pegs, the traditional method, which Gifford's nevertheless had tested at Southampton University to see that a universal medieval practice had not been mistaken. The peg method proved to be much stronger and more tolerant than they thought. Each peg, pulled to breaking point on a jig, bowed almost an inch before it broke. When they cut the joints open, the inch-thick pegs were bent, Downes remembers, 'like a double knuckle'.

The resulting joint at the top of the pendant post, at least in its final form, could then be described as follows: 'Central pegged, stop-end tenon, with reduced pegged bridle-bearing and face-scribed housings to purlins with haunched top tenons.' The reality was as much of a maze as the language. This was the most complicated joint they had, but it was only one, if you include all the rafter to purlin joints (the relatively simple 'housed and scribed shoulders, with reduced-width, pegged soffit tenon and diminished haunches'), of over 1200 in the roof as a whole.

The detailed design and tender documents for the St George's Hall ceiling were ready by the last days of December 1994. The quantity surveyors had estimated that this enormous, complicated roof, with many uncertainties still hanging over it, might cost some way over £1 million. That indeed, when the tenders came in early in the New Year, was precisely where most of the bids clustered: £1.1, £1.3 million. But one of them, from Capps and Capps in Herefordshire, leading experts in the field, came in hundreds of thousands of pounds lower than that. 'This is very unusual,' the project manager Simon Jones of GTMS says. 'Three or four tenders very close together and one that is a very great deal cheaper. The dilemma you face then as a professional is: if the market is telling you that three or four think it is worth one thing and the other guy thinks its's worth half that, has he got it wrong? Mistakes do happen. Has he screwed up?'

They went back to Capps and Capps and at that stage, Jones continues, 'we don't say how far out he is but we say "Look, your tender is very attractive, we would just like to understand a bit more about it. Just to check you've included this and included that and not left anything out so that we don't have any problems down the line." Roger Capps was cooperative and convinced the quantity surveyors Bucknall Austin that he had incorporated everything we wanted and that was the price of the job.' Capps and Capps were awarded the contract at the price they had quoted.

In March, the beautiful, straight Sarnesfield timber was selected and the felling began. Individual trees were selected, as had always been Roger Capps's intention, for particular members in the ceiling. By making that precise selection, waste was kept to a minimum and helped Capps keep his price down. The only problem, at least to start with, was finding enough grown bends from which to cut the curved braces. Bob Goodman from Capps and Capps was scouring the country for naturally curving wood. Steve Potter, the estate manager at Sarnesfield, wasn't pleased: 'To be honest, that annoyed me a bit. I'm trying to grow these trees straight and all they wanted was the bloody things bent!' Some bends were to be had from the buttresses of the Sarnesfield trees, where the trunk curves out to meet the ground, but most of them came from Wales, where, as Roger Capps says, 'the timber is a lot wilder'.

Through the spring and summer of 1995 Capps and Capps cut and shaped the timber at their yard in Llowes. They had decided from the start that they would cut the pieces by hand. It would have been perfectly possible, and much cheaper, to have used a computer-controlled router. But for both Capps and Downes the precision finish of router-cut wood was not what was wanted. Capps compares that effect to Victorian work 'in which the shadows fall straight and the result is perfect but as dead as a dodo'. This was a piece of work which Capps and Capps wanted to do as well as it could be done. They were prepared to pour their all into it and that meant, among other things, that the job had to be hand-finished. With great ingenuity Capps and Capps invented a system by which a mechanical saw, making a large number of parallel cuts to a pre-defined profile, could take out much of the waste, while leaving the final quarter of an inch or so to be removed with a scratch-stock, a medieval tool used to cut mouldings, and hand-planes.

Using these techniques, half a trial truss was made and erected in their yard and approved. The sheer scale and weight of the pieces was daunting, although they had worked on even bigger pieces in the past, and the way in which mouldings from different pieces met and ran together proved difficult to get right. Many small changes were made on instructions from both the architect and the engineer but there was no sign yet that anything might go wrong.

Roger Capps had not specifically included in the contract any payment for developing the design. He knew there would be some design development but assumed that it would not go on very long and that any cost incurred that way would be made up by the increases in productivity that would result from it. In fact, as the design was developed, changes in detail were being made to the roof, for both aesthetic and structural reasons, for six months after Capps and Capps had begun work on the job. The cost implications of those alterations were to have serious effects as work progressed.

By mid-September 1995 the elements of the first trusses were ready to come up from Hereford. Simon Jones, the project manager, watched apprehensively. 'They raised the pieces on to the working platform and the first truss was fiddled into position at the west end of the hall.' Principal rafter raised and held, wall post fitted beneath it, pendant post hung from top chord, lancet panel fitted between wall post and pendant post, raking strut below lancet panel, lower arch strut below that, main arch strut fitted beneath it, purlins and wall plates attached and rafters laid between purlins. As they were working on the truss, they realized the survey of the hall was four inches out, only the first of many unwelcome surprises: there were previously unknown voids behind the plasterwork on the north wall; the west and east walls were not parallel; the south wall bowed outwards along its length. All of these factors were to complicate and slow the work, inevitably incurring costs en route.

The first truss eventually went up, but they could not get the second truss to slot in neatly with all the purlins and the two wall plates that were coming down the hall from the first truss. Everyone had assumed that with the right set-up you could simply slot it on, but the precision required in three dimensions and the way in which the still wet timber was behaving meant that, while everything was working on paper, nothing was working on site.

The project manager watched in agonized apprehension. As Simon Jones remembers it, 'One truss went up, two up, back down to one up, two up again, up and down, up and down. The job went nowhere. No one could work out how to do it. That was when we really began to be concerned. We had a very, very key component of the job and very, very critical for the critical path. Time was ticking and we had this very, very serious problem.'

'What we hadn't realized,' Roger Capps now says, 'and I don't think anyone could have realized, is that what had been drawn from theory would not work in practice. If you have a rigid jigsaw, there has to be something that slots in last. In this design, everything had to slot together simultaneously. With timbers that are 25 inches in diameter, nothing could be sprung in. Nothing gives at that size.' Capps and Capps got on with making all the purlins and all the wall plates at Llowes but cutting no joints because the system wasn't working. On site, Bob Goodman was struggling manfully with a difficulty he had never encountered before. 'These were huge timbers and the design was asking for them to be fitted together in a way like joinery or furniture. Higgs and Hill were saying to us "get all the trusses up, don't worry about the rest", but it didn't work like that. That was the problem. Each set of purlins had to be enclosed in the joints of the new truss as that truss was being assembled. You couldn't install the truss first and drop the purlins in later. That wasn't how it was designed nor the joints cut.'

The men from Capps and Capps, working on their high platform close up underneath the outer steel structure they called 'the supermarket roof' felt they were in a world of their own. 'It was almost as if we were under siege,' Capps says. 'Here we were, dealing with this huge and difficult problem, craftsmen in a sea of people doing fast-track building below us. I felt at times that everything was against us. We were lucky to have only a single accident. The foreman dropped a purlin on to his finger, only from an inch or so, and the weight of it crushed the finger so that when he got to hospital there was nothing to sew together.'

Even the green oak was doing its best to frustrate them. 'On a Friday afternoon,' Bob Goodman remembers, 'we were fitting a joint and we got it up and we said, "All right, we'll peg that up on Monday." But, come Monday, the wood had moved and the joint wasn't working and we'd have to start all over again. I had never lost sleep over a job in my life, but this one was different. I even woke up that Christmas night in a panic. It was this Sword of Damocles business: this wonderful job which gets you lots of publicity. But if it goes well, people won't even remember it. The only reason that anyone will remember it is if it goes badly.'

Even apart from the 'last piece of the jigsaw' problem, design changes had also been imposed on the roof by Gifford's, the engineers. The point at which these roofs usually fail is at the ridge. The eaves push out, the ridge settles and the structure becomes unstable. To avoid anything like that Gifford's introduced two elements. Steel rods or hangers were suspended from the steel roof to hold each truss from above. Bob Goodman of Capps persuaded Gifford's that the steel rods should not be tightened up so that the oak could carry its own weight and in that way tighten its own joints. The hangers in the void above the ceiling are attached to the timber but only loosely; they are simply there to catch a truss if in future there is some danger of it settling. Those involved with the green-oak carpentry disparage the idea that the hangers are necessary but Gifford's were thinking of their liability.

In the centre of each truss they also introduced what is known by the beguilingly simple name of an elbow. It is a large and very heavy, curved piece of timber – and the curve cannot be cut out of a straight section; the curve must be grown if the drying grain is not to split the piece open – which is attached to the principal rafters as they come up to the ridge which Gifford's saw as the main danger. The means of fixing the elbow was described as 'two folding wedges in a double-ended stop-splayed and tabled scarf, with under-squinted transverse key and four face pegs'. As that might suggest, the fitting of the elbow turned out to be one of the most difficult operations on the whole job.

It was, apart from anything else, an immense physical struggle. Each elbow is a very heavy piece of wood, weighing three hundredweight before it is cut and, because St George's Hall is not square – it tapers westwards and unexpected variations had appeared in the wall lines themselves – the elbows and the five complicated joints each of them contains, with twenty-two internal faces, could not be cut off-site. The elbow could only be fitted by measuring it off against the principal rafters once they had been installed. As Bob Goodman says, 'It was a large lump of wood. You had to put it up there, mark it, bring it back down, cut it again, put it back up there again, and so on and on.'

Capps and Capps were adamant from the start that they would do their best by the job. They realized that the development costs in particular were hitting them very hard and that money was beginning to look very tight indeed. 'Bob Goodman and I decided', Roger Capps says, 'that, if there was ever going to be a choice between leaving the job partly finished and cutting corners, by using routers, say, then we'd choose the first. We would never cut corners at Windsor, or anywhere else come to that.'

The project managers for their part, coming from a very different

Some idea of the scale of the work involved in the St George's Hall ceiling. The carpenter sits on the top chord and hand-planes the main arched strut, one of the many curved members which had to be cut from a branch that had grown with that curve. With this material, a great deal of work had to be done on site.

metropolitan business culture, were seeing time and money slip away. They thought that Capps and Capps might be on the point of hitting them with a big claim. 'The construction business is usually very adversarial by nature,' Simon Jones of GTMS explains. 'Once you hit a problem, if you are in bad contractual relationship with your contractor or your subcontractor, they see that problem as a potential commercial gain.' Nothing could have been further from the mind of Roger Capps but the suspicion was rising in the mind of Simon Jones.

Giles Downes, Capps and Capps, and Richard Swift at Gifford's were all working on the problem, and by February the technical difficulty had at last been resolved. The change sounds simple. Instead of having the purlins fully housed, that is to say entirely surrounded by the mortises of the other elements in the truss, they managed to redesign all the

joints so that the purlins could be dropped in from above. This meant that the trusses could be put up first and the purlins slotted in afterwards. The major aspect of the three dimensional juggling – getting the nine longitudinal members in at the same time as the twenty-five different components of the truss spanning the hall – had been removed.

Just as the technical problems were overcome, another, potentially disastrous, factor appeared. Over the first five trusses, with all the difficulties, the design changes, the extra labour and the extra time, Capps and Capps had been incurring huge additional costs. At a meeting in Windsor that March, attended by Phil Rowley the Contracts Manager from the main contractor Higgs and Hill, Richard Swift the engineer from Gifford's, Giles Downes the architect, Roger Capps, and both Chris Watson and Simon Jones from GTMS, the project managers, the crisis came out into the open. Roger Capps said, 'Look, I've got a real problem.' He was getting into difficulties. Basically he was running out of money. Giles Downes pointed out that the necessary changes to his design had changed the original scope of the works. Payments to reflect that must be made to Capps on the basis of the relevant project manager's instructions. This standing up to be counted by Downes was something for which Capps was immensely grateful, and the payment to Capps for those changes was put in train.

Jones and Chris Watson of GTMS then met Capps at Windsor later in March. An air of apprehension hung over the Project Team. There was a chance of one of the most important elements of the Restoration Project going badly wrong. As far as the outside world was concerned, and as it heard during a Press Day held that spring, everything was proceeding smoothly, on time and to budget. That was not strictly the case.

Roger Capps said simply, 'My bank won't support me.' He wanted to keep the company afloat until he could get to truss 8 or 9 and leave the project with a clean finish. The bank had extended his overdraft and he had a piece of land he could sell. 'The way it's looking,' he told the project managers, 'I can only survive another two or three months. That's probably the best I can do for you.'

It was Roger Capps's idea to bring his bank manager, from the Royal Bank of Scotland, up to site, to show him what was going on, and to enthuse him with what Capps and Capps were trying to do. It was an effort to extend the Windsor factor to the bank itself, to ask them to pull the stops out too. The bank manager came, talked to the project team and was generally supportive. But, of course, there were limits to what he could do.

The structure of the ceiling half complete. High on their scaffold platform, almost shut off from the rest of the site, the men from Capps and Capps felt they were in an almost private world of medieval craftsmanship, away from anything else that was going on at Windsor at the same time.

Simon Jones, imagining the worst, as his experience with the worst of the building industry had led him to do, felt he was facing a conundrum here. 'Was this a real problem,' he asked himself, 'or was I having the wool pulled over my eyes? Had Capps simply made a mistake in his tender and was now trying to come the sob story in the hope of getting help? Or was there a real danger of the company going bust and the job being left dangling?'

The letter of the contract, which Capps and Capps, like all other firms here, had signed, allowed the project manager to force them to finish the work on the terms initially agreed. They could, if they wanted to, call his bluff, refuse any extra money and so risk driving his business into bankruptcy. 'My impression and conviction was', Jones now says, 'that this was a man who was probably going to let his business go under. He wasn't pretending to us. He would go so far, but then he'd pull the plug.'

It was impossible, under the contract, according to the Desk Instruction on which the Royal Household runs its finances and in terms of the psychology of managing a project like this, simply to give Capps an *ex gratia* payment to save him from his difficulties. 'We have a contract,' Simon Jones said at the time, 'and we have to pay within that contract. There is no latitude to say, "Well, this is a special case." We have to be tough and we have to be seen to be acting in accordance with all the rules. Auditors are going to be crawling all over this one day and we have to keep the audit trail clean. And, if we go soft on this one, there'll be a queue of people saying, "Can I have some more money, please? I need another half a million, please." We must be prepared to let Roger Capps go bust or it will be an open door on claims.' Capps says that Jones was 'fighting his own shadows. There was an atmosphere of distrust over this at the time; of course they had to look on the worst side of the case but I was telling them exactly what was going on.'

It was a delicate moment. The project managers felt they had to keep Capps and Capps going as long and as productively as they could. At the same time, they had to be putting into position all the contingency plans in the event of Capps crashing out of the job. Jones was in a dilemma and felt he could not be entirely honest with them: 'I was saying to Roger, "I want to help you, I will help you, we will do what we can to keep you afloat," while sitting in a room with him looking at him eye to eye. The reality was at the same time I had people in the next room preparing for him going broke.' The quantity surveyors were drawing up an ingeniously designed tender document to put out to other companies for the remaining trusses of the St George's Hall ceiling. As

Capps and Capps completed each truss, the page describing it was torn out of the new tender document that was kept waiting in the wings.

Simon Jones was acting as the shoulder to cry on, but he was also pushing Phil Rowley at Higgs and Hill, the main contractors, to give Capps and Capps a very hard time indeed. As a result they were being ferociously demanding on site. 'This was a tough-cop, soft-cop game we had to play,' Jones says. The people at Capps and Capps ended up feeling alienated from Higgs and Hill – 'they called us the Welsh farmers; it was a culture clash,' Bob Goodman remembers and Roger Capps reinforces that: 'We had a complete intellectual block with Higgs and Hill. I sometimes think they thought we were hanging doors.'

On the other hand, they admired the generosity of understanding that Chris Watson of GTMS in particular displayed. 'The project managers', Capps now says, 'were as accommodating as they could be, but I know they could not overstep the mark. They provided the men with free digs in the mews at Windsor and they were generous with their ideas and getting things to work. But of course we knew the game they were playing. We're businessmen. And if you've got what you think is incurable cancer and someone tells you, "You're looking pretty well today", well ... we know the score. It would have been inconceivable for them not to have been preparing for our going bust.'

In reality, GTMS was in a savage dilemma. 'We could see', Jones says, 'that with a hundred thousand or so we could nursemaid him through to the end. The problem was that the price we would get back from an alternative supplier was probably going to be three or four times that. The rules say you have to let the man go bust. But it was very obvious that it was going to be very, very expensive to let him go bust.'

Michael Peat was riding the project manager particularly hard about this, and the questions would come banging down the telephone: 'What measures have you taken? How are you preparing for this? What are you putting in place? What are you doing about it? How are you planning for the future?'

In the end, the quantity surveyors agreed to revalue a large number of the changes that had been made. They went down to Llowes and measured the difference in the time it took for the mouldings and joints as originally quoted for and as eventually executed. Everything Capps claimed was legitimately based on a change of design. They never claimed for any development money because that had already been allowed for in their original contract. The £437,461 that had been quoted for the St George's Hall ceiling rose to £548,731. Capps and Capps are

still in business, the ceiling is up in St George's Hall and it is certainly the largest, most elaborate and most complex green-oak structure erected since the sixteenth century. In their original programme they had hoped to get it up in six and a half months. Eventually, it took two weeks short of a year. But when, in September 1996, it was complete, and the scaffolding was still there so that you could walk the length of the hall, among the giant oak trusses, in and out of them like a series of vastly overscaled booths at a fair, the marvel of what had been achieved was obvious: a richly authentic structure, perfectly capable of acting as the roof itself, a net of heavy oak sculpture deeply in the tradition of what would have been here in the fourteenth century, and just as meticulously cut and moulded.

The worries over the cracks, or shakes, in the timber had evaporated. Those very deep mouldings had brought about an unpredicted but felicitous effect. The oak members were narrowest in section on the line that ran between the deepest grooves which the mouldings had made in their surface. It was in those grooves, hidden in the shadow, unapparent from the floor, that the shakes appeared, simply because that was the line of least resistance. Had those mouldings, it occurred to Giles Downes, actually been developed in the Middle Ages as a means of controlling the shakes that would always have developed in green timber? There was no telling, but it was at least another symptom of that concordance between the aesthetics of Gothic, the emphasis on the incised line, and the inherent qualities of the material in which they were expressed.

It was now certain that, with the brilliantly polychromatic shields of the Knights of the Garter glittering on the panels between the trusses, the ceiling would appear rich, dignified and perfect, the precise embod-

St George's Hall was always intended to be the secular headquarters of the Order of the Garter, and the remaking of the heraldic element in the decoration was a central part of the brief. The new ceiling shields form a more accurate record than anything that was there before and provide the glitter for a room whose whole purpose is celebration.

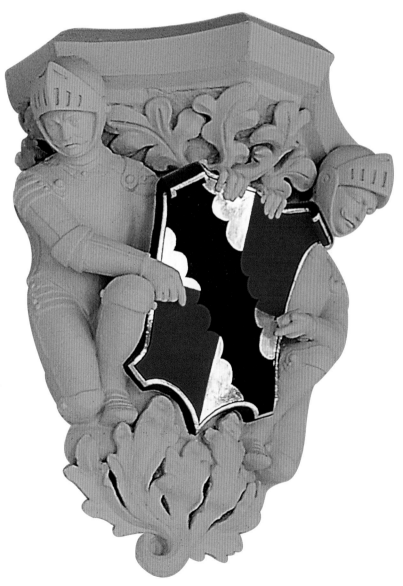

One of Wyatville's Kneeling Knight Corbels in St George's Hall restored by the Cliveden Conservation Studio.

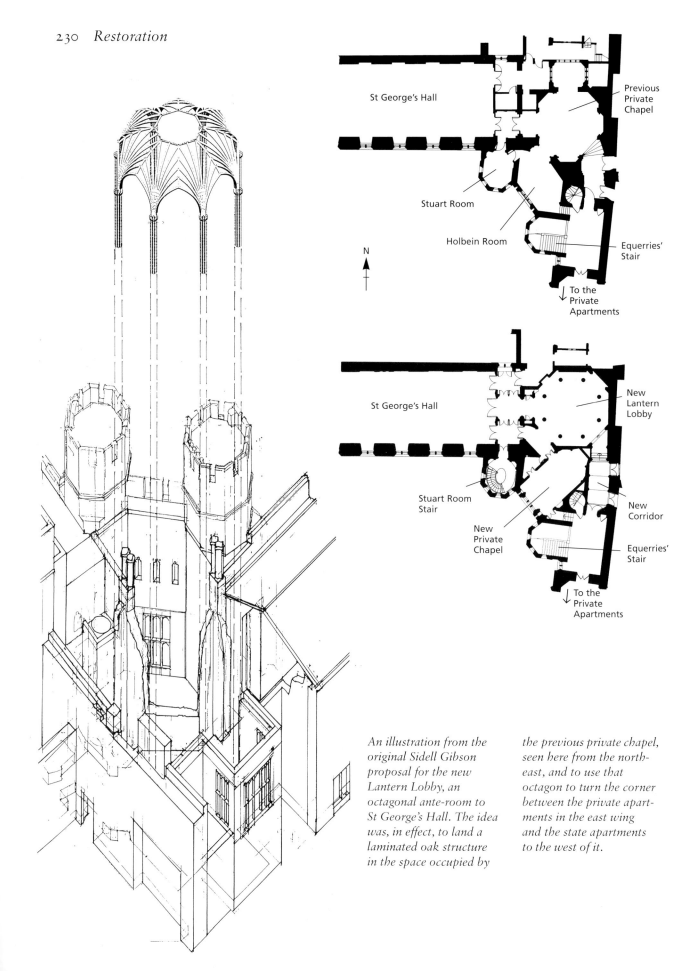

St George's Hall

Previous Private Chapel

Stuart Room

Holbein Room

Equerries' Stair

N

↓ To the Private Apartments

St George's Hall

New Lantern Lobby

Stuart Room Stair

New Private Chapel

New Corridor

Equerries' Stair

↓ To the Private Apartments

An illustration from the original Sidell Gibson proposal for the new Lantern Lobby, an octagonal ante-room to St George's Hall. The idea was, in effect, to land a laminated oak structure in the space occupied by the previous private chapel, seen here from the north-east, and to use that octagon to turn the corner between the private apartments in the east wing and the state apartments to the west of it.

iment of everything Giles Downes had envisaged two years earlier. This is now the roof for 'an idealized medieval king's banqueting hall'. The new floor is, at least in part, made from oak donated by the Garter Knights to the Castle. The kneeling-knight corbels have been meticulously restored to their appearance in 1828. The armoured mounted figure of the King's Champion, high on the balcony of the screen at the east end, re-enacts the last moment the Champion's armour was worn: at George IV's Coronation Banquet in Westminster Hall, itself a Gothic extravaganza which looked back to medieval precedent and directly prefigured Wyatville's work at Windsor.

Few places in the world can have such an involved and almost pleated relationship to their own past as this room, and the new Downes ceiling is another turning over of that historical fabric, another layer added to the layered layers that preceded it. When the Prince of Wales saw the result, he was thrilled. 'An absolutely stunning roof,' he wrote to Michael Peat, 'a masterpiece.'

For all its drama and its central position in the imagery of Windsor, and for all the courage, persistence and ingenuity which the making of the ceiling eventually involved, it represented only a small proportion of the architect's task in redesigning this part of the Castle. The site of the Private Chapel where the fire had begun; the screen separating it from St George's Hall which had been vaporized in the fire; and the two small ruined spaces beside it, the Stuart and Holbein Rooms: all these awaited a new fate.

Downes's first submission for these rooms, developed in long conversations with his partner Paul Gibson, the two of them poring over masses of images and details of the great Gothic buildings of Europe, had been respectful of the historic fabric. This 'minimum intervention' had been a conscious decision – it had in fact been part of the brief – but it had serious implications for the planning of any new proposal. The old Private Chapel was surrounded by thick, largely nineteenth-century walls and their presence governed the planning of Sidell Gibson's first proposals for the area.

The central task there, as everyone realized, was to improve the circulation, the route from the Grand Corridor and private apartments on the east side of the castle through to St George's Hall and the other State Apartments on the north of the Upper Ward. An octagon would turn that corner. If Gothic were the chosen idiom, a fan vault would bridge that octagon, coming down on the eight attached columns at the angles. Very little sidelight is available in the middle of that knot of ancient

structures and so the vault would have to be top-lit with a glazed lantern rising above the roofline. The basic strategy for the space was in this way clearly determined by the function of the building, the character of the surrounding spaces and the shape of the ruins that had been left by the fire. In Sidell Gibson's original submission to the Restoration Committee they showed this graphically: the octagon landing (see page 232), as if from space, to restore the ruin.

The main disadvantage of this rather respectful approach was that their new octagon was forced southwards of its ideal position by the remaining structures and as a result could not be centred on St George's Hall. Other submissions had not been quite so deferential in their approach and with a more cavalier attitude to historic fabric had advocated large-scale demolition of the nineteenth-century work which would allow the ante-room to be aligned with the central axis of the hall. The Duke of Edinburgh's Restoration Committee had liked that suggestion very much, as well as the proposal to have a balcony running around the octagon. A balcony would need a stair for access and, in addition, the Duke and his committee were drawn to the idea of replanning the area of the Holbein Room to accommodate a new Private Chapel.

The new East Screen in St George's Hall, replacing what had been incinerated during the fire. When the central doors are closed, it acts as a visual end-stop to the room. When they are open, it becomes a processional archway between the Hall and the Lantern Lobby beyond it.

Downes was asked to incorporate all of these ideas in a revised version of his scheme.

He was delighted. It introduced an element of complexity and richness; a stair is an inherently beautiful thing; and the possibility of making a third space, as an extension of the progression that was already there from St George's Hall to the octagon, was deeply appealing. He leapt at the opportunity.

Downes had begun his architectural career in the office of the uncompromising and brilliant modernist Norman Foster. It was there, Downes says, that he absorbed a central lesson. 'I didn't learn how to approach design as anything other than a system. It was system, all systems. I learned about the overriding importance of little details, of the need to understand materials and the ways in which they can be manipulated, but particularly how to get a system going, a system which is going to cover all the answers and to carry continuity through the design.'

Only in the late 1970s when Downes joined the Sidell Gibson partnership – Paul Gibson had been with him at Foster's – did he begin to examine pre-modernist architecture. It was a revelatory experience. 'To me, it was like opening a door on to a massive, beautiful world of all the things I had seen, but which I had discounted and said "I can't use this because it's old."'

That now changed and he started to design buildings that drew on the vernacular tradition. Was he not frightened of being labelled a pasticheur? 'Of course I was, but we knew what we were doing, which was to analyse what was important and what was relevant about these other models. What does pastiche mean, when used like that? It means a cheap copy without understanding. Analysis, interpretation, relevance, that's what's important. There's nothing new. You're always using a model, whether it's from ten years ago, two months ago, fifteen years ago or 100 years ago. There is very little which comes clean out of your head. The secret is breadth of understanding and a concern for detail. That's what makes good architecture.'

It is this double inheritance – the rather stripped, cool and systematic coherence of modernism sewn into a reinterpretation of the Gothic tradition – which gives Downes's work at Windsor its unique qualities. He had never built a Gothic building before and so immersed himself in every book he could find on the subject, returning to the mathematical treatises by medieval architects on the geometrical means of setting out an arch, an octagon, a vault or a building.

Talking about the forms of tracery in his neo-Gothic balustrade and

door panels, the architect mingles that geometrical understanding with the intuitive involvement of the draughtsman's eye: 'For an idea to work like this, it needs to be a bit like a mathematical formula. It needs to be elegant, with a simplicity and a directness to carry it on through and be all of a piece. But all these are drawn by hand. I found the eye was much easier than trying to work out a sort of rationale of what shapes I was actually using.' So it is not mathematical in that sense? 'Well, it starts from geometry but the proportions tend to arrive just naturally. On many, many parts of this building I have simply drawn the curves again and again and again until they look right to me, forty or fifty pages in an A3 pad full of nothing but curves. And it is very easy afterwards to look at them and discover the golden mean in what you have done but if it is there it is always the eye that has brought you to that point.'

A. W. N. Pugin remarked famously about the heavily encrusted Fonthill style of medievalist architecture that 'A man who remains any length of time in a modern Gothic room and escapes without being wounded by some of its minutiae, may consider himself extremely fortunate.' That is the quality which Downes has erased from his designs here and he has imposed instead an extraordinarily beautiful, almost vegetable sinuosity and liquidity of form. The emphasis is always on the fluency of movement between parts. The architecture of the lantern lobby, chapel and stair, all of which is almost entirely in carved oak, seems to have been poured into a mould. 'What I've done', Downes says, 'is avoid florid decoration. The structure itself is the decoration, based on Gothic geometry that related to natural plant forms. You are trying for elegance through spareness of detail and that requires immense discipline.'

The so-called lily heads for the new octagonal Lantern Lobby in the Venables workshop (left), being installed at Windsor (centre) and seen from the high-level working platform (right). Nothing was more important to the architect than a sense of natural flow between the elements of the structure.

That discipline and that combination of clarity with sensuous refinement of form is apparent in every detail. In the mouldings around the many doorways he has re-adopted a medieval practice which the Victorians had abandoned. 'I never liked the way the Victorians did it,' he says. 'They always ran the same moulding all the way round the opening. That was the obvious way to do it, bland and boring. I was in Salisbury, looking at the tracery in the cloisters there. And then in Fairford and in Westminster Abbey and when you look you notice that they very rarely take the moulding in the head of the arch down into the vertical. Generally, the jambs of the doors have a simpler profile which echoes but doesn't actually match the head of the arch. In Salisbury, it actually slides from one form to another: a simple jamb just slips into a heavily recessed moulded head, which has a very rich double hollow in it. I thought, "Wow, that's nice," and so I've worked it out here.'

To achieve the effect has been a long, fiddly struggle for the specialist plasterers A. G. Joy, but the result is subtly beautiful. The jambs of the doorways have a gently curvilinear profile, a tactile and visually easy surface at eye level, but above your head they transmute imperceptibly into something fuller and deeper, with full-bodied roll-mouldings and rich, strong-shadowed hollows. It is the best of both worlds.

His first scheme for the octagonal Lantern Lobby was relatively simple, but the introduction of a balcony in some ways disrupted it. The replanning was not complicated. Downes simply shrank his original by 18 per cent overall, bringing the eight columns in towards the centre of the room.

Once the columns were free of the walls, they took on a fuller life than before. They are made of laminated oak vanes glued on to a tulip-wood and plywood core. These vanes and the spaces between them read as the wooden, Gothic equivalent of the flutings on a classical column. Those spaces are filled with shallow oak webs. In an effect that matches the plaster mouldings around the doorways, each of those webs both narrows and shrinks away from the surface of the column as it gets higher so that, as the vanes begin to turn over, becoming the ribs of the vaults over the balcony and the central space of the lobby, they grow sculpturally richer, emerging from the column itself. Each column head with its ribs attached becomes like the flower of an arum lily, a smoothly moulded openness slowly emerging from the stem.

This continuous, composite structure of column-cum-vault, with no strong division between the two, as there would be in a classical version of the arrangement, is a central element in the fluency of the space. The liquid continuity between floor, vault and lantern, which Downes was wanting to achieve, depended on that line running uninterrupted through the structure. The problem was that a balcony, with its strong horizontals, would cut it in two. Sir William Whitfield, the architect and member of the Prince of Wales's Design Committee, was firmly against a balcony for that very reason, 'for the loss of verticality' it would involve.

Downes struggled long and hard to emphasize the vertical elements and to restore the sense of natural flow that the balcony was disrupting. Difficulty summoned inventiveness: the balcony was pushed to the back of the columns so that from the central space their oak vanes would read as continuous flow-lines; the balustrading became a mass of verticals in two planes, folding over at the top into double-thickness Gothic tracery and at the bottom sliding past the floor-line of the balcony to the arches supporting it; and the springing points of these arches were made to emerge almost from the back of the column, twisting and turning as they did so, in a way that directly mimicked the emergence of a side-branch from the trunk of a tree. At the springing point of the arch, the oak vanes on either side were to be eased apart, as if the arch had pushed its way out between them, and to close back together again afterwards so that the eye would run on up to the vault and the glazed lantern that crowned it.

In a thousand details, the geometry was tortured in this way to achieve naturalness of effect. The curves, hand-drawn but later transferred to computer, became very complicated, some of them a combination of five different radiuses from five different centres. The mouldings on the ribs themselves are designed to evolve as your eye moves upwards, a lightening of the form in the way that the branches of a tree lessen towards the crown. The designed tolerance of the structure, which was more like a huge piece of furniture than part of a building was a single millimetre throughout.

After the tendering process had been gone through, this immensely challenging job went at the end of 1995 to Henry Venables Ltd of Stafford. They had made the new laminated oak roof for York Minster after the 1984 fire and, through the agency of Peter Ross of Arup Associates, had advised Giles Downes in the spring of 1994 when he was first developing his ideas for Windsor.

Now the drawings had arrived. Venables had never seen anything like it. 'It was like a bunch of great big dock leaves,' Roger Venables, the Chairman, says. 'And the most difficult thing about it is the complete absence of repeats. No rib is the same distance from any other. No angle is the same as any other.' The eight columns are in fact identical and the springing points and ribs come out in four pairs, but the essential point is true: ease of effect meant complexity of construction.

Venables produced shop drawings to interpret the architect's drawings and to test his measurements. Richard Smith, Venables's setter-out, could not find a single instance in which Downes had got it wrong. 'I lived and breathed it,' Smith says, 'for twelve months. When I first saw it, I thought, "How were they ever going to do this?" Like the webs between the vanes. They have to be tapered in two dimensions and scalloped all the way up. And then there have to be two little channels at the edges of those infills. That is a challenge for any machinist. Matt Jones did it. He made it work.' Using the soft wood of an American poplar known as tulipwood, a mock-up was then made of one of the 'lily heads'.

There was a great deal of learning to be done and the job went slowly to start with. 'It's all been difficult,' Ron Eaton says in the joiners' shop. 'Very, very difficult to get your head round. But it's like a book: the story comes out as you read on.' Of all the problems, the achievement of a liquid quality in carved oak was the most difficult. Each of the ceiling ribs as they come down on the column had to be carved and coaxed into a smooth relationship with its neighbour as they clustered around the top of the shaft. They were to look like gathered reeds held together by a bronze band, but carved-oak elements don't naturally bunch like reeds. It was taking seven man-weeks per lily head to put the oak vanes on. Only one man could work it at a time because each vane partly covered its neighbour. The joiners could not understand the way in which the arch supporting the balcony was to emerge from the vanes of the column by smoothly pushing them aside. 'We just couldn't picture what he had in his mind,' Eaton says. Downes came to Stafford and made a model in plasticine of what he wanted.

By early October 1996 some good progress had at last been made. The geometry had been understood, the system of construction established, three columns had been made and installed at Windsor and all the components for the ribs of the vaults had been manufactured. Templates for other parts had also been cut. They were all in the Construction Shed at the Venables plant in Stafford, a big building on whose floor a full-size plan of the Lantern Lobby had been drawn out, ready for the pieces to be assembled. It was the only shed at Venables which did not have a sprinkler system installed.

CROSS REFER TO DRAWING NOs.356/400-404
FOR LANTERN DETAILS

1.632   1.642   1.676

3.065

7.400

10.000

On the evening of 11 October 1996, a Friday, Roger Venables was on holiday in Pembrokeshire. 'The phone rang. It was one of my sons. He said, "Don't worry, but we've had a fire. And what's worse it's the Windsor stuff."' A forklift truck, parked in there for the night, had somehow fused, created a spark and set the whole shed and its contents alight. Everything that was in there was destroyed or made useless. The Fire Brigade had arrived quickly and soon put the fire out but the water damage to those oak pieces that had not been burnt was irremediable. Venables couldn't trust the performance of oak that had received such a dousing. Many months' work worth about £350,000 had been lost.

That evening, hearing of the fire, the men who had been working on the job came in to see what they could do. 'We were broken-hearted,' David Dutton, the Production Controller, says. 'Everything we had done was lost. It was total devastation. I just had to walk away for a few moments to gather my thoughts. It was very emotional. All the lads came in and the fire officer said, "Get out what you can," and we were dancing round trying to get stuff out like flies round jam pots. Some was salvaged but it was a very small amount.'

Venables sent a fax to Windsor over the weekend and on Monday morning Chris Watson, the project manager, came into his office in the Lord Chamberlain's Upper Stores to find it sticking out of the fax machine and his schedule shot to pieces. The next day he and Phil Rowley from the main contractors Higgs and Hill went up to Venables for a crisis meeting. Rowley, as the man responsible for getting sub-contractors to perform, was anxious. 'I like programmes,' he says, 'I like bar charts, I live on bar charts. They give me a certain level of comfort and that stops the anxiety. But now, into my programme, all of a sudden, here's this thing that's gone way out of control. It wasn't my fault but I knew at the end of the day it would still come on my desk, so I needed to get back in control of it pretty damn quick.'

It wasn't a happy meeting and the entire programme had to be rejigged. Venables had to increase the number of men on the job from eighteen to thirty, other projects of theirs were to be starved of labour, but it still meant a massive hole kicked in the Windsor schedule. The Lantern Lobby was due to have been installed by March 1997. After the fire that date slipped to early July. It didn't mean the restoration job as a whole would be late but it did mean that virtually all the time-contingency that had been built into the programme had been absorbed. Plasterers, floor layers and decorators all had their timetables squeezed at the end of the job. There was no room, as Rowley says, 'for any more hiccups'. Only by December 1996 were Venables back up to the point where they had been before the fire and throughout the spring and early summer they were pushing hard, straining to meet the new deadline. The atmosphere in Stafford was tense but on the site of the Lantern Lobby itself, where the oak should have been coming in, all was quiet. The project managers decided to move the installation of the new floor forward to fill the gap.

The precise nature of the floor of the Lantern Lobby had been a contentious issue from the first. The Duke of Edinburgh had not liked Sidell Gibson's original floor suggestions, thinking them 'over-fussy', and the question had moved through a whole series of options in the two years since the question was first raised. The Duke of Edinburgh in particular had been concerned that there should be carpets; parquet or stone floors would be both noisy and slippery.

The architect was keen nevertheless to have a non-carpeted floor and by August 1995 the proposal was to have a stone floor throughout the new lobby, with the same central design as suggested for the original marquetry floor, but with the tongue of the Garter emblem facing towards St George's Hall. Still the Duke was discontented and in December 1995 the Prince of Wales asked Michael Peat if there 'would there be *any* chance of *combining* the designed stone floor with a carpet so that, in years to come, it would be possible to choose between a stone floor or a carpet (which, I dare say, will be nothing like as interesting)?' The Duke was happy with that idea 'provided that the carpets are fixed in such a way that they don't slide about'.

The conclusion of the discussion was that a stone floor should be installed, but that a carpet with a large Garter Star woven into it should be used when it is thought necessary. The floor itself, according to Giles Downes's design, carries a heavy symbolic freight. From the start, he had wanted, as he says 'to commemorate the spiritual elements in the origins of the Order of the Garter'. He took his inspiration from the Cosmati stone pavement made for Henry III in the thirteenth century in Westminster Abbey, which in geometrical and numerological terms describes the myth of the Creation. Downes's pavement is as far as possible made of English stones, including a centrepiece of Duke's Red Marble from the Duke of Devonshire's estate at Chatsworth in Derbyshire. The piece was given by the Duke, a Garter Knight himself, from a small store of it at Chatsworth, the only remaining fragments from a mine long since worked out. It is set within a pavement of Purbeck Thornback flagstones. Although the masons who laid the famous West-

The stone floor of the Lantern Lobby embodies in a complex numerological scheme something of the spiritual aims behind the original foundation of the Order of the Garter. It is made, as far as possible, of English stones.

minster pavement for Henry III came from Rome, the centre of their craft was in northern Italy, in the marble hills near Carrara. That is where these English stones were sent in 1996 to be made into the decorative floor of the new Lantern Lobby.

Downes's design consists of a series of concentric bands. 'The outermost has a four-way geometry, which stands for the material world. That pattern is used as the background for the next band, which is twenty-six octagons, the original number of the Knights of the Garter, including the Sovereign and the Black Prince. The knights were originally divided into two tournament teams of thirteen, a highly significant number, representing among other things Christ and the twelve apostles. The twenty-six octagons are interlinked, as if holding hands. Eight is the number for spiritual regeneration, so there are twenty-six figures here, standing together in a group intent on spiritual renewal. Within that is a band of six-way pattern, which represents the spiritual world. You could say that they are stepping from one world to the next, the material to the spiritual. Set in that band, you have the Round Table, which like the one at Winchester is a series of alternating black and white segments. Within that again you have another band of sixty-one lozenges: sixty is the number for time and sixty-one is the number beyond time, encompassing the motto and badge of the Order, which symbolizes their aims. In the very centre, you have a silver disc, which represents wisdom.'

Of the two rooms alongside the new Lobby, it was clear from the start that the staircase up to the balcony should occupy the smaller of the two, the Stuart Room, and that the Holbein Room should be swept away and replaced with a new Private Chapel. The staircase continues the themes on which the Lantern Lobby is based. It is elliptical in form, and its bronze handrail swirls down to a newel post in the form of five rush leaves, their tops just bending over to accept the handrail as it curls to a finish. The balustrade itself, another liquid exercise in Downesian Gothic geometry, repeats the interlaced tracery of the balustrade in the Lobby, but this time, of course, on the rise.

The joiners at Taylor Made Joinery in Suffolk made the staircase. Jonathan Wright, the Contracts Manager, explains how the balusters, although largely cut with a five-axis computer-controlled router, could only be finished by hand. 'The tracery had got to travel up the balustrade and still look right. To get that, to get it looking even, as though it belongs there, needs a little bit of give and take and you can only get that with hand-carving. The thing of it looking right on some-

The liquidity of the Downesian ideas for Windsor reaches one of its highpoints in the newel post at the foot of the elliptical staircase in the Stuart Room, where the balustrade curls to a spiralling conclusion and the newel itself is made of five rush leaves, their tops just bending over to accept the handrail.

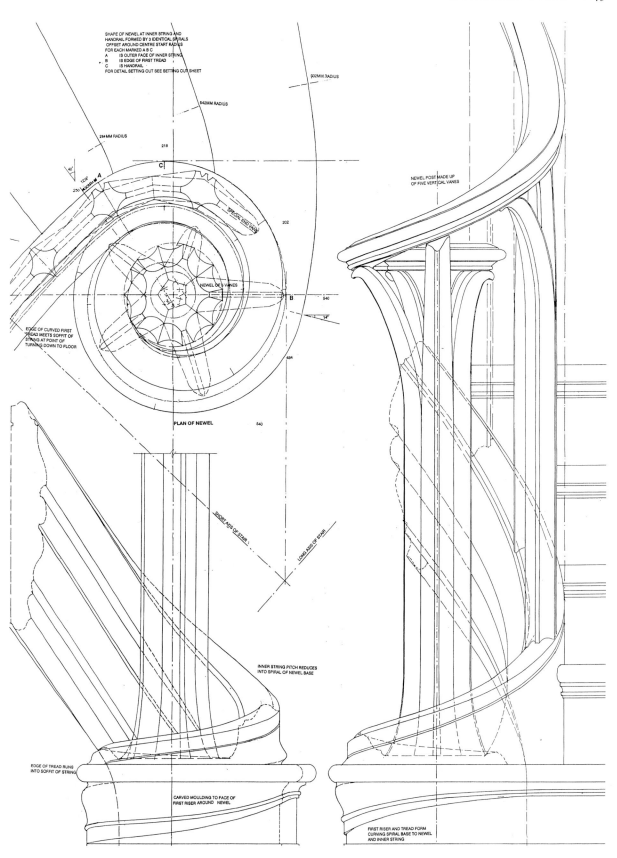

SHAPE OF NEWEL AT INNER STRING AND
HANDRAIL FORMED BY 3 IDENTICAL SPIRALS
OFFSET AROUND CENTRE START RADIUS
FOR EACH MARKED A B C
A   IS OUTER FACE OF INNER STRING
B   IS EDGE OF FIRST TREAD
C   IS HANDRAIL
FOR DETAIL SETTING OUT SEE SETTING OUT SHEET

932MM RADIUS

542MM RADIUS

284MM RADIUS

218

202

SPIRAL END VANE

NEWEL OF 5 VANES

540

14°

484

EDGE OF CURVED FIRST
TREAD MEETS SOFFIT OF
STRING AT POINT OF
TURNING DOWN TO FLOOR

PLAN OF NEWEL

540

NEWEL POST MADE UP
OF FIVE VERTICAL VANES

SHORT AXIS OF STAIR

LONG AXIS OF STAIR

INNER STRING PITCH REDUCES
INTO SPIRAL OF NEWEL BASE

EDGE OF TREAD RUNS
INTO SOFFIT OF STRING

CARVED MOULDING TO FACE OF
FIRST RISER AROUND NEWEL

FIRST RISER AND TREAD FORM
CURVING SPIRAL BASE TO NEWEL
AND INNER STRING

thing like this is more important than getting the dimensions right. And it is not everyone who can do it. You need the confidence on a job like that. If you've got it, it all runs through, it just flows through. And if you haven't, it doesn't.'

The final Downesian space in Windsor is the new Private Chapel. It is a little jewel-box. No more than thirty people will be able to fit in there for an Easter Day service and it has the qualities of privacy and preciousness which you would associate with an oratory, a place of prayer. This too has had a difficult design history. Downes's first conception was for a roof consisting entirely of angels' wings. The Ark of the Covenant is decorated with angels' wings and that had been in his mind. It was rejected by the Design and Restoration Committees as being 'too much' and so Downes adapted it, fought for it, had a model made, took it to St James's Palace and showed it to the Prince of Wales, but he still failed to convince. Robert Kime said – a point which Giles Downes now accepts – that in most of what he had done he had 'turned the structure into decoration; in this case [he was] trying to turn the decoration into the structure'.

Downes, impressively, swallowed this Puginesque rebuff, gained the respect of the project team by doing so, and tried again. Taking his sketchbook on holiday in France, he had to ask himself: what can I do with it? 'I had to keep the shape. The shape was a given. The fan vault was an obvious option because you needed to arch over the central space of the chapel, but they also wanted openings high on each side, one for the choir loft and one for the organ. A fan vault would create the necessary shapes.'

It was too obvious, though, too much of a repetition of the Lantern Lobby. Then, thinking again about his feathered wings, he thought, 'Hang on, if the feathers were stripped to their quills, and I used the vocabulary of the crossing-over tracery in the balustrades, then that might work.'

Returning from France, he came across a description of the Henry VIII chapel vaulting at Hampton Court. It looked at first like a stone fan vault, but was actually a ceiling made entirely in oak and suspended from hidden structural members above. Downes realized that, if he brought the real structure, which in this case would be a stepped arch,

The vaulting in the new Private Chapel is not a stiff repetition of inherited forms but a moulding and squeezing of that inheritance into forms that Gothic has never taken before.

down to the visible level of the ceiling, he could combine something of both the stepped-arch trusses in St George's Hall and the balustrade tracery of the Lantern Lobby into a ceiling which had both a real rhythmic and structural strength to it and the sinuosity of form he was looking for. In the design he then came up with, it is as though the arches are the bass line of the music, and the extraordinary, continuous and closely moulded net of tracery, laid over the whole of the chapel ceiling, the melody running over and above it. This is the highpoint of Downesian Gothic. Nowhere does this architecture become more ingenious or more vegetable than in the interlacing of the oak ribs in the Private Chapel.

'It took a long time,' Downes says, 'drawing these ribs again and again and again by hand for one bay until I got the balance right between their turning and spreading and a sense of evenness, of naturalness.' The result is a vault that comes to a tight geometrical precision at the centre and emerges from very orderly straightforwardness in the outer bays but which, in mid-range between these two, develops a superbly easy fluidity, as if the oak ribs have been extruded from the nozzle of a tube. The surface across which they are laid is geometrically complicated. As Downes says, 'If you had a barrel vault, made it in rubber and blew very hard, that is the shape you'd get. That's why it's got tension. It is a curved curve.'

Needless to say, the cutting of oak to fit a curved curve is about as deep a challenge as architectural joinery could present. The experts at Taylor Made confess that it could not have been done without Computer Aided Design. Each of the six bays of the chapel, which is not a big room, has over a thousand different pieces of oak built into it. They were all assembled, bay by bay, in the Taylor Made workshops, laid over a mock-up of the vault, each piece fixed with hidden bolts to make a self-sustaining net. The amount of bench labour was phenomenal, deeply underestimated by Taylor Made in their tender for the job. The key difficulty was the need to keep the moulding on each rib perpendicular to the floor. In a straight vault, that would have been no problem. But as the ribs moved across a surface that was curving through all three dimensions they were forced, as the Contracts Manager, Jonathan Wright puts it, to 'bend the mouldings over to keep them straight'.

The unintelligibility of that phrase is a measure of what they were being asked to do. But the justification is in what they have produced. As this room stood ready in the last months of restoration for its final dressing of stained glass, altar and altarpiece, you could watch, almost as if it were mobile, the wonderful play of form across the chapel ceiling, a rippling of life across the curved surfaces. This was what Downes had meant to create, tradition which goes beyond tradition, taking it to places that tradition has never been and making demands of the craftsmen to which the craftsmen, using all the modern techniques at their disposal, have been happy to respond.

Just outside the chapel, above the Stuart Room stair, the new plaster vault has a central boss in the form of a green man. Oak leaves sprout from his mouth, and his face, like many medieval green men, has a bearded, sombre quality. Only slowly do you realize: it is a portrait of Giles Downes.

The green-man boss on the vault above the Stuart Room stair, a portrait of the architect Giles Downes, whose work at Windsor aims to establish the relationship of organic to architectural form.

8 Restoration

The original programme had envisaged an end to the job in the spring of 1998. In the summer of 1996, although nothing was announced to the outside world, the idea was mooted in the Household, and the decision finally taken in the autumn, that the fire restoration project should be brought to a conclusion the following year.

November the 20th 1997 was both the fifth anniversary of the fire and the Golden Wedding of the Queen and the Duke of Edinburgh. A party to mark that anniversary in the restored apartments of the Castle would suit an occasion which might well be one of the outstanding celebrations of the reign. It also had the advantage, from the point of view of the project managers, of being a strikingly visible target for the contractors and subcontractors to aim at, a deadline of such public prominence that no one could contemplate overrunning it. The new completion date was the Windsor factor *in excelsis*: an end to the project which if successfully met would be a triumph and if missed a disaster.

Programmes were adjusted. The elements on the bar charts by which the project managers visualized their future progress had previously stepped calmly out across the winter of 1997/98, one task succeeding another, not too much going on at one moment and with plenty of time allowed for the Royal Collection to arrange the interiors after the contractors had left. Now those elements were being squeezed from both ends. Those jobs which were to have taken place in the last months of the project were shuffled back to meet the new deadline. The charts, from being a shallow staircase bringing the job smoothly into a rather understated landing, now looked steeper and sharper, with much more going on at once. As Phil Rowley, Contracts Manager for Higgs and

The lantern, with glass by John Reyntiens, crowns the lily-head vaults in the Lantern Lobby. A collar of traceried, nodding arches in plasterwork articulates the point where the form of the lobby moves through the roof and up into the glazed light of the lantern beyond.

Hill, said at the time, 'You just have to look at one of these charts to see what sort of programme it is. Is it a 35°, 45° or 60° programme? In some ways, the shallower the better, for the contractor anyway. This used to be a 35° programme. It has now got a lot steeper. People think that you can drive a job full steam up to the end and finish it there, bang, the Normandy landings approach, everyone on the beach at once. Well you can't. A job has its own natural time. There are 200 men on site, a thousand activities, 80 subcontractors. You can't have this Normandy thing. If you do, you start to lose control.'

The new programme introduced a certain tension into the project team. Far from a gentle winding down to an easy conclusion, the Windsor job would now be wound up to its highest pitch yet. Hugh Roberts, Director of the Royal Collection, recognized at the time 'that all of this meant a pretty bleak atmosphere for the project managers, having to put the screws on everyone. It will be all right in the end but the lead up to it has been very tough and it has required some very tough words and very tough negotiating, but that's the price you have to pay for keeping something to budget and to schedule. The polite term is decisiveness and the harsh term is ruthlessness. It's an inevitable part of it.' Certainly, relationships in several parts of the project became strained in the last few months.

It was decided that one area in particular should come, at least temporarily, into full operation well before the final handover. The Great Kitchen and all the rooms clustered around it for food handling, food storage and food preparation, filled with elaborate equipment, had to be tested in a full dry run well before it was used in earnest. The reception for the Queen's Golden Wedding in November was to be for at least 600 people, most of them eating and drinking as well as dancing. It would have been lunacy to try out the restored kitchens for the first time on that day.

The trial run, serious enough without being on a vast scale, was set for Garter Day, Monday 16 June, and for the Ascot Week that follows it, during which the Queen has a house party at Windsor. The climax of Garter Day is the service in the afternoon in St George's Chapel and the procession of the Sovereign and the Garter Knights down from the Upper Ward through the crowds clustering in the Lower Ward to the great west door of the chapel. It is the day when Windsor Castle is *en fête*, when its dedication to the Order is made most apparent and when it takes on the air most obviously of a small self-contained village community celebrating its highpoint of the year. Temporary beribboned

The Crimson Drawing Room in the days before it was finally opened. Protective polythene still covers Sir Gerald Kelly's portrait of George IV and two of Sir William Beechey's portraits of George IV's sisters, on either side of the fireplace. The restored early nineteenth-century gilt bronze and cut glass chandelier was brought to this room only in the 1920s by Queen Mary. More than three-quarters of the facets hanging here had been salvaged from the ashes.

The Great Kitchen with its final lighting scheme installed, designed to provide modern levels of brightness above Wyatville's restored kitchen tables without impinging too much on the view of the medieval roof and lantern.

stands are built in the gardens of the Military Knights like the structures you see in Sienna for the Palio. Entrance is by ticket only. The Garter Knights themselves, for all that they are among the most distinguished people in the country, look like the members of a medieval guild dressed up for the occasion. (The procession, even if with ancient antecedents, was invented or re-invented after the war by the Queen's father.) It is the moment in which you see Windsor Castle most clearly as a sort of national village, as grand as England gets, with hedges of burnished swords and breastplates along the lane down which the Garter Knights walk and an enormous royal standard floating over the Round Tower,

The Victorian Great Kitchen, portrayed here in Frederick Bishop's The Wife's Own Book of Cookery, *1856, used both modern standard gas-lamps and the gothic, elm-topped kitchen furniture Wyatville had installed here in the 1820s. The tables were rehabilitated, and their legs lengthened to a modern working height, during the restoration.*

but rather intimate and homely at the same time, as near as England comes to a fiesta for the 9000-odd guests and friends and their children and grandchildren gathered there to watch.

Before this procession, the Garter Lunch is held in the Waterloo Chamber. It was this in June 1997 which was to provide the test for the restored kitchens. The week previously, the project managers had ensured that all contractors were out. Long and at times difficult discussions had been held about how to light the kitchen. The architects, interior designers and English Heritage had all been keen for the lighting to impinge as little as possible on the beautiful historic interior which they had done so much to re-create. Nineteenth-century drawings of the kitchen in operation showed gas-lamps fitted to standards above each of the work tables, and for a while it looked as though something resembling them might now again be installed. But the Household's F Branch – 'F' stands for Food, as against 'G' for General and 'H' for Housekeeping – felt that was entirely the wrong approach. Andrew Jarman, once Banqueting Manager at Claridges and now Head of F Branch, makes the point: 'There are health and safety implications here and that has to be the underlying consideration. It is a kitchen. The fact that it has been there for 700 years or whatever is irrelevant. I have got to look after my people and, if you are going to employ people from the hotel world, I would argue that we apply the same sort of safety regulations to Windsor Castle as to any hotel kitchen.'

Although this was accepted in principle, the actual method of providing the necessary intensity of light at worktop level, without totally disrupting the look of a kitchen whose roof was 40 feet above the floor, had not been found by the time Garter Day came round. Hideous, temporary fluorescent light fixtures had been installed along both sides of the Great Kitchen to satisfy the health and safety requirements.

There was an initial hiccup. The week before Garter Day, after the workmen had finished, the entire kitchen was subjected to a deep and thorough clean by cleaning professionals. Gas was turned on to the cookers, some of them adapted from the cast-iron charcoal grills installed here in the 1820s. They are probably the oldest working kitchen appliances in the country and had been meticulously restored by the historic kitchen specialist, Tim Martin. Steam was provided for the Cleveland Steamer, flown in from America, and water and electricity for the bain-marie. The electric insect-killer was installed and turned on. The large new walk-in fridge, as big as most people's sitting rooms, was brought down to the required temperature. The salamander grills, the hobs and fryers, the hot trolleys, the roasting ovens and the proving ovens, all were ready to roll. The June sunshine streamed in through the windows of the green oak lantern, bouncing off the high, limewashed masonry of the walls, suffusing this beautiful room with a beautiful light. The Wyatville furniture had been rehabilitated, the legs of the work-tables raised to a modern height, which aims to avoid the back trouble that is endemic among chefs, and the elm worktops had been cleaned and repaired. The new stone floor had been coated in a highly polished and highly cleanable finish after the Royal Chef, Lionel Mann, with the benefit of thirty-seven years' experience in the royal kitchens, had dramatically demonstrated to the architects, with red wine, blackcurrant and beetroot juice, precisely what a kitchen floor has to be impervious to. The restored kitchen looked, to a lay eye, as marvellous a tool as anyone could wish for and as neat a sewing of modern requirements into a historic building as has ever been achieved.

The pastry kitchen – occupying the rooms in which George III had been incarcerated during his madness – was not yet up and running. As a result, the teas for Ascot week – bridge rolls and sandwiches, jam and

Sunlight pours through the south side of the lantern in the restored Great Kitchen. One of the large air-handling units with which the room is ventilated is hidden behind the grille at the far end. For many, the restoration of the Great Kitchen was the most successful part of the whole project.

cream sponges, honey fingers and fruit scones – would still have to be brought from the Palace kitchens in London. There was also a question over the ice-cream maker, whether its capacity was adequate. But the whole of the lunch itself could, with the equipment available, be made here.

Then the brigade of chefs, fourteen of them, arrived from London. It was a ticklish moment, with all the potential for disaster. The chefs and the Head of F Branch took one careful look at the kitchen and said they were going back to London. There was no way they could cook the Garter Lunch in there. It was filthy. 'You could taste the dust in the air,' Lionel Mann, the Royal Chef said. 'You could taste it in your mouth standing in the kitchen and you would certainly have been able to taste it in the food. We are not here to produce dusty food.'

Hurried negotiations were held between the project managers and F Branch. The problem had been dust migrating into the kitchen from other parts of the site. F Branch gave them twenty-four hours to sort it out and a battery of contract cleaners was instantaneously wheeled in for the deepest of deep cleans.

A day later, Mann and Jarman pronounced themselves content, and the lunch for seventy-two in the Waterloo Chamber, as well as the 250 staff lunches to be served in the restored Undercroft between 11.15 am and 1 pm, could go ahead. Paupiettes de saumon fumé aux fruits de mer, suprême de volaille avec risotto aux champignons sauvages, followed by Vacherin Cardinal for pudding and then cheese, emerged from the Great Kitchen that Monday morning with a calm and ease that was a pleasure to witness. The new air-handling units hummed from the lantern. The chefs' briefcases, with their own sharp knives and pepper grinders, sat open on the Wyatville sideboards. Peter Matthews, the Senior Sous Chef, said 'It's like we've never been away.' Taffy Gwynne Jones, another Sous Chef who has been there nearly thirty years, thought that the Windsor kitchen was the best of all the royal kitchens to work in. 'I know you could get a block of flats in here,' he says, 'but I love the place. It's more homely and friendly than the Palace. At the Palace it's more spread out but here you're all together. It's big, it's very tiring on the feet, you have to walk a long way, but I don't think there's a kitchen like it.'

This Garter Lunch was, in a way, the first fruit of the restoration. The sight of the medieval kitchen with the chefs' hats bobbing up and down over their work tables; the smells of the chicken and risotto wafting around the room; the astonishing calm with which professional chefs

St George's Hall awaits its final dressing. The suits of armour removed in the week before the fire on stretchers have still to be reinstalled on the 'wall corbels' that run the length of the Hall. The portraits, busts and furniture have yet to clothe and soften the room. But the visual effect of Giles Downes's design is clear. The stepped arches of the trusses provide a rich sculptural shape, a head and shoulders, to a room that had previously been a long and rather dreary box.

produce over 300 lunches; the sight upstairs of the Waterloo Chamber, still with half the great sequence of Lawrence portraits missing from their frames – they had been removed during the fire – but with the 60-foot long table laden with so many cut flowers that the huge room smelt like a spring garden: all of this in itself seemed to justify the whole, difficult, gritty and agonized process of the restoration. It was a foretaste of completion.

That was of course an illusion. The rest of the fire-damaged area was still far short of being finished or dressed. On all fronts it was being driven towards an end that still seemed a long way off. The Green Drawing Room was furthest advanced and the restored Carlton House Trophies went back up on the doors in late June. The new silk was going up on the walls of the Crimson Drawing Room and the painting and gilding was being completed in the State and Octagon Dining Rooms as well as the Grand Reception Room. In St George's Hall, half the repainted shields of the Garter Knights were in place, the new oak floor was approaching completion and the joinery for Giles Downes's new east screen was installed but wrapped in plastic for protection. His vast new oak doors from Taylor Made Joinery lay in boxes on the floor of St George's Hall. The Stuart Room stair was in except for its handrail, and the wooden vault of the new Private Chapel was complete. The immensely complex joinery of the Lantern Lobby was, after the fire the previous winter at the Venables plant in Stafford, still months behind its original schedule. Here was a clenched little net of scaffolding and oak members, among which the joiners were striving to make this huge, precision piece of architectural furniture go neatly together in the narrow gap between the scaffold platform and the bulky air-conditioning and other service ducts above them. It had become the tensest part of the site.

Despite the tight limits within which the whole job was now set, the project managers had been feeling relatively comfortable. Budget, schedule and quality were still looking all right. Even with all the additional costs associated with the Undercroft, the Royal Collection work, the elaboration of the Giles Downes schemes and the late changes to the Kitchen Court building, it looked as though their private budget limit of £35.5 million would not be breached. Most of the contingency fund had been taken up, but that was to be expected and they were certainly still far below the initial publicly declared target of £40 million.

Then a bombshell hit them. The quantity surveyors, Bucknall Austin, were having difficulty keeping up with the number of design changes the project was still generating. They were also becoming uneasy about

In the Lantern Lobby, Giles Downes's organic, lily-head vault emerges and grows from the column-stalk that gives rise to it. You can make out the careful staggering of the joints in different ribs, designed so that no horizontal joint-line should appear with which to break the eye's smooth movement from floor to lantern.

what the final cost would be. Almost 3500 Project Manager's Instructions, some of them with up to twenty separate parts, had been issued since the beginning of Phase 3B in April 1994. Bucknall Austin reckon that about 30,000 instructions were given, some affecting the same piece of work three or four times, over the course of the job. Each of them had to be separately evaluated and costed. This number of changes is unprecedented. The Household had required all costs, and all changes to costs, to be apportioned to the relevant package of works. In addition to the original £8.5 million contract for Phase 3B, the rest of the works had been divided into 240 separate packages. This subdivision of a project is also unprecedented. About sixty to eighty packages is the industry norm for a job of equivalent value. Bucknall Austin's monthly cost reports on an average job of this value are thirty pages long. At Windsor, they reached 290 pages.

Until about February 1997, Bill Bladon of Bucknall Austin says they were 'having difficulties keeping up with cost-checking changes to the design. But we were unwilling to admit defeat and I felt there was probably enough residual money hidden away in contingencies and provisional budgets for us to be able to achieve the target.'

In early June, the main contractors, Higgs and Hill, through whom all claims for payment come, told the Quantity Surveyors that on their calculations the projected final account would not be less than £28 to £28.5 million, which with all the other project costs would total £37.5 to £38 million, blowing away the £35.5 million internal target. Contractors always want to make large claims on projects of this kind and the Quantity Surveyors always knock them down, but in this case Bucknall Austin, still dealing with the uncertainty of costs yet to be incurred at the end of the project, anything up to £400,000, could not get the Higgs and Hill figure towards the Household's target.

The project managers were devastated by the news, and a series of bitter meetings was held. Bucknall Austin had already begun a major cost update and review of disputes with Higgs and Hill, and they produced a report on the full cost risk to the Household in July. The figure they came up with was less than Higgs and Hill's estimate but still a long way outside the Household's target.

An independent Quantity Surveyor from the project managers' parent company, Gardiner and Theobald, was brought in to produce an independent audit. and as the dust settled what had happened seemed less drastic. The system of Rolling Final Accounts, established in the early days of the contract, meant that no extra claims could be made beyond what had already been finally agreed up to December 1996. The final projected sum would be no more than about £36.5 million, an overrun of 3–4 per cent against the internal target and a saving of around 9 per cent on the declared budget of £40 million.

Looking back on it now, Bill Bladon says, 'I can understand why things became fairly heated at the time, but I believe this independent audit has brought about some level of understanding of the intense pressures that we have been working under. This was a unique project with unique problems. Although the timing of our advice could have been better, the final cost is incredibly good value for money. And if you

The exotic upper landscape of the State Dining Room ceiling, studded with 'Ascot hat' bosses, as one of the architects called them, seen in one of the mirrors with which the room is lined. Page 48 shows what this room looked like five years earlier.

The gilded plaster vault of the Octagon Dining Room, with the carved bosses and corbels now in place. The appearance of this room immediately after the fire, with the vault utterly destroyed, can be seen on page 42.

compare apples with apples, and disregard all those additional works not within the original brief, the final costs are almost identical with our original estimate for the project.'

Michael Peat, the Keeper of the Privy Purse and the person with ultimate responsibility for the project, partly blames himself for being too easily mollified when he expressed concerns that Bucknall Austin's costing did not seem to be keeping pace with the job. 'On the other hand,' he points out, 'the only issue is how far below budget, which is £40 million, we are going to be. And to come in below budget for a job of this nature, size and complexity is, as far as I am aware, unprecedented. A lower internal target was set, to give a safety margin and to encourage tight cost control, and failing to meet that was unsatisfactory and disappointing. If a target is set, it should be met. But, in a broader context, coming so well within the £40 million budget can only be seen as an extremely good outcome.'

As the financial question was being sorted out in the early autumn of 1997, the great apartments themselves began to be dressed for their opening day. For the new private chapel, an altarpiece of the Holy Family by the early sixteenth-century follower of Raphael, Berto di Giovanni, was installed above a new altar designed by David Linley, the Queen's nephew. The chapel itself was furnished with a set of giltwood chairs originally made by Pugin for the State Dining Room but which even in the 1820s turned out to be too heavy for that use. Stained glass by Joseph Nuttgens was installed in the south-west window of the chapel according to a design that followed an initial outline drawing by the Duke of Edinburgh. In the lower half, St George pierces a dragon from whose mouth fire emerges to engulf the Castle. A fireman and a salvage worker struggle in the smoke, whose tendrils reach towards the upper half. There the Castle, seen from a distance on its woody hill, emerges from the flames, and a sense of light and renewal floods the scene.

In the Lantern Lobby next door, the superbly substantial tournament armour belonging to Henry VIII, previously at the other end of the state apartments, is set to stand on the central axis of St George's Hall, visible, at least when the doors in the east screen are open, seventy yards away down the length of the Hall which itself is glittering with the polychromatic heraldry of the Garter Knights and lined with suits of armour. Around the other sides of the octagonal lobby, the Royal Collection has arranged some of Windsor's richest treasures in display cases whose cumulative effect is of pure exuberance and spectacle: silver and silver-gilt buffet plate, candelabra and vases, George IV's col-

lection of Renaissance and early nineteenth-century display cups, elaborated nautilus shells, a tankard covered in cameos, a huge German ivory cup and cover. Together these create what Hugh Roberts, the Director of the Royal Collection, calls 'a *Schatzkammer*, a *Wunderkammer*, a treasure house. Previously there has been some reticence about putting this silver on display, except during a State Banquet when the whole lot comes out. But this will look marvellous.'

In the sequence of state apartments created by George IV, the idea has been to put back what had been there before the fire, but in its best possible condition. Every piece of furniture was re-upholstered. Some of the chairs had been what Hugh Roberts calls 'rather violently upholstered, like pouffes or balloons', and these have been brought back to a more reasonable state. The porcelain cabinets in the Green Drawing Room were cleaned, the mounts washed, the veneer repaired. The Green Drawing Room carpet had shrunk by a few inches after its sousing during the fire and so a new border a few inches wide has been woven to fill the gap. Other carpets have been cleaned, 'titivated' or replaced with patterns nearer the Georgian original. A new replica Pugin sideboard in rosewood veneer has been made to replace the one in the State Dining Room destroyed in the fire. An enormous painting of the family of Frederick, Prince of Wales, by George Knapton has now taken the place of the destroyed Beechey in that room, the new picture being squeezed though the window with an inch and a half to spare, even after one stone transom of the window had been removed.

Slowly, as the rooms filled in the autumn of 1997, as the paintings were hung again on the silk wall panels where they had been before, the apartments which had seemed, even with their curtains in place, too enormous to be usable, or even very pleasant to be in, over-stimulating in their gilded richness, started to become human again. Hugh Roberts had to allay fears about the nature of the rooms as they would finally seem. 'I've spent a lot of time saying to various people, "Please don't form a view of this room at the moment. Wait until it's furnished, till everything's back in. Before then, it will be too bright, too pink, too red." Putting things in a room adds a balancing layer to the whole thing. They knock it back in a funny way.'

The last few weeks of the work, frantic as they were, with questions of paint type and colour still being decided, of the precise sorts of render to be applied to exposed medieval masonry or the level of brightness in the bulbs on the restored chandeliers, were nevertheless a time in which people who had devoted the best part of five years to this job could begin to look back on it with some perspective.

For Chris Watson, project manager, sitting at the centre of the web in his office on the top floor of the Lord Chamberlain's Upper Stores at Windsor, the whole experience revealed with absolute clarity that there is 'no Red Adair for situations like this, no one great hero who can come striding into a disaster like this and sort it out. Anyone who reads the story of what happened here during the restoration will see a whole

The Green Drawing Room was the first of the principal apartments to approach completion. The great Louis XVI Sèvres service, made immediately before the French Revolution and bought by George IV in 1811, was put back into the cabinets which had begun life as bookcases in Carlton House. The eighteenth-century candelabrum by François Desjardins and Jean-Jacques Caffieri is a representation of 'Autumn', and the mirror is a mid-eighteenth century rococo fantasia in the style of Chippendale. The Carlton House Trophies dazzle on the doors.

series of necessary things at work. People have been decisive. They have never said "That's not my problem." There has been very little passing of the buck. They have been professional, in the sense that there hasn't been a stupid over-intellectualizing of what needs to be done. The benefit is that the job has gone with a swing. We've never been bogged down and we haven't, on the whole, had people faffing on for hours about the ten different ways of doing something and at the end of all that finding that they don't know the best way of going about it. It's been realistic in that way, and the architects have played a large part in that. You might expect an architectural practice famous for its expertise in historic buildings to become very precious about using authentic materials in every nook and cranny. But they haven't. They embraced the idea of Equivalent Restoration from the start and have gone with that. That has been enormously important in the success of the project.'

It is easy to see that for a building project this has been well done – for Michael Peat it is simply the result of applying modern management techniques to an industry that has not always been subject to them – but it is more difficult to judge what history will think of this restoration. It is certainly extraordinarily careful, neither pedantically re-creating the past, nor throwing over the historical context in which it is set. Both Giles Downes and the architects from Donald Insall Associates have been meticulous in their efforts to release the vitality of the two traditions in which they are working. There is a sense in all those rooms not of formality and stiffness but of great optimism and gusto. It is almost as if the rooms continue to hold the great mass of thought, imagination and energy that has been poured into them over the last five years. If history treats this project well, that liveliness is what will remain.

Donald Insall himself finds a human or even medical analogy the most useful. 'I have always seen a building as a person,' he says. 'Or at least as a living thing, in the sense that it expresses like a shell the needs, habits and even the imaginations of its living occupants. It learns and retains what time and experience do to it. You have to ask how a building became what it is, how it has acquired its character. And if you look at Windsor before the fire there was a lot there which was clogging and confusing it. If it had been a person, you would have said that person was being handicapped, held back from being a healthy, vital soul.'

Seen in that way, the fire and the restoration have had an extraordinarily salutary effect on Windsor Castle. A new clarity, a new vigour, a new coherence, a new confidence and, as a result, a new sort of beauty now emerges from the restored corner of the Upper Ward. As Donald

Squeezed to within an inch of its life, the portrait of Frederick, Prince of Wales and his family by George Knapton enters the State Dining Room by a window adapted for the purpose, to take its place on the west wall where the giant portrait of George III by Sir William Beechey had been destroyed during the fire.

Insall says, the five years of the project have left Windsor 'a much healthier being. Its circulation is better and it breathes more easily. It has benefited immeasurably from an army of people, studying and understanding the organism, applying selective assessment to what is positive and what is hindering it, as a doctor would a patient, seeing it not as a chance amalgam of parts but as something with a life and a future.'

Windsor has been restored to health. On the north side of the Lantern Lobby, on the site of the sanctuary in the old private chapel, the restored remains of the Victorian reredos to the altar have been reinstated but now bearing an inscription. The reredos was put back in place during August 1997 and for the last few months of the restoration project waited there, wrapped up, for its unveiling day. The inscription reads as follows:

THE FIRE OF 20TH NOVEMBER 1992
BEGAN HERE

— • —

RESTORATION OF
THE FIRE-DAMAGED AREA
WAS COMPLETED
FIVE YEARS LATER,
ON 20TH NOVEMBER 1997
THE 50TH
ANNIVERSARY OF
THE WEDDING OF
HER MAJESTY
QUEEN ELIZABETH II
AND
HIS ROYAL HIGHNESS
THE DUKE OF
EDINBURGH

The curtains and pelmet designed by Pam Lewis for the bay window in the Crimson Drawing Room. The pelmet, consisting of swags with overdrapes in a crimson poppy-leaf silk damask, with bells between each swag and a long tail at the side, is enriched with a heavy hanger-fringe and tassels of spectacular construction. The swags and bells are hung from carved and gilded rosette pins.

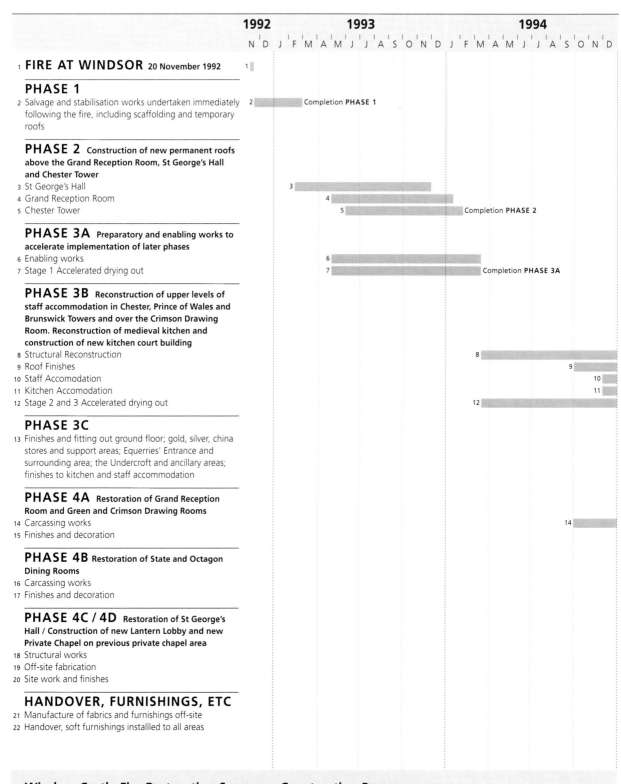

	1992	1993	1994
	N D J	F M A M J J A S O N D J	F M A M J J A S O N D

1 FIRE AT WINDSOR 20 November 1992

PHASE 1
2 Salvage and stabilisation works undertaken immediately following the fire, including scaffolding and temporary roofs — Completion **PHASE 1**

PHASE 2 Construction of new permanent roofs above the Grand Reception Room, St George's Hall and Chester Tower
3 St George's Hall
4 Grand Reception Room
5 Chester Tower — Completion **PHASE 2**

PHASE 3A Preparatory and enabling works to accelerate implementation of later phases
6 Enabling works
7 Stage 1 Accelerated drying out — Completion **PHASE 3A**

PHASE 3B Reconstruction of upper levels of staff accommodation in Chester, Prince of Wales and Brunswick Towers and over the Crimson Drawing Room. Reconstruction of medieval kitchen and construction of new kitchen court building
8 Structural Reconstruction
9 Roof Finishes
10 Staff Accomodation
11 Kitchen Accomodation
12 Stage 2 and 3 Accelerated drying out

PHASE 3C
13 Finishes and fitting out ground floor; gold, silver, china stores and support areas; Equerries' Entrance and surrounding area; the Undercroft and ancillary areas; finishes to kitchen and staff accommodation

PHASE 4A Restoration of Grand Reception Room and Green and Crimson Drawing Rooms
14 Carcassing works
15 Finishes and decoration

PHASE 4B Restoration of State and Octagon Dining Rooms
16 Carcassing works
17 Finishes and decoration

PHASE 4C / 4D Restoration of St George's Hall / Construction of new Lantern Lobby and new Private Chapel on previous private chapel area
18 Structural works
19 Off-site fabrication
20 Site work and finishes

HANDOVER, FURNISHINGS, ETC
21 Manufacture of fabrics and furnishings off-site
22 Handover, soft furnishings installled to all areas

Windsor Castle Fire Restoration Summary Construction Programme

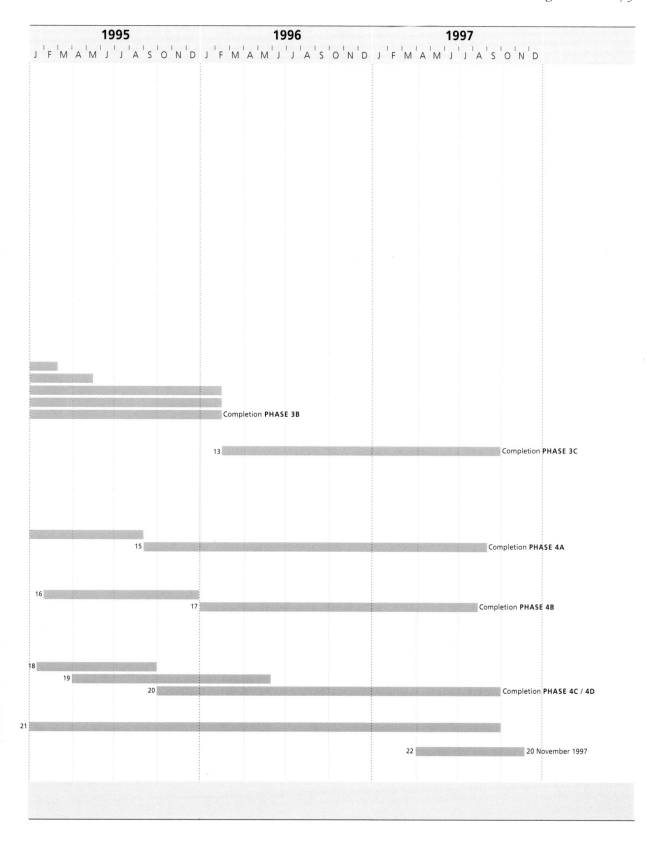

1995 1996 1997

J F M A M J J A S O N D J F M A M J J A S O N D J F M A M J J A S O N D

Completion **PHASE 3B**

13 Completion **PHASE 3C**

15 Completion **PHASE 4A**

16

17 Completion **PHASE 4B**

18

19

20 Completion **PHASE 4C / 4D**

21

22 20 November 1997

Acknowledgements

Apart from those mentioned in the Preface, there are many people I have spoken to and relied on both for information and more importantly for clarifying the complex web of detail which a project of this kind generates.

Both the Prince of Wales and the Duke of Edinburgh were kind enough to take time to answer my questions and read the book in draft. In the Royal Household, apart from Michael Peat, I would also like to thank Lord Airlie, the Lord Chamberlain; Sir Robert Fellowes, the Queen's Private Secretary; John Tiltman, Director of Property Services; Major Jim Eastwood, Superintendent of Windsor Castle; Suresh Dhargalkar, one-time Superintending Architect in the Royal Household; David Plunkett, Clerk of Works at Windsor; Annette Wilkin, the Housekeeper at Windsor; Lionel Mann, the Royal Chef, and Peter Matthews and Taffy Gwynne Jones, Sous Chefs; Andrew Jarman, Assistant to the Master of the Household, F Branch; Marshall Smith, in charge of the Castle's own fire brigade; Oliver Everett, Royal Librarian; and the Constable and Governor of the Castle, General Sir Patrick Palmer and his wife Joanna.

At the Royal Collection, apart from its Director, Hugh Roberts, I am grateful to Sir Geoffrey de Bellaigue, Hugh Roberts's predecessor as Director; Caroline Paybody and Amelie von Pistohlkors in the Director's office; Dickie Arbiter, the Director of Media Affairs; Viola Pemberton-Pigott and Cliona Bacon, conservators; and to Gwyneth Campling who runs the Royal Collection's picture library. In the Prince of Wales's office, Stephen Lamport, the Private Secretary, Sandy Henney, the Press Secretary, and Amanda Neville, the Information Officer, have all been unfailingly helpful.

As members of the Restoration Committee not mentioned elsewhere, I would like to thank Sir Jocelyn Stevens of English Heritage, and the architects Richard MacCormac and Francis Duffy. Of the Prince of Wales's Design Committee, I thank John Martin Robinson, Giles

Worsley and Sir William Whitfield. Roderick Gradidge, John Outram and Sir Colin Stansfield-Smith, all architects who were invited to submit schemes for the restoration, discussed them generously with me.

Of the consultants, I would like to thank Simon Jones at Gardiner & Theobald Management Services and Suska John and Nadia Gulamali, both of whom worked with Chris Watson in the GTMS office in Windsor. At Donald Insall Associates, the architects, Donald Insall himself has been of enormous help, while Alan Frost, John Dangerfield, Peter Riddington and Peter Cooke have all given unsparingly of their time and insights. Giles Downes and Maria Tindall of the architects Sidell Gibson have been equally generous with theirs as have John Coleman and Stephen Batchelor of Bowyer Langlands Batchelor, architects on the early phases.

Bill Bladon at the Quantity Surveyors Bucknall Austin and David Cross at the Quantity Surveyors Northcroft; Richard Swift, Richard Fewtrell and Roger Davies at Gifford and Partners, the structural engineers; Clive Dawson and Cliff Nursey at Hockley and Dawson, the structural engineers on the early phases; Doug Oughton and David Waterhouse at the mechanical and electrical engineers Oscar Faber; Brian Ridout of Ridout Associates; Tim Hutton at Hutton + Rostron; Ken Winch, the Kitchen Consultant; Pam Lewis, the expert in historic textiles; Robert Kime, the interior designer; Maureen Lovering of Scott Lovering, conservators of salvaged materials: all gave me large amounts of their time.

At English Heritage – in addition to John Thorneycroft and Sir Jocelyn Stevens – Geoffrey Parnell, Steven Brindle, David Batchelor and Brian Kerr have all been immensely generous with their knowledge of the Castle. For a highly fruitful suggestion about the context of the fourteenth-century transformations at Windsor I would like to thank Professor John Stevens of Magdalene College, Cambridge. At the Royal Berkshire Fire Brigade my thanks go to David Harper and Lynn Ashfield.

From the two main contractors, my thanks are due to John West, Jim Gillam and Les Broome of Wallis's and Phil Rowley of Higgs and Hill. Among the specialist subcontractors my grateful acknowledgements go to: Laurence Beckford; Peter Begent; Jane Brighty; Roger Capps; Ian Constantinides; Drummond Cuthbert; Paul Dennis; Ray Dudman; David Dutton; Ron Eaton; Ron Edwards; Paul Ferguson; Bob Goodman; David Gunton; David Harrison; Jim Hill; Paul Humphreys; Richard Humphries; Jack Jenner; Matt Jones; Philippa Kain; Peter Kightley;

Sue Levy; Tim Martin; Nigel Matthews; Tony Mileham; Joe Nuttgens; Christine Palmer; Richard Pelter; Steve Potter; Trevor Proudfoot; Dick Reid; Richard Smith; Mike Stoakes; Keith Taylor; Brian Turner; Aasha Tyrrell; Roger Venables; Catherine Woodforde; and Jonathan Wright.

My thanks at Penguin/Michael Joseph, to my editor Susan Watt, to Mark Handsley, Helen Ewing, the designer, Lily Richards and Cecilia Mackay the picture editors, all of whom have been a huge pleasure to work with. My agent Caroline Dawnay at Peters Fraser and Dunlop and her assistant Annabel Hardman have been constantly sustaining in their support and encouragement. Marian Richards, finally, orchestrated with great efficiency the transcription of many hours of taped interviews.

Restoration Committee

The Duke of Edinburgh, *Chairman*

Hayden Phillips, *Department of National Heritage (now the Department for Culture, Media and Sport)*

Sir Jocelyn Stevens, *English Heritage*

Lord St John of Fawsley, *Royal Fine Arts Commission*

Richard MacCormac/Francis Duffy/Robin Nicholson, *Royal Institute of British Architects*

The Earl of Airlie, *Lord Chamberlain*

Sir Geoffrey de Bellaigue, *Royal Collection*

Michael Peat, *Keeper of the Privy Purse*

John Tiltman, *Royal Household Property Section.*

Design Committee

The Prince of Wales, *Chairman*

Stephen Lamport, *Private Secretary to the Prince of Wales*

Robert Kime, *Interior Designer*

John Martin Robinson, *Architectural Historian*

Dmitri Porphyrios, *Architect*

The Earl of Snowdon

Giles Worsley, *Architectural Historian*

Alan Baxter, *Structural Engineer*

Sir William Whitfield, *Architect*

Hugh Roberts, *Royal Collection*

Bryan Jefferson, *Department of National Heritage*

Michael Peat, *Keeper of the Privy Purse*

John Tiltman, *Royal Household Property Section.*

Appendix

Consultants and Contractors

CONSULTANTS

Acoustic Consultant Phase 4D
Hann Tucker Associates

Archaeological Recording
Central Archaeology Service

Architect Phases 1 & 2
Bowyer Langlands Batchelor

Architect Phases 4C & 4D
Sidell Gibson Partnership

Archive of Recovered Materials
Scott Lovering

Carpet Consultant Phases 3, 4C & 4D
Mr D. Luckham

Carpet Designer Phase 4B
Mr J. Richards

Carpet Supplier Phase 4B
Afia Carpets

*Co-ordinating Architect & Architects for Phases
3, 4A & 4B*
Donald Insall Associates

Environmental Consultant Phases 1 & 2
Ridout Associates

Environmental Consultant Phases 3 & 4
Hutton + Rostron

Environmental Health Consultant Phase 3
The PWT Environmental Consultancy

Fire Adviser Phases 1 & 2
Mott MacDonald

Heraldic Consultants Phase 4C
Mr P. Begent
Mr H. Chesshyre

Heraldic Librarian Phase 4C
Ms C. Cross

Historic Interiors Phases 4A & 4B
Ms P. Lewis

Interior Design Consultancy
Mr R. Kime

Lighting Consultant Phase 3
Mr G. Carter

Lighting Consultant Phases 3 & 4B
Mr C. Marsden-Smedley

Lighting Consultant Phases 4C & 4D
Mr M. Brill

Project Manager Phases 3 & 4
GTMS

Quantity Surveyor Phases 1 & 2
Northcroft Chartered Quantity Surveyors

Quantity Surveyor Phases 3 & 4
Bucknall Austin

Services Consultant Phases 1 & 2
H. L. Dawson & Partners Ltd

Services Consultant Phases 3 & 4
Oscar Faber Group Ltd

Structural Engineer Phases 1 & 2
Hockley & Dawson Consulting Engineers

Structural Engineer Phases 3 & 4
Gifford & Partners

Wood Carving Co-ordination
Mr D. Reid

CONSERVATION

Carpet Conservation
Carpet Conservation Workshop
Textile Conservation Studio

Chandelier Restoration
Sargeant Restorations

Fireplace Metalwork
Nimbus Conservation Ltd

Furniture Restoration
Charles Perry Restorations Ltd

General Conservation
Hirst Conservation

Metalwork Conservation
Taylor Pearce
Plowden & Smith Ltd

Picture Conservation
Hamilton Kerr Institute

Plaster Conservation
Cliveden Conservation Workshop Ltd

Stone Restoration
CDL Stone Restoration

CONSTRUCTION AND ENGINEERING

Air Handling Equipment
Gill Airvect

Asbestos Removal
Amity Insulation Services Ltd
European Asbestos Services

Asphalt Roofing
Coverite Ltd

Builders' Work
Diacore Concrete Cutting Ltd

Cleaning
Ambassador Services
Excellence
Sleetree Ltd

Crane Hire
Beck & Pollitzer Crane Hire

Dehumidification Equipment
Aggreko
Munters Moisture Control Services

Demolition
Demolition Company Partnership

Drain Survey
Morgan Collis Group Ltd

Dry Lining
Kitson Insulation Contractors Ltd

Drying Equipment
P. T. E. Airflow

Electrical Installation
Lowe & Oliver Ltd

Fire Fighting Installation
Wormald Fire Systems

Fire Insulation
F. P. Ninety Three Ltd

Fire Proofing
Construction Coating Co.

Fire Shutters
Lycetts (Burslem) Ltd

Flue Linings
Kedddy-Poujoulat (UK) Ltd

Hoist Installation
UK Lift Company Ltd

Labour Supply
Garde Construction Services Ltd

Laundry Equipment
Anglowest Distributors

Lawn Restoration
G. Burley & Sons Ltd

Lead Roofing
Anglia Lead
Farren & Sons Ltd
K J A Plumbing
Richardson Roofing Company Ltd

Lift Installation
Apex Lift & Escalator Engineers Ltd

Lightning Conductors
A. W. Elliot & Co. Ltd

Main Contractor Phases 1 & 2
Wallis Ltd

Main Contractor Phases 3 & 4
H. B. G. Higgs & Hill Special Contracts Ltd

Mechanical Installation
F. G. Alden Heating

Precast Concrete
Technostone Ltd

Safety Fixings
Centuryan Safety Services

Scaffolding Contractors
Palmers Ltd

Security Alarms
Secom plc

Site Services
Andrews Sykes Hire
Wysepower Ltd

Skip Hire
Lanz Group

Specialist Cutting
W. T. Specialist Contracts Ltd

Steel Decking
Richard Lees Steel Decking Ltd

Structural Steel
F. R. Gittins & Sons Ltd
H. Young Structures Ltd

Structural Work
Keltbray Demolition Ltd

Waterproofing
Sword Sealant Services

DECORATIONS

Bobbins
Mr M. Cobb

Carpet Fitting
Linney Cooper

Curtain Fabric
Abimelech Hainsworth

Curtains to Phases 4A & 4B (part)
Albert E. Chapman Ltd

Curtains to Phase 4B (part)
Milne Associates

Decorating & Gilding
Campbell, Smith & Co. Ltd

Decorating & Gilding Phases 4A & 4C
Hare & Humphries Ltd

Decorating & Gilding Phase 4B
Hudson White Ltd

Decorations & Heraldic Painting
International Fine Art Conservation Studio Ltd

Fitting-out Materials
Caleys
Arthur Sanderson & Sons
Warner Fabrics

Floor Coverings
Abbeywood Floor Coverings Ltd

Floor & Wall Tiling
J M Tilers Ltd

General Decoration
Cousins Ltd

Needlework
Royal School of Needlework

Passementerie
Wendy Cushing Trimmings
Smith & Brighty Ltd
G. J. Turner & Co.

Silk
The Gainsborough Silk Weaving Co. Ltd
The Humphries Weaving Company Ltd

Sun Blinds & UV Film
Sun-X (UK)

Wood Flooring
Rodan Flooring Company

GLASS

Decorative Windows
Paul Antony Mirrors

Forest Glass
Mr W. Walker

Glass
N & C Glass Ltd
South East Glass Ltd

Secondary Glazing Kitchen Court
Baydale Architectural Systems Ltd

Special Glass
Daedalian Glass Ltd
Gilbert & McCarty

Stained Glass
John Reyntiens Glass

Stained Glass Windows
The Stained Glass Studio

KITCHEN EQUIPMENT

Cold Rooms
Capital Refrigeration Services Ltd

Dishwasher Repair
B. H. M. Group Services

Fitted Kitchen
Stoneham

Kitchen Consultant
Winch & Associates

Kitchen Equipment Supply & Installation
Holmes Catering Equipment

Kitchen Ventilation
Kitchen Ventilation Services

Restoration of Historic Kitchen Fittings
Context Engineering

Storage Kitchen Equipment
Ronald Crafter Associates

Supply of Kitchen Equipment
Garland Catering Equipment

LIGHTING SUPPLY

Lighting Supply
Chelsom Ltd
Dernier & Hamlyn
Directorate Engineering Support (Army)
Kensington Lighting Co. Ltd

METAL

Decorative Ironwork
The Blacksmiths Shop

Door Furniture
N T Yannedis Ltd

Memorials
Valley Forge

Metalwork
Estuary Maintenance
Gazeway Fabrication
Marsh Brothers Engineering Services
Moizer & Co. Ltd

Wrought Ironwork
Paul Dennis & Sons Ltd

Wrought Iron Recycling
The Ironbridge Gorge Museum Trust

PHOTOGRAPHIC AND VIDEO

Filming Record
BCA Film & Television

PICTURE HANGING

Phoenix Fine Art

PLASTER

Cast Plaster Ceilings
Hayles & Howe

Decorative Plaster Ceilings & Cast Plaster
A. G. Joy & Sons
St Blaise Ltd

General Plastering
Kent Plastering Ltd

Plaster Mouldings
Troika Architectural Mouldings Ltd

Wall Plastering
Hodgson Plastering Contractors

REMOVALS

James Bourlet Inc. UK Ltd
Momart
Reeves of Petersfield

STONE

Decorative Stone Supply
FREDA srv

Lime Products
The Lime Centre

Stone Flooring
Cathedral Works Organisation (Chichester) Ltd
Stone Cladding International Ltd

Stone Masonry
J. Joslin
PAYE Stonework & Restoration Ltd
Stonewest Ltd
Universal Stone Ltd

WOOD AND JOINERY

Cabinet Making
NEJ Stevenson

Carving
Linford Bridgeman
The Paul Ferguson Workshop
Mr T. Hilliard

Carving & Gilding
Carvers & Gilders
W. Thomas Restorations

Furniture Makers
David Linley Furniture Ltd

Hardwood Flooring
David Gunton Hardwood Floors

Joinery
Ashby & Horner Joinery and Interiors Ltd
A. V. Specialised Joiners
E. B. Barnes
Dovercourt Joinery
Harleyford Joinery
Howard Brothers
F. J. Mitchell
Rattee & Kett (Mowlem)
S. G. Joinery Constructors Ltd
Taylor Made Joinery (Bildeston) Ltd
Henry Venables Ltd
Wallis Joinery

Joinery & Carving
Herbert Read

Mouldings
Clerk & Fenn (incorporating George Jackson & Sons)

Oak Flooring
Durabella Ltd

Structural Joinery
Capps & Capps Ltd
Carpenter Oak & Woodland Co. Ltd

Timber Supply
John Boddy Timber Ltd
East Bros (Timber) Ltd

Grateful acknowledgement is made to the following sources for providing pictures (numbers refer to pages):

Bridgeman Art Library/Lambeth Palace Library: 122. Building Research Establishment: 49. John R. Bustin: frontispiece, 37, 38, 45 (shell of St George's Hall), 48, 65, 68, 150. English Heritage: 42, 43, 46, 50, 51, 52, 56, 67, 82, 83, 111, 112, 115, 119, 124, 131. English Heritage/John Thorneycroft: 1, 61, 86–7 (Mark Fisher & Stuart Hopps' scheme), 96, 132, 165, 173. Mark Fiennes: 252. Gifford & Partners: 147 (Kitchen roof projection), 161. Roderick Gradidge: 88. Tim Graham: 73, 85. Higgs & Hill: 180, 188–9 (all pictures), 192–3, 216 (stacked rafters; craftsmen at work), 228–9 (ceiling shield sequence), 234–5. HRH The Prince Philip, Duke of Edinburgh: 264. Hockley & Dawson: 27, 89 (drawing of shallow-pitched roof). Hutton & Rostron: 142. Donald Insall Associates: 146 (photograph of roof timber), 152, 155 (excavation of Kitchen Courtyard), 156 (all pictures), 158–9, 160, 162, 168–9, 177, 183, 186, 196, 201 (fire-damaged trophy). Pamela Lewis: 204, 205. MacCormac Jamieson Prichard: 87 (Richard MacCormac's scheme). Imre Makovecz: 97. John Outram Associates: 98 (John Outram's scheme). PA News: 21 (all pictures), 25, 35. Palmers Scaffolding: 44–5 (scaffolding design). Photographers International: 2, 14, 19, 128, 182, 223. Rex Features: 31, 32–3. The Royal Collection: 7, 8, 9, 59, 93, 104, 107, 126, 127, 135, 149, 155 (Kitchen Courtyard steel frame), 172, 175, 179, 195, 201 (restored trophy), 202, 209, 210, 212, 215, 225, 229 (kneeling knight corbel), 232, 247, 248, 251, 252, 255, 256, 259, 261, 262, 265, 267, 268, 271. Sidell Gibson Partnership: endpapers (design for Lantern Lobby floor), 103, 216 (architect's drawing), 230 (plan for ribbed octagon vault), 238, 241, 243, 245. Christopher Smallwood Architects: 101. Colin Stansfield-Smith: 98–9 (Stansfield-Smith's scheme).